PRINCIPLES OF ACCOUNTING FOR NON-ACCOUNTING PROFESSIONALS

PRINCIPLES OF ACCOUNTING FOR NON-ACCOUNTING PROFESSIONALS

Lee Tat Man

Nanyang Technological University, Singapore

With the contributions of:
Brian C. L. Lee

Dean, School of Electrical and Electronic Engineering
Nanyang Technological University, Singapore

PRENTICE HALL
New York   London   Toronto   Sydney   Tokyo   Singapore

First published 1994 by
Prentice Hall
Simon & Schuster (Asia) Pte Ltd
Alexandra Distripark
Block 4, #04-31
Pasir Panjang Road
Singapore 0511

 © 1994 Simon & Schuster (Asia) Pte Ltd
A division of Simon & Schuster International Group

All rights reserved. No part of this publication may be
reproduced, stored in retrieval system or transmitted in any form,
or by any means, electronic, mechanical, photocopying, recording or
otherwise, without prior permission in writing from the publisher.

Cover photograph by Hans Neleman and The Image Bank

Printed in Singapore

1 2 3 4 5   98 97 96 95 94

ISBN 981-3026-99-5

Prentice Hall International (UK) Limited, *London*
Prentice Hall of Australia Pty. Limited, *Sydney*
Prentice Hall Canada Inc., *Toronto*
Prentice Hall Hispanoamericana, S.A., *Mexico*
Prentice Hall of India Private Limited, *New Delhi*
Prentice Hall of Japan, Inc., *Tokyo*
Editora Prentice Hall do Brasil, Ltda., *Rio de Janeiro*
Prentice Hall, Inc., Englewood Cliffs, *New Jersey*

Dedicated to my wife Anne and my parents

Contents

Preface   xi

PART ONE   FINANCIAL ACCOUNTING PROCESS

1 Accounting Equation and Accounting Rules   3
    Introduction   3
    The accounting equation   3
    Accounts and accounting rules   4
    Classification of accounts   8
    Practice problems   9

2 Bookkeeping and Accounting Cycle   11
    The six major groups of accounts   11
    The general journal   12
    Ledger accounts   15
    The accounting cycle   19
    Practice problems   21

3 Trial Balance and Adjustment of Accounts   24
    Trial balance   24
    Adjustment of accounts   24
    Accounting entries and methods of depreciation   28
    The worksheet   30
    Practice problems   34

4 Closing of Accounts   37
    Recording closing entries   37
    Profit and loss and retained earnings accounts   39
    Post-closing trial balance   40
    Practice problems   41

PART TWO FINANCIAL REPORTS AND SPECIFIC ISSUES

5 Presentation of Financial Statements   45
- Profit and loss statement — 45
- Statement of retained earnings — 46
- Balance sheet — 47
- Generally accepted accounting principles — 49
- Practice problems — 51

6 Accounts of Merchandising Firms   52
- Special journals and analytical cash book — 52
- Subsidiary ledgers — 54
- Posting of special journals — 55
- The treatment of opening and closing stock — 56
- The perpetual inventory system — 59
- The income statement — 60
- Practice problems — 61

7 Statement of Sources and Application of Funds   64
- Working capital — 64
- Flow of funds — 65
- Statement of sources and application of funds — 67
- Practice problems — 74

PART THREE COST ACCOUNTING AND COST CONTROL

8 Classification and Control of Costs   79
- Cost centre and cost classification — 79
- Inventory control and economic reorder quantity — 80
- Direct wages and direct expenses — 85
- Absorption and apportionment of indirect costs — 86
- Practice problems — 92

9 Job Order Cost Accounting and Process Cost Accounting   95
- Cost accounts in the general ledger — 95
- Cost-of-production report: weighted-average method — 99
- Cost-of-production report: FIFO method — 101
- Practice problems — 103

10 Break-even Analysis and Marginal Costing   107
- Break-even chart — 108
- Profit/volume graph — 109
- Principles and application of marginal costing — 113
- Practice problems — 116

PART FOUR   MANAGEMENT ACCOUNTING

11   Budgeting and Business Forecast — 123
- Budget centres and master budget — 123
- Flexible budgets — 124
- Methodology of business forecasting — 126
- Practice problems — 130

12   Standard Costing and Analysis of Variances — 133
- Principles of standard costing — 133
- Classification of sales and cost variances — 134
- Mathematical and graphical representation of variances — 135
- Accounting entries of variances — 146
- Practice problems — 147

13   Analysis of Financial Statement by Ratios — 150
- Profitability ratios — 151
- Liquidity ratios — 153
- Finance ratios — 154
- Stock market ratios — 155
- Practice problems — 159

14   Capital Budgeting and Discounted Cash Flow Methods — 165
- Capital budgeting methods — 165
- Net present value method — 167
- Internal rate of return method — 168
- Compound interest and annuity formulae — 174
- Practice problems — 177

PART FIVE   COMMERCIAL FINANCE

15   Bank Loans and Financial Instruments — 183
- Types of bank loan: overdraft, term loan and mortgage loan — 184
- Import/export transaction by letter of credit — 186
- Documentary collections by D/P and D/A — 189
- Import finance by trust receipt and bank guarantee — 197

16   Business Organisations — 199
- Sole proprietorship — 199
- Partnership — 200
- Limited company or corporation — 202

APPENDICES

A	**Some Cost and Management Accounting Problems and Solutions**	**209**
	1. Transfer pricing among cost centres	209
	2. Buy or make decision	215
	3. Production and sales strategy	218
	4. Cost reduction by automation	224
	5. Cost of loss of production	226
	6. Replacement of obsolescent equipment	232
	7. Cost of acquisition of a company	236
B	**Answers to Practice Problems**	**242**
	Bibliography	**251**
	Index	**253**

Preface

It has long been my desire to write a book on accounting for non-accounting professionals since I started lecturing on the subject Financial Accounting to third-year electrical engineering students in 1983. Heavy teaching commitments and other priorities delayed this endeavour until I was given the opportunity to take my sabbatical leave at the University of Technology, Sydney in 1992.

My quest for a suitable accounting textbook for engineering students began when I started teaching this subject. Thus far, my search has been in vain. Accounting books inevitably fall under one of the following two categories: sketchy delineation for casual readers with insufficient coverage of the subject to substantiate teaching at the undergraduate level or a standard text for accountancy students which rarely contains less than one thousand pages. The latter is usually prescribed as a textbook but students, naturally, find it intimidating. Further, they are not prepared to spend too much time reading wordy paragraphs on a subject which is not their major. This book will, I believe, fill the current gap in available texts on the subject.

As a trained engineer and a qualified accountant, I am presenting the subject of accounting to non-accounting students with a different approach and perspective. I hope this book will help to bridge the gap between accountants and students of other professional disciplines.

The content of this book will cover broadly the three areas of accountancy: financial accounting, cost accounting and management accounting. The book also explains the essence of import/export finance and the different types of business organisations. Most of the accounting topics essential to management decision making are included to provide a working knowledge for a management position. Mathematical and graphical presentations are used as far as possible in the introduction of basic accounting concepts. As for the topic of financial accounting, it is my belief that basic ideas of journal entries through to trial balance and financial statements must be grasped as a prerequisite to management accounting. A reader of financial statements is in no position to appreciate its real significance if he does not even know how those statements are derived. Quick-fix type of management courses for instant managers usually only teach the interpretation of accounts without going through the accounting cycle. That is obviously putting the cart before the horse. A non-accounting professional may not need to know the finer details of bookkeeping but he must realise the exact meanings of debit, credit and the accounting equation.

Practice problems are found at the end of each chapter. Only representative questions incorporating all major principles covered in that chapter are set out. All the exercises should be attempted in order to have a good grasp of concepts and procedures taught in each chapter. After all, the maxim 'practice make perfect' has been even more strongly advocated in the teaching of accounting compared to other subjects.

As readers of this book are expected to apply what they learn mostly in the areas of cost and management accounting, some case studies are included in Appendix A. The application of principles expounded in this book for the solution of these problems will highlight the more sophisticated management problems and challenges confronting business managers.

Professor Brian Lee has contributed significantly to Part Five of this book on commercial finance and business organisations by bringing to it his considerable experience as a successful industrialist. His encouragement and critical comments on the book are deeply appreciated. I am also indebted to my former students for their feedback over the years when I was teaching this subject. Thanks are due to Professor Warren Yates and Professor Vic Ramsden of University of Technology, Sydney for providing the conducive environment for me to complete this project. Ms Jerene Tan and Ms Ang Lee Ming of Prentice Hall have provided efficient editorial assistance and Mrs Frances Tsui has rendered her excellent typographical service. To them I am most grateful.

Lee Tat Man

PART ONE

FINANCIAL ACCOUNTING PROCESS

Chapter 1

Accounting Equation and Accounting Rules

Business will play the rules of the game – whatever they are – as long as those rules are not changed halfway through the game.

Richard L. Lesher

Introduction

Accounting theory and practice arose from the need to record and monitor the financial performance of commercial enterprises. With the increase in economic activities and growth in the size and complexity of commercial corporations, the accounting system has evolved over the past few hundred years into the present highly structured one. The fundamental objective of accounting, however, remains to provide information essential to the efficient conduct and evaluation of the activities of an organisation.

In today's context, accounting information is essential for the following purposes:

- Use inside the organisation for effective planning, control and decision making by management.
- Use outside the organisation to discharge the accountability of the company to investors, creditors, government agencies, etc.

The Accounting Equation

The whole system of accounting has developed from the basic tenet of a single equation. It is surprising that so much can be built on so simple an axiom involving only three terms in an arithmetical equation:

$$\text{ASSETS} = \text{LIABILITIES} + \text{CAPITAL}$$

Before proceeding, some specific terms used by accountants must first be introduced:

- **Assets:** these are resources such as cash, equipment, stock, etc., in a company.
- **Interest:** by obtaining a share of a company or the right to claim from a company, we say in accounting the party has acquired an 'interest' in the company.
- **Creditor:** a person to whom a company owes money.
- **Equities:** the 'interests' of various parties (the owner/shareholders and the creditors) in the assets of a company.

Thus, liabilities and capital in the accounting equation can now be defined as creditors' equity and owners' equity in a company respectively. In term of resources, assets are the resources of a company while liabilities and capital are legitimate claims on these resources by creditors and owners.

The accounting equation can be readily appreciated if we compare it with many physical laws of nature such as the laws of conservation of energy and matter. What the equation implies is simply that something cannot be created from nothing and an effect must always have its cause. Thus, assets in a company must be acquired either by contribution of the owner or owing to external parties. The matching of assets to liabilities plus capital is maintained at all times in an accounting system. The accounting equation is actually expressed in the form of a balance sheet of a company as shown in Chapter 5.

To illustrate the accounting equation in terms of some typical transactions in a company, let us consider example 1.1 which is self-explanatory.

The example bears out the principle that every change in one item of the accounting equation will be matched by a corresponding change in another. If the increase (or decrease) is on one side of the equation, there will be an increase (or decrease) on the other side and vice versa. On the other hand, an increase (or decrease) may also be matched by a decrease (or increase) in other items on the same side of the equation. In any case, algebraic balance is always maintained. Transaction 7 is essentially made up of two transactions: one to reduce liabilities by repaying $1,000 to the bank; another to pay the interest expense of $10 to the bank. The cash asset, therefore, is reduced by $1,010. Transactions 5 and 6 are both expenses that effectively reduce the assets of the company and at the same time lower the owner's equity by the same amount.

Accounts and Accounting Rules

The method of recording business transactions as shown in example 1.1 is not particularly useful for practical application in a real-life situation. Since assets,

Example 1.1

Transaction	ASSET		=	LIABILITIES		+ CAPITAL
	cash	+ inventory	= owe to bank	+ owe to creditor	+ owners' equity
	$	$	$	$	$
1. Owner invests $5,000 in the business	+5,000				+5,000
2. The company borrows $3,000 from the bank	+3,000		+3,000		
3. The company buys goods on credit		+500		+500	
4. The company buys goods with cash	−200	+200			
5. The company pays salaries	−4,000				−4,000
6. The company uses inventory		−300			−300
7. The company repays part of loan plus interest charge	−1,010		−1,000		−10
8. The company collects cash for services to customers	+6,000				+6,000
9. The owner withdraws cash for personal use	−400				−400
End-of-period balance	8,390 +	400	= 2,000 +	500 +	6,290
	Total assets = 8,790		Total equities = 8,790		

liabilities and capital comprise many classes of information, such a system of recording will result in an extremely long, multi-column document.

The ingenuity and experience of businessmen driven by the need to record business data has led to the development of the existing bookkeeping and accounting system. It is based on the accounting equation modified by the following two rules: (a) the T-account and (b) the debit/credit rule.

The T-account

Every class of information is considered as an account which falls under one of the categories of assets, liabilities or capital. The various items in example 1.1 also fall under these three broad classifications. At the same time, instead of using a plus or minus sign to indicate an increase or decrease of an item, the T-format of an account is one which is represented as a page divided into left and right sides:

Account name
Left side (Debit)	Right side (Credit)

The left side of an account is termed 'debit' and the right side is 'credit'. Depending on the nature of the account, an increase or decrease in an account is now represented by a debit or credit entry.

The difference between the sum total of the two sides of an account is called the *balance*. If the account has a debit balance, it means the left side exceeds the right side by that amount. A credit balance means the opposite is true. It must be emphasised that 'debit' and 'credit' are only used to designate the two sides of a T-account and have no other meaning by themselves. Although a debtors' account will have a debit balance and creditors' account a credit balance, these are not how the terms were originally derived.

Although the above rule seems more troublesome compared to simply putting a plus or minus sign together with a figure, it is much more efficient in practice in compiling the account balance. The mathematical operation will only require the summing up of the debit side and credit side separately before calculating the difference. It is more systematic and results in less mistakes as compared to a mixed operation of addition and subtraction. The separate debit and credit total amounts also provide additional information about changes in the account during that particular period being accounted for.

The debit/credit rule

In order to de-couple the various terms in the accounting equation so that they do not have to be written with all the signs in a linear format, a rule must be formulated to recognise the fact that assets are separate from liabilities and capital which are on the other side of the equation.

Firstly, the accountant has a choice to represent an increase in an asset account by either a debit or credit entry as this is solely arbitrary. Traditionally, the debit-side has been chosen for this and this has since been adopted universally. With this convention established, increases in liabilities and capital accounts must be represented by credit entries in order to reflect that these accounts are on the other side of the equation. These rules are shown as follows:

Asset accounts		=	Liability accounts		+	Capital accounts	
+	−		−	+		−	+
(Debit)	(Credit)		(Debit)	(Credit)		(Debit)	(Credit)

With the above rule in place, the equal and plus signs of the accounting equation can now be dispensed with. An increase in an asset account reflected by a debit entry will be matched by a credit entry in either a liability/capital account or in another asset account. In the first case, an increase in assets corresponds to an increase in liabilities or capital while in the latter case, one asset is substituted by another. In both instances, a debit entry gives rise to a credit entry which is the basic 'double-entry' principle of bookkeeping. Obviously we are no longer concerned about which side of the accounting equation these accounts belong to provided the double-entry rule is followed. Since every debit amount corresponds to an identical credit amount, the debit total must necessarily be equal to the credit total all the time. This is essentially a way of expressing the accounting equation in a more general form using the accounting rules developed.

Finally, there are instances when changes may occur on accounts at the same side of the accounting equation. The double-entry rule can also apply without necessarily considering the equation at all.

To summarise:

1. Increase in asset accounts are *debit* entries. (Consequently asset accounts always have debit balances as assets in a company will not be a negative amount.)
2. Increase in liabilities and capital accounts are *credit* entries. (Consequently liabilities and capital accounts always have credit balances.)

The principles so far developed will now be illustrated using the same data in example 1.1. The number placed before every figure in example 1.2 corresponds to the transaction number in example 1.1.

Example 1.2

	ASSET ACCOUNTS Cash					**LIABILITY ACCOUNTS** Bank			
		$			$		$		$
(1)		5,000	(4)		200	(7)	1,000	(2)	3,000
(2)		3,000	(5)		4,000				
(8)		6,000	(7)		1,010			Balance: 2,000	
			(9)		400				
		14,000			5,610				
Balance: 8,390									

	Inventory				Creditors		
	$		$		$		$
(3)	500	(6)	300			(3)	500
(4)	200						Balance: 500
	700		300				
Balance: 400							

CAPITAL ACCOUNT
Capital

	$		$
(5)	4,000	(1)	5,000
(6)	300	(8)	6,000
(7)	10		
(9)	400		
	4,710		11,000
		Balance: 6,290	

It can be seen clearly from example 1.2 that instead of keeping all the information together in a single spreadsheet, accounts can now be physically separated. Each account may occupy a number of pages in a book or may be kept in separate books of record. Generally, a *ledger* is a book containing all the accounts of a company. In the case of a computerised accounting system, each account will be a data file stored on magnetic disk or tape.

Classification of Accounts

As explained earlier, accounts can generally be classified into assets, liabilities and capital. How detailed the accounting information is depends on the needs of the company. The following accounts are commonly used:

Asset accounts
Fixed-asset accounts: land and building
plant and machinery
motor vehicles
Current-asset accounts: cash
shares in public-listed companies (or investment in public companies)
debtors (or accounts receivable)
inventory (or stock)
prepayment (or payment in advance)

Liability accounts
Creditors (or trade creditors): recording the amount owed to supplier
Bank (or owing to bank): normally the amount of overdraft
Accrued expenses: accrued rent account, accrued salary account, etc. which are records of expenditure incurred but not yet due and without bills for payment
Income tax payable: income tax owing to the government
Dividends payable: announced distribution of profit to shareholders of a company but not yet paid
Long-term loan: usually mortgage loan secured by fixed assets

Capital accounts
Capital (or invested capital or shares issued)
Retained earnings: the accumulated profit kept in the company
Revenue accounts (sales account and/or service fee account)
Expense accounts (accounts for purchases of goods and acquiring services)
Owner's withdrawals (or dividends)

The relationship of retained earnings with revenue, expense and withdrawals accounts as well as how these are tied to capital will be explained further in Chapter 2.

Practice Problems

1.1 A company has the following items among its assets, liabilities and owner's equity at the end of a month:

	$
Cash	10,000
Accounts receivable	11,000
Land and building	44,000
Creditors	8,000
Long-term loan	15,000
Capital	42,000

The following transactions occurred during the following month:

1. Collected $6,000 from debtors.
2. Purchased a machine for $10,000 by paying half in down-payment and the rest owed to the supplier to be paid in 60 days.
3. The owner withdrew $1,000 in cash.
4. Paid creditors an amount of $4,000.
5. Purchased office equipment on credit for $3,000.

6. Returned office equipment with purchase price of $1,000 later and received the same credit against the amount owed.

You are required to list all the accounts in a tabular form as in example 1.1 and record all the transactions to show their effects on the company's assets, liabilities and capital.

1.2 Re-work the above problem by recording in the T-account format. Confirm that the total debit balance is equal to the total credit balance.

1.3 Re-write the account balances listed below into two columns with the left column for debit and right column for credit. Confirm that the total debit balance is equal to the total credit balance.

	$
Cash	4,870
Accounts receivable	23,700
Inventory	31,250
Office stationery	450
Prepaid insurance	2,430
Equipment	38,500
Accounts payable	3,200
Capital	65,000
Withdrawals	9,000
Sales	298,600
Purchases	220,000
Retained earnings	3,200
Long-term loan	5,000
Income tax payable	3,000
Salaries	42,000
Rental expense	3,600
Advertising expense	750
Insurance expense	1,250
Office stationery expense	200

Chapter 2

Bookkeeping and Accounting Cycle

The self-made manager in business is nearing the end of his road. Despite his own blind faith in the practical, he is already hiring professionally trained engineers, chemists, accountants, and hygienists ... He must himself turn to professional education, or surrender control to those who do.

Richard J. Walsh

The Six Major Groups of Accounts

While the classification of asset and liability accounts can be easily understood from their account names, capital accounts require some further clarification. Capital is related to invested capital, retained earnings, revenue, expenses and owner's withdrawals as follows:

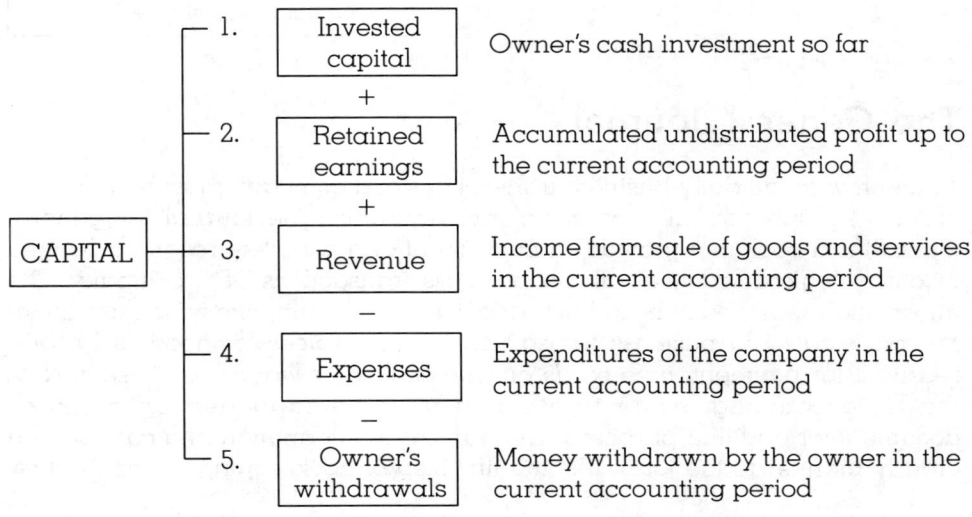

11

Items 1 and 2 are essentially owner's equity (or shareholders' fund) in a company from direct investment and undistributed profit accumulated throughout the years of operation. Although their sources are different, they are basically funds belonging to the owner and can be grouped as simply owner's capital.

Items 3, 4 and 5 all apply to the current accounting period and eventually become the retained earnings of that period to be accumulated with item 2 for the next accounting period:

> Retained earnings from the current period
> = Net income (or profit) from current operation
> − Owner's withdrawals (or dividends)
> = (Revenue − Expenses) − Owner's withdrawals

Expenses and owner's withdrawal both reduce the amount of owner's equity in the company. They are therefore debit entries since increase in capital accounts is credit according to the accounting rule. Among capital accounts, owner's capital and revenue accounts always have credit balances while expenses and withdrawals accounts always have debit balances. To summarise, the accounting equation can be expressed in six major groups of accounts:

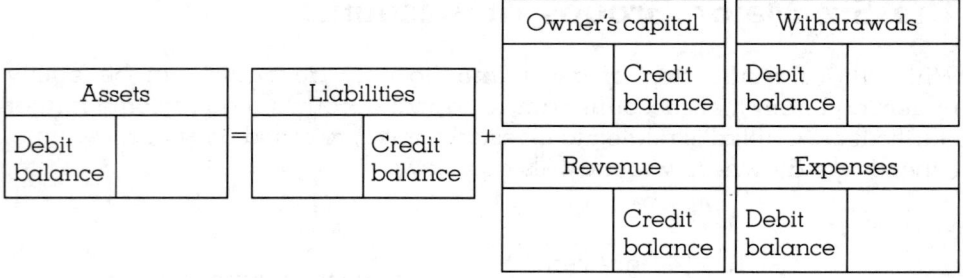

The General Journal

To begin with, all daily business transactions of a company must be recorded orderly for subsequent processing into accounts. The journal (or general journal) is a book that provides a permanent and complete record, arranged in chronological order, of all the business transactions of a company. The information recorded is based on various *source documents* which are initial records created in business transactions, e.g., *invoices* for goods sold, *bills* received for payment, *time cards* or *time sheets* for wages of workers. Note that in accounting, every transaction must be supported by a source document for auditing purposes. The transfer of information in a concise and orderly manner to the journal is the first step of bookkeeping. Since the task is repetitive and routine, a bookkeeper instead of an accountant is responsible for recording and processing these data.

The general journal of a company in its first two months of operation may hypothetically be like example 2.1.

Example 2.1

Date		Account titles and explanation	LP	Debit	Credit
June	1	Cash Capital Issue 6,000 shares for cash invested		60,000	60,000
	2	Office stationery Cash Purchase office stationery		720	720

	5	Office premises
		    Cash
		    Accounts payable
		Purchase office premises with part payment by cash, balance payable within 90 days
				57,000	36,000
					21,000

	10	Accounts receivable Office premises Sell a portion of the office space at cost, due within 3 months		6,000	6,000
	14	Office equipment Accounts payable Purchase office equipment on credit		5,400	5,400
	20	Cash Accounts receivable Collect part of payment for office premises sold		1,500	1,500
	30	Accounts payable Cash Make partial payment for office equipment		3,000	3,000

Date		Account titles and explanation	LP	Debit	Credit
July	1	Advertising expense Cash Paid for newspaper advertisement to recruit staff		360	360
	1	Unexpired insurance Cash Purchase 3-year fire insurance policy		540	540
	1	Cash Unearned consulting fee Collect in advance service fee for July–December		1,800	1,800
	1	Cash Loan payable Borrow 3-month loan from bank at 6% annual interest		3,000	3,000
	6	Cash Consulting fee earned Collect fee for service provided		2,250	2,250
	16	Advertising expense Accounts payable Order newspaper advertisement, payable in 30 days		270	270
	20	Accounts receivable Consulting fee earned Consulting fee for service provided to be received in 60 days		3,390	3,390
	30	Office salaries expense Cash Pay office salaries for July		2,100	2,100
	30	Utilities expense Accounts payable To record liability for July utilities expense		144	144
	30	Dividends Cash Pay dividends at 30 cents per share		1,800	1,800

The following points should be noted:

1. The entries of account titles are offset in positions to indicate that the account on the left (the first one) is to be debited and the account offset to the right (the second one) is to be credited.
2. A column titled LP is left empty. This stands for Ledger Page (or sometimes called Folio) and is for recording the account numbers when the figures are eventually transferred to the respective accounts.
3. A general journal is not an account. It only serves as a data-collecting point so that all the accounts will eventually be updated using the information recorded. Direct entry of data to accounts in a manual accounting system without a general journal will be extremely messy and make it difficult to check for mistakes made. In a modern computerised accounting system, there is no necessity for a single general journal as accounts are updated by various data files created by batch or online operation.

Ledger Accounts

Information recorded in the general journal will be used at regular intervals (say daily) to update the accounts kept in the ledger. The process of copying journal entry information to the ledger is called *posting*.

After the posting of each transaction information to an account, the account number (or ledger page number where the account is located) will be entered into the LP column of the general journal. This serves to indicate that posting has been made and also facilitates checking for mistakes in the future. Similarly the page number of the general journal from which the information is transferred from will be entered in the Reference (or Posting Reference) column in the corresponding account.

All resulting accounts after posting from the general journal will be as shown in example 2.2.

Example 2.2

Cash						Account no. 1	
Date		Explanation	Ref.	Debit	Credit	Balance	
						Debit	Credit
June	1	Issue 6,000 shares for cash		60,000			
	2	Purchased office stationery			720		
	5	Part payment for office premises			36,000		
	20	Collected part payment for office premises		1,500			
	30	Part payment for office equipment			3,000	21,780	

Cash
Account no. 1

Date		Explanation	Ref.	Debit	Credit	Balance Debit	Balance Credit
July	1	Paid for newspaper advertisement			360		
	1	Purchased 3-year fire insurance			540		
	1	Collected service fee in advance		1,800			
	1	Borrowed 3-month loan		3,000			
	6	Collected service fee		2,250			
	30	Paid office salaries			2,100		
	30	Paid dividends			1,800	24,030	

Accounts receivable
Account no. 2

Date		Explanation	Ref.	Debit	Credit	Balance Debit	Balance Credit
June	10	Sold part of office space		6,000			
	20	Collect part payment for office premises sold			1,500	4,500	
July	20	Consulting fee for services provided		3,390		7,890	

Office premises
Account no. 20

Date		Explanation	Ref.	Debit	Credit	Balance Debit	Balance Credit
June	5	Purchased office premises		57,000			
	10	Sold part of office space at cost			6,000	51,000	

Office equipment
Account no. 25

Date		Explanation	Ref.	Debit	Credit	Balance Debit	Balance Credit
June	14	Purchased office equipment on credit		5,400		5,400	

PART ONE   FINANCIAL ACCOUNTING PROCESS

Accounts payable						Account no. 30	
Date		Explanation	Ref.	Debit	Credit	Balance	
						Debit	Credit
June	5	Purchased office premises, due in 90 days			21,000		
	14	Purchased office equipment			5,400		
	30	Partial payment for office equipment		3,000			23,400
July	16	Newspaper advertisement, payable in 30 days			270		
	30	Utilities expense			144		23,814

Capital						Account no. 50	
Date		Explanation	Ref.	Debit	Credit	Balance	
						Debit	Credit
June	1	Issued 6,000 shares for cash			60,000		60,000

Dividends						Account no. 51	
Date		Explanation	Ref.	Debit	Credit	Balance	
						Debit	Credit
July	30	Paid dividends at 30 cents per share		1,800		1,800	

Consulting fee earned						Account no. 61	
Date		Explanation	Ref.	Debit	Credit	Balance	
						Debit	Credit
July	6	Collected cash for service provided			2,250		
	20	Consulting fee receivable in 60 days			3,390		5,640

Advertising expense						Account no. 70	
Date		Explanation	Ref.	Debit	Credit	Balance	
						Debit	Credit
July	1	Newspaper advertisement paid in cash		360			
	16	Newspaper advertisement payable in 30 days		270		630	

Office salaries expenses						Account no. 72	
Date		Explanation	Ref.	Debit	Credit	Balance	
						Debit	Credit
June	30	Office salaries for July		2,100		2,100	

Utilities expense						Account no. 74	
Date		Explanation	Ref.	Debit	Credit	Balance	
						Debit	Credit
June	30	Utilities expense for July		144		144	

Office stationery						Account no. 27	
Date		Explanation	Ref.	Debit	Credit	Balance	
						Debit	Credit
June	2	Purchased stationery with cash		720		720	

Unexpired insurance						Account no. 24	
Date		Explanation	Ref.	Debit	Credit	Balance	
						Debit	Credit
July	1	Purchased 3-year fire insurance		540		540	

Unearned consulting fee						Account no. 35	
						Balance	
Date		Explanation	Ref.	Debit	Credit	Debit	Credit
July	1	Collected in advance fee for July–December			1,800		1,800

Loan payable						Account no. 40	
						Balance	
Date		Explanation	Ref.	Debit	Credit	Debit	Credit
July	1	Borrowed 3-month loan, 6% interest		3,000			3,000

It will be useful at this stage to review the journal entries of example 2.1 and trace how the posting to ledger will result in the accounts in example 2.2. At the same time, readers should try to relate each transaction to the accounting equation expressed as six major groups of accounts at the beginning of this chapter. Data in these two examples will continue to be used in examples in the next two chapters to illustrate the accounting process up to final accounting statements. Understanding all these typical transactions will go a long way in appreciating the whole bookkeeping and accounting process.

The Accounting Cycle

The previous sections have explained how accounting data are processed to update ledger accounts. At the end of an accounting period, a *trial balance* is prepared to verify the correctness of all the posting. This involves the summing up of both the debit and credit balances of the ledger and confirming that they are equal. Adjustments are then required to take into consideration information which has not originated from source documents but which will render the account figures more accurate. Accounts of revenues, expenses and withdrawals will then be 'closed' as these are recording 'period' figures which finally will be merged to produce the retained earnings for that accounting period. A 'post-closing' trial balance will confirm that all accounts are properly finalised and prepared for the next accounting period. Management reports in the form of *financial statements* are then produced. The whole *accounting* cycle is summarised in Figure 2.1.

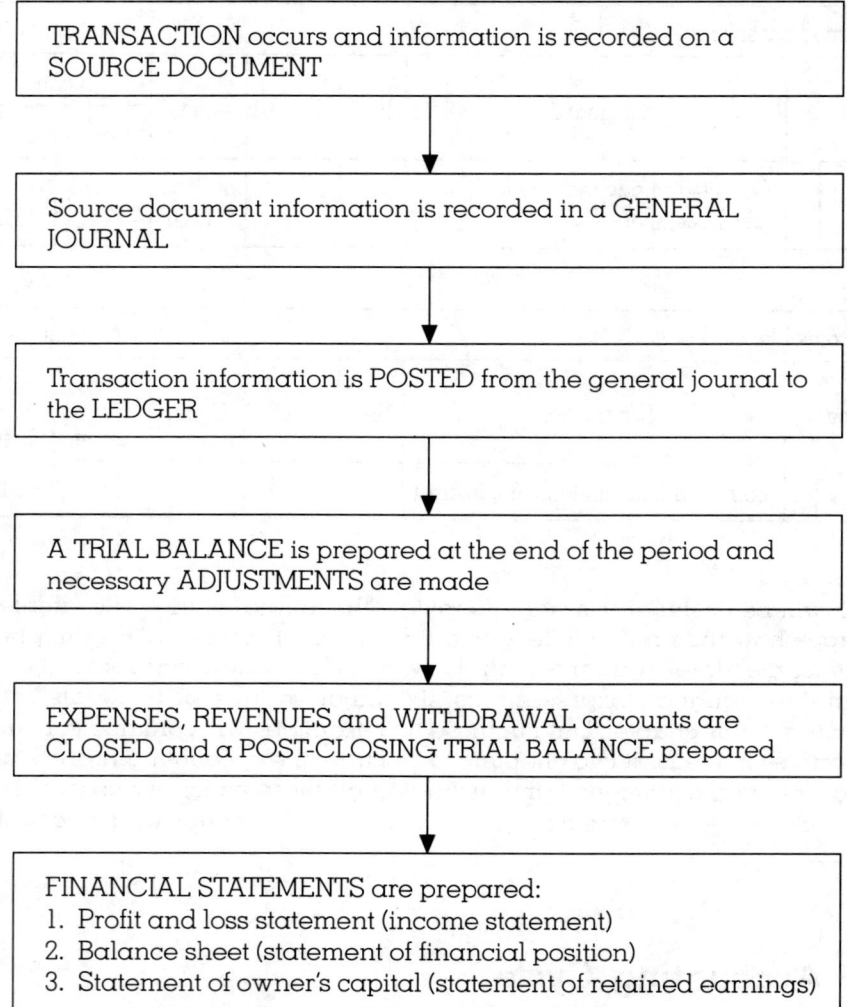

Figure 2.1 The accounting cycle

An accounting cycle is completed within an accounting period which may be a month, three months, or a year in length. Annual accounting period with twelve months is the norm. It is not unusual however, for large corporations to have half-yearly or even quarterly accounting periods. In our example for illustration purposes, the accounting period comprises only two months, i.e., June and July.

Practice Problems

2.1 A consulting firm was set up with a capital of $50,000 on 1 July and has the following transactions in the first month of its operation:

July 2 Paid rent for July, $900.
     4 Purchased equipment on credit, $6,000.
     8 Collected $1,500 in cash for services performed for a client.
     9 Paid $200 for an advertisement on newspaper.
    16 Completed work and billed a client for $2,500.
    16 Purchased office stationery for $500 cash.
    17 Received $1,000 from a client for services performed.
    19 Paid $3,000 to the supplier of equipment bought on 4 July.
    21 Received part payment of $1,500 from client billed on 16 July.
    26 Owner withdrew $2,000 in cash.
    31 Paid $3,600 salaries to employees.

You are required to record the above transactions in tabular form under the following account titles grouped under assets, liabilities and capital as in example 1.1:

    Cash   Owner's withdrawals
    Accounts receivable   Service fee
    Equipment   Rent expense
    Office stationery   Advertising expense
    Accounts payable   Salaries expense
    Capital

Verify that the end-of-period balances are correct.

2.2 Rework the above problem by recording in the T-account format. Confirm that the total debit balance is equal to the total credit balance.

2.3 A lawyer set up a law firm in July and completed the following transactions in that month:

July 1 Invested $5,000 in cash and $1,000 worth of law books in the firm.
     1 Rented a furnished office by paying $2,000 which is two months' rent in advance.
     2 Purchased more law books costing $800 with $100 down payment. The remaining $700 is recorded as accounts payable to be paid by monthly instalment.
     3 Purchased office stationery on credit, $100.
     4 Paid the premium on an insurance policy giving one year's protection, $480.
    10 Completed legal work for a client and collected $500 of fee.

July 14 Paid for the office stationery purchased on 3 July.
   16 Completed legal work and billed a client for $900.
   20 The lawyer paid his home telephone bill of $50 using the cheque of the law firm.
   26 Received $900 from the client billed on 16 July.
   27 Completed legal work and billed a client for $600.
   30 Paid telephone bill of the legal practice, $100.
   31 Paid salary of the office secretary, $1,200.

You are required to:

1. record all transactions in a general journal;
2. open the following accounts: cash, accounts receivable, prepaid rent, unexpired insurance, office stationery, law library (asset), accounts payable, capital, withdrawals, legal fees earned, salaries expense and telephone expense.
3. post the entries in the general journal to these accounts as in example 2.2.

2.4 A company which started its business on 1 July has the following transactions in the first month of operation:

July 1 The owner invested $15,000 in cash and a car having a market value of $8,000.
   1 Paid office rent for July, $1,000.
   2 Paid advertising cost to newspaper, $200.
   3 Purchased office equipment costing $4,000 with 10% down payment and the balance to be paid within 30 days.
   6 Collected $400 of service fee for services rendered to a client.
   7 Paid for office stationery, $150.
   7 Collected $500 of service fee for services rendered to a client.
   9 Purchased office equipment costing $1,400 on credit.
   12 Completed services and billed a client $1,200.
   17 Paid travel expenses, $300.
   18 Paid the balance owed to supplier of equipment purchased on 3 July.
   20 Collected $600 of service fee for services rendered to a client.
   22 Received partial payment of $500 from the client billed on 12 July.
   25 Completed service for a client and billed $800.
   28 Paid utilities bill, $350.
   29 Paid travel expenses, $250.
   30 The owner withdrew $1,500 in cash for personal use.
   31 Paid salaries to employees $1,600.

You are required to record the above transactions in a general journal. Set up the necessary accounts and post the entries in the general journals to these accounts.

2.5 Entries in the T-accounts of a company in the first month of its operation are:

	Cash					Service fee earned	
Aug. 3	45,000	Aug. 4	600			Aug. 9	1,100
9	1,100	11	200			14	1,400
19	800	16	1,800			20	1,500
20	1,500	17	1,000				
		23	500		Capital		
		24	1,200			Aug. 3	45,000
		26	700				
		31	1,600				

	Accounts receivable				Owner's withdrawals		
Aug. 14	1,400	Aug. 19	800	Aug. 26	700		

	Office equipment			Salaries		
Aug. 7	2,500		Aug. 31	1,600		

	Motor vehicle			Prepaid rent		
Aug. 16	6,000		Aug. 4	600		

	Accounts payable				Travel expenses		
Aug. 17	1,000	Aug. 7	2,500	Aug. 23	500		

	Loan payable				Advertising expense		
Aug. 24	1,200	Aug. 16	4,200	Aug. 11	200		

Using the dates to identify each transaction entered in the T-accounts, record the transactions in a general journal.

Chapter 3

Trial Balance and Adjustment of Accounts

The executive exists to make sensible exceptions to general rules.

Elting E. Morison

Trial Balance

A trial balance is normally produced to confirm that there are no errors in the bookkeeping process. It is a list of all the accounts in the ledger with their current balances. The total credit balance should be equal to the total debit balance. The trial balance of the ledger in example 2.2 is as shown in example 3.1.

If the trial balance is not correct, errors may have been introduced at the recording into the general journal or during posting to the ledger. A common technique to trace the wrong entry caused by posting twice to the debit or credit side is to divide the difference in debit and credit totals by two and then try to spot that figure in the general journal. Multiple errors, however, are not so easily traced. Another problem is the case of wrong posting to the debit (or credit) side which is countered by an identical incorrect posting to the credit (or debit) side. In such a case, the trial balance will appear to be correct even though two accounts have been wrongly recorded.

Adjustment of Accounts

In order to present the financial position of a company more accurately so that the *accrual concept* is recognised, accounts must be adjusted even though these adjustments have not originated from source documents. The accrual concept requires revenues and expenses to be entered in the period they materialise rather than according to cash received or paid or whether a record has been made.

Example 3.1

Account no.	Account title	Debit	Credit
1	Cash	24,030	
2	Accounts receivable	7,890	
20	Office premises	51,000	
25	Office equipment	5,400	
30	Accounts payable		23,814
50	Capital		60,000
51	Dividends	1,800	
61	Consulting fee earned		5,640
70	Advertising expense	630	
72	Office salaries expense	2,100	
74	Utilities expense	144	
27	Office stationery	720	
24	Unexpired insurance	540	
35	Unearned consulting fee		1,800
40	Loan payable		3,000
		94,254	94,254

Two basic types of adjustment are necessary:

- A business transaction has taken place, but the information has not yet been recorded in the account. This may be either unrecorded expense or unrecorded revenue:
  - Unrecorded expense: such as wages of employees between the last payday and the end of the recording period.
  - Unrecorded revenue: such as services which have been provided but for which bills have not been sent to the client.
- Transaction information has already been entered in the accounts but the balances need to be corrected to reflect recent developments. This may be either for cost or revenue apportionment:
  - Cost apportionment: such as depreciation on the cost of a building or equipment.
  - Revenue apportionment: such as part realisation of fee received in advance for service extending into the future.

All these adjustments will have to be recorded in the general journal for subsequent posting to the ledger. Using the accounts in example 2.2 and with additional information on adjustment, the necessary entries in the general journal are shown in example 3.2. All additional accounts created are underlined.

Example 3.2

Unrecorded expenses. The company has borrowed $3,000 on 1 July at 6% annual interest. Accrued interest expense for July is therefore $3,000 × 0.06/12 or $15. As the nature of interest is different from other expenses, two new accounts are created to record this adjustment:

July	31	Interest expense Interest payable (Interest expense for July)	15	15

Although a salaries payment of $2,100 has been recorded on 30 July, there are some employees whose payday is later than the account closing date. The amount owing to these employees (or accrued salary) is $180:

July	31	Office salaries expense Office salaries payable (Salaries owed to employee)	180	180

Unrecorded revenue. Service has started in mid-July for a client who agreed to pay $240 every middle of the month in arrear. The client is therefore not to be billed until mid-August. The accrued revenue at the end of July is recorded as follows:

July	31	Consulting fee receivable Consulting fee earned (Revenue accrued for service in July)	120	120

Note that a new 'consulting fee receivable' account has been created instead of the fee being debited to the 'accounts receivable' account. This is because the latter account only records amounts which has already been billed to clients.

Cost apportionment. Fire insurance premium of $540 was paid on 1 July for a coverage of three years. The insurance expense for one month in July is therefore $540/36 or $15.

July	31	Insurance expense Unexpired insurance (Insurance expense for July)	15	15

A stock check on 31 July showed that $600 of office stationery still remained. Thus $120 out of the total $720 of office stationery purchased on 2 June has been used.

July	31	Office stationery expense	120	
		Office stationery		120
		(To record consumption in June–July)		

The office premises purchased for $51,000 on 5 June has a life span of twenty years. The drop in value of the office after using it for two months from June to July is therefore $51,000 × (2/240) or $425 using the method of straight-line depreciation. More about depreciation will be discussed in the next section.

July	31	Depreciation expense: office	425	
		Accumulated depreciation: office		425
		(To record depreciation for June–July)		

Similarly, the depreciation expense for office equipment purchased for $5,400 on 14 June with a life span of ten years will be $5,400 × (2/120) or $90. It will be too trivial to base depreciation on days so that rounding off to the nearest month usually suffices.

July	31	Depreciation expense: office equipment	90	
		Accumulated depreciation: office equipment		90
		(To record depreciation for June–July)		

Revenue apportionment. A service fee of $1,800 has been received on 1 July in advance for service to be provided in July to December. Since service for one month has been rendered up to 31 July, consulting fee earned should be $1,800/6 or $300.

July	31	Unearned consulting fee	300	
		Consulting fee earned		300
		(Fee earned for service in July)		

Accounting Entries and Methods of Depreciation

Among all the adjustments of accounts, depreciation requires more elaboration. First of all, it is noted that unlike other cost apportionment (e.g., insurance and office stationery expenses) an accumulated depreciation account is created instead of directly reducing the asset value by a credit entry. The idea is to retain the original cost of the asset in record. The current value (or book value) is the original cost minus the accumulated depreciation. This is important for fixed assets which are usually of high costs and have to be disclosed in details in accounting reports. It certainly will not look realistic to have say, a factory originally costing 1 million recorded simply as $50,000 in the account. The accumulated depreciation account, which always has a credit balance, is actually a *contra account* which acts to reduce the debit balance of the corresponding asset account when the two are read together. An asset account, on the other hand, records the original cost of asset and remains unchanged until a new purchase or the sale of an asset takes place.

The three accounts relating to a fixed asset are therefore as follows:

Asset A	Accumulated depreciation, A	Depreciation expense, A
a	b	c
	c	
	(b + c)	

The next thing about depreciation is that it is not a cash transaction involving payment for depreciation expense. It is only a means of apportioning the costs of fixed assets throughout their life spans. Assets have originally been acquired using a company's resources or resulting in liabilities to outside parties. Depreciation essentially charges out part of the revenue as an expense within the company so that the profit figure will be lowered. This serves to restrain the distribution of profit to the owners or shareholders so that a pool of cash can be accumulated for paying back external borrowing which has financed the acquisition of fixed assets or to replace the fixed assets at the end of their life spans.

There are many methods of apportioning the cost of an asset throughout its life. Four of the more frequently used methods are:

1. straight-line method
2. sum-of-the-years'-digits method
3. declining-balance method
4. units-of-production method

The straight-line method is the simplest and most widely used. The asset's depreciable cost is allocated equally to each accounting period in its estimated useful life. Thus:

$$\text{Annual depreciation} = \frac{\text{Cost} - \text{Estimated residual (or salvage) value}}{\text{Estimated useful life in years}}$$

The sum-of-the-years'-digits method is an accelerated depreciation method such that more depreciation expense is charged to the early years of an asset's useful life. The depreciation expense in year j for an asset with a life span of n years is:

$$\text{Depreciation (year } j) = (\text{Cost} - \text{Residual value}) \times \frac{n - (j - 1)}{\sum_{i=1}^{n} i}$$

$$= (\text{Cost} - \text{Residual value}) \times \left[\frac{n - (j - 1)}{n(n + 1)/2}\right]$$

The denominator in the equation is the sum of digits representing the years throughout the asset's useful life. The numerator is the number of years remaining in the asset's life at the beginning of the period under consideration.

The declining-balance method is also an accelerated depreciation method. Under this method, the depreciation expense for each period is determined by multiplying a fixed depreciation rate to the asset's book value. The fixed rate is some multiple of the straight-line rate. When it is twice the straight-line rate, the depreciation is called the *double-declining-balance* method. In that case:

$$\text{Annual depreciation} = \text{Book value} \times \frac{2}{n}$$

$$= (\text{Cost} - \text{Accumulated depreciation}) \times \frac{2}{n}$$

The units-of-production method is used when an asset's service life can be better estimated in terms of output rather than years. This method is usually used for machinery and motor vehicles. Depreciation in a particular year will be:

$$\frac{\text{Annual}}{\text{depreciation}} = \frac{\text{Cost} - \text{Estimated residual value}}{\text{Estimated units of productive output}} \times \frac{\text{Units produced}}{\text{in that year}}$$

The choice of a depreciation method depends on company policy and how accurately the method reflects the physical depreciation of an asset. The government usually only allows certain depreciation methods to charge out depreciation expenses for income tax purposes. The straight-line method without residual value is normally prescribed and different assets are assigned different life spans in the computation. Companies, however, may still choose whatever methods of depreciation in their accounts for their own use. However, these accounts usually have to be adjusted in the computation of income tax. In any case, accelerated depreciation does not mean that tax is avoided. It just defers tax payment as depreciation expenses are charged out early but eventually there will be less expenses to offset against profit in later years. It does encourage investment in fixed asset as the cost of purchase is in effect reduced by tax relief expeditiously.

The Worksheet

The adjustments discussed earlier can be quite tedious so that mistakes may be made and some adjustments may be overlooked. A worksheet is therefore employed to present a clear overall picture of ledger accounts and all necessary adjustments. It is a large columnar paper on which the ledger accounts are listed, adjusted, balanced and arranged in the general form of financial statements. Modern-day spreadsheet computer programs lend themselves readily to the formulation of an accounting worksheet. As a matter of fact, one of the first commercial applications of microcomputers was in this area.

Using the data of examples 3.1 and 3.2, the worksheet of example 3.3 is obtained. The following points on the worksheet should be noted:

1. It is a ten-columnar worksheet because there are ten columns of figures. In practice, the two columns of adjusted trial balance may be omitted. The resulting worksheet will then be an eight-columnar worksheet.
2. The 'Adjusted trial balance' columns are the results of merging the 'Trial balance' and 'Adjustment' columns to show the resulting net debit and credit balances under the respective accounts. The 'Income statement' columns are make up of all accounts under the revenue and expense categories. The remaining four major groups of accounts in the accounting equation, i.e., assets, liabilities, capital and withdrawals, are grouped under the 'Balance sheet' columns.
3. The trial-balance, adjustment and adjusted-trial-balance columns all have debit totals equal to credit totals. The income statement columns, however will either have a debit or credit balance. In this example, the credit balance of $2,341 represents the operating profit in that period. The debit entry of $2,341 under the income-statement column and the corresponding credit entry under the balance-sheet column effectively transfer this profit figure to the balance-sheet column. Since all the accounts in the accounting equation are included in the income-statement and balance-sheet columns, equality of debit and credit total in the income-statement columns (i.e., $6,060) automatically implies that the debit total and credit total under the balance-sheet columns will be equal.

4. There are usually opening balances for accumulated depreciation accounts and retained earnings account. No opening figure is given in this example because there is no carrying down from the previous period as the company has just been set up.
5. A worksheet is not an account. It only serves as a working paper for review and adjustment of accounts before the relevant data are properly recorded into the general journal. This step may be omitted if it is deemed unnecessary.

Example 3.3

Ledger accounts	Trial balance Debit	Trial balance Credit	Adjustment Debit	Adjustment Credit	Adjusted trial balance Debit	Adjusted trial balance Credit	Income statement Debit	Income statement Credit	Balance sheet Debit	Balance sheet Credit
Cash	24,030				24,030				24,030	
Accounts receivable	7,890				7,890				7,890	
Office premises	51,000				51,000				51,000	
Accumulated depreciation: office		0		425		425				425
Office equipment	5,400				5,400				5,400	
Accumulated depreciation: office equipment		0		90		90				90
Office stationery	720			120	600				600	
Unexpired insurance	540			15	525				525	
Accounts payable		23,814				23,814				23,814
Loan payable		3,000				3,000				3,000
Unearned consulting fee		1,800	300			1,500				1,500
Capital		60,000				60,000				60,000
Retained earnings		0				0				0
Dividends	1,800				1,800				1,800	
Consulting fee earned		5,640		300		6,060		6,060		
				120						
Advertising expense	630				630		630			
Office salaries expense	2,100		180		2,280		2,280			
Utilities expense	144				144		144			
	94,254	94,254								

Example 3.3 (contd)

Ledger accounts	Trial balance		Adjustment		Adjusted trial balance		Income statement		Balance sheet	
	Debit	Credit	Debit	Credit	Debit	Credit	Debit	Credit	Debit	Credit
Insurance expense			15		15		15			
Office stationery expense			120		120		120			
Depreciation expense: office			425		425		425			
Depreciation expense: office equipment			90		90		90			
Interest expense			15		15		15			
Interest payable				15		15				15
Office salaries payable				180		180				180
Consulting fee receivable			120		120				120	
			1,265	1,265	95,084	95,084	3,719	6,060	91,365	89,024
Net income							2,341			2,341
							6,060	6,060	91,365	91,365

CHAPTER 3 TRIAL BALANCE AND ADJUSTMENT OF ACCOUNTS

Practice Problems

3.1 The following account balances of a company are listed in alphabetical order:

	$		$
Accounts payable	3,200	Loan payable	2,500
Accounts receivable	5,000	Owner's withdrawals	1,400
Advertising expense	500	Rent expense	3,000
Building	20,000	Repair expense	300
Capital	?	Salaries expense	5,000
Cash	1,800	Telephone expense	600
Consulting fee earned	16,000	Travel expense	1,200
Equipment	7,000	Unexpired insurance	400
Interest expense	200	Utilities expense	1,300

Determine the balance in the capital account and prepare a trial balance listing the accounts in a more logical order for the preparation of financial statements.

3.2 Refer to the data in problem 2.3 and take note that at the end of the period:

1. an inventory check showed that office stationery costing $50 has been used,
2. one month's rent expense has been incurred,
3. one month's insurance coverage has expired.

Open additional accounts and prepare general journal entries to record the necessary adjustments. Post the adjustment entries to all relevant accounts and prepare a trial balance using the results of problem 2.3.

3.3 A machine costing $85,000 has an estimated useful life of five years and an estimated residual value of $5,000. The total number of units that can be produced is 360,000 within the machine's useful life. Estimated production in the five years are:

Year 1	50,000 units
Year 2	75,000 units
Year 3	90,000 units
Year 4	80,000 units
Year 5	65,000 units

Calculate the annual depreciation of the machine based on the following methods:

1. straight-line method
2. units-of-production method
3. sum-of-the-years'-digits method
4. double-declining-balance method

3.4 A company is in the business of performing research and preparing financial analyses for business organisations and government agencies. Much of its work is done through a computer service centre for which payment is made on an hourly basis. The company adjusts and closes its accounts monthly. The account balances at the end of a month were as follows before adjustments were made:

	$
Cash	71,760
Research fees receivable	–
Prepaid office rent	28,800
Prepaid computer rental expense	42,960
Office supplies	4,200
Office equipment	25,200
Accumulated depreciation: office equipment	600
Loan payable	24,000
Accounts payable	8,760
Interest payable	–
Salaries payable	–
Unearned research fees	114,600
Capital	50,000
Retained earnings	33,820
Dividends	2,400
Research fees earned	16,200
Office salaries expense	5,040
Research salaries expense	58,320
Telephone expense	2,640
Travel expense	6,660
Office rent expense	–
Computer rental expense	–
Office supplies expense	–
Depreciation expense: office equipment	–
Interest expense	–

Other data are given as follows:

(a) The amount in the prepaid office rent account represented office rent for eight months paid in advance at the beginning of the month when the lease was renewed.
(b) During the month, 220 hours of computer time were used at a cost of $180 an hour.
(c) Office supplies on hand at the end of the month were determined by count to amount to $840.
(d) Office equipment was estimated to have a useful life of seven years from date of purchase.
(e) Accrued interest on loan payable amounted to $96 at the end of the month.
(f) Services to clients amounting to $76,440 performed during the month were chargeable against the unearned research fees account.
(g) Services to clients who had not made advance payments and had not been billed amounted to $35,280 at the end of the month.
(h) Salaries earned by research staff but not paid amounted to $5,160 at the last day of the month.

You are required to prepare a ten-column worksheet using the above data of the month.

Chapter 4

Closing of Accounts

Profitability is the sovereign criterion of the enterprise.

Peter Drucker

Recording Closing Entries

Three of the six major groups of accounts, i.e., revenue, expenses and withdrawals measure activities in a current accounting period. They must be closed (i.e., reset with zero balance) at the end of the period so that activities for the upcoming period can be properly accumulated and measured. The process is as follows:

(a) To close the revenue and expenses accounts so that they will start afresh in the next accounting period, their closing balances are transferred to a Profit and Loss account (P & L A/C) by debiting the revenue accounts and crediting the expense accounts.
(b) The resulting balance in the profit and loss account is the net income which will be transferred to a retained earnings account. The profit and loss account (which has been created solely as a temporary account to compute the net income for that period) will therefore be closed.
(c) The withdrawals (or dividends) account is also closed by transferring the balance to the retained earnings account which represents the accumulated undistributed profit kept by the company.

The following diagram illustrates this process more clearly. Account balances are shown as numbers without brackets around them. Figures in brackets represent double-entries transferring account balances to other accounts.

```
      Revenue              Expenses            Profit and loss
    (1) |   1             2  | (2)             (2) |   (1)
        |                    |                 (5) |    5
```

```
        Withdrawals         Retained earnings
          3 | (3)                      |   4
            |                      (3) |  (5)
            |                          |   6
```

The number 5 represents the credit balance in the profit and loss account which is eventually transferred to the retained earnings account. All the accounts have a zero opening balance for the next period except the retained earnings account which has a new credit balance represented by the number 6.

The following two points should be recognised by now:

1. Double-entry can be used to transfer a figure from one account to another. It is not just applicable for recording transactions posted from the general journal.
2. The worksheet in the previous chapter has already incorporated the account closing process with the profit and loss account represented by the income statement column. The net income has been transferred to the balance-sheet column where the retained earnings account and balance-sheet figures are incorporated.

The necessary entries for account closing are recorded in the general journal as shown in example 4.1.

Example 4.1

Date		Account titles and explanation	LP	Debit	Credit
July	31	Consulting fee earned		6,060	
		Profit and loss account			6,060
		(to close the revenue account)			

Date		Account titles and explanation	LP	Debit	Credit
July	31	Profit and loss account		3,719	
		Advertising expense			630
		Office salaries expense			2,280
		Utilities expense			144
		Insurance expense			15
		Office stationery expense			120
		Depreciation expense: office			425
		Depreciation expense: equipment			90
		Interest expense			15
		(to close the expense accounts)			
	31	Profit and loss account		2,341	
		Retained earnings			2,341
		(to close the profit and loss account)			
	31	Retained earnings		1,800	
		Dividends			1,800
		(to close the dividends account)			

Profit and Loss and Retained Earnings Accounts

After posting the closing entries from the general journal, the profit and loss and retained earnings accounts will be as shown in example 4.2.

Example 4.2

Profit and loss						Account no. 100	
Date		Explanation	Ref.	Dr	Cr	Balance	
						Dr	Cr
July	31	Closing consulting fee earned account			6,060		
	31	Closing expenses accounts:					
		Advertising expense		630			
		Office salaries expense		2,280			
		Utilities expense		144			
		Insurance expense		15			
		Office stationery expense		120			

Profit and loss						Account no. 100	
Date		Explanation	Ref.	Dr	Cr	Balance	
						Dr	Cr
July	31	Depreciation expense: office		425			
		Depreciation expense: equipment		90			
		Interest expense		15			2,341
	31	To retained earnings account		2,341			0

Retained earnings						Account no. 52	
Date		Explanation	Ref.	Dr	Cr	Balance	
						Dr	Cr
July	31	Balance b/d			0		
	31	Closing P & L A/C			2,341		
	31	Closing dividends A/C		1,800			541

A few abbreviations used in bookkeeping are introduced here:

Dr	debit
Cr	credit
P & L	profit and loss
A/C	account
b/d	brought down

The first entry in the retained earnings account showing the zero credit balance brought down is not necessary in this case but is included for illustrative purposes. The credit balance of $541 however will be carried down (or c/d) to the next period. If it has been an operating loss, it will result in a debit balance. It may also be carried down to the next period as a negative credit balance. Instead of a minus sign, bookkeepers normally put a bracket around a figure to indicate it is negative.

Post-closing Trial Balance

After the account-closing procedure has been completed, a post-closing trial balance is necessary to confirm that all records have been entered properly to prepare the ledger accounts for the next accounting period. Since accounts under the revenue, expenses and withdrawals categories have already been closed (i.e., having zero balance), only the remaining three major groups of accounts (i.e., assets, liabilities and capital) are expected in the trial balance.

All the account balances (with the exception of the retained earnings account) should be identical to what appear in the balance-sheet columns of the worksheet.

The post-closing trial balance of our working example is shown in example 4.3.

Example 4.3

A/C no.	Account title	Dr	Cr
1	Cash	24,030	
2	Accounts receivable	7,890	
20	Office premises	51,000	
22	Accumulated depreciation: office		425
25	Office equipment	5,400	
26	Accumulated depreciation: equipment		90
27	Office stationery	600	
24	Unexpired insurance	525	
30	Accounts payable		23,814
40	Loan payable		3,000
35	Unearned consulting fee		1,500
50	Capital		60,000
31	Interest payable		15
32	Office salaries payable		180
3	Consulting fee receivable	120	
52	Retained earnings		541
		89,565	89,565

Practice Problems

4.1 The following T-accounts belong to a service company at the end of an accounting period:

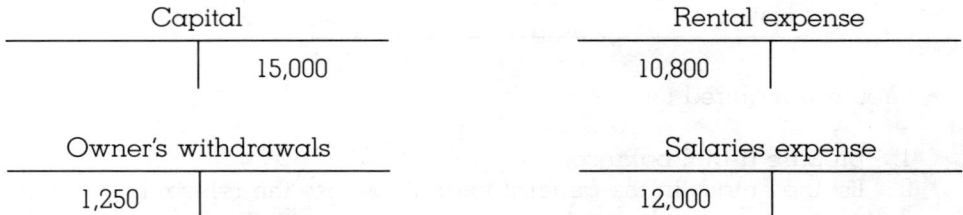

CHAPTER 4 CLOSING OF ACCOUNTS

Service fee earned		Insurance expense	
	35,000	800	

Depreciation expense	
1,500	

Set up the profit and loss and retained earnings accounts and perform the necessary entries to complete the accounting cycle. Label every double entry with a number.

4.2 The accounts of a company at the end of a period after making the necessary adjustments are:

	$
Accounts receivable	15,200
Motor vehicles	10,700
Accumulated depreciation: motor vehicles	2,200
Equipment	36,400
Accumulated depreciation: equipment	6,700
Depreciation expense: motor vehicles	1,100
Depreciation expense: equipment	3,600
Office salaries expense	8,200
Sales salaries expense	21,450
Legal expense	2,500
Service fee earned	69,510
Rent expense	6,000
Owner's withdrawal	8,000
Office stationery expense	1,000
Advertising expense	3,500
Accounts payable	12,715
Utilities expense	3,380
Travel expense	4,940
Capital	50,000
Telephone expense	2,890
Insurance expense	1,320
Cash	10,945

You are required to:

1. prepare a trial balance,
2. list the entries in the general journal to close the relevant accounts,
3. prepare a post-closing trial balance.

PART TWO

FINANCIAL REPORTS AND SPECIFIC ISSUES

Chapter 5

Presentation of Financial Statements

The executive of the future will be rated by his ability to anticipate his problems rather than to meet them as they come.

Howard Coonley

While the recording of business transactions in the general journal and the posting to ledger accounts are done by bookkeepers, adjusting and closing accounts are usually the jobs of an accountant. One of the most important tasks of the accountant, however, is to summarise all the information and to present in an accurate but concise manner the financial position of a company in financial statements. These statements are not part of the accounts but are vital to management decision making and for the discharge of disclosure obligation to external parties.

Profit and Loss Statement

This statement is also called the income statement. It provides information about the profitability of the operation of a company in a certain period. The operating results of a business are summarised by matching the revenue earned during a given time period with the expenses incurred in obtaining that revenue. It is an orderly presentation of the figures contained in the profit and loss account in an easy-to-understand format. All these data are also obtainable from the income statement column of the worksheet.

There are differences in style of presentation especially for large corporations with multiple sources of income and expenditure. A typical format using data developed so far is shown in example 5.1.

Although the profit and loss statement attempts to present the operating profit of a company as accurately as possible, it does not reflect gain not evidenced by accounting transactions. This includes the value of relationships built up with the clients and the improved image of the company and so on. Errors may also be introduced in determining the amount of depreciation of fixed assets since the depreciation method chosen may not realistically reflect the rate of physical deterioration and changes in market price. Finally, the valuation of closing inventory in order to determine the cost of goods used in that period is at best an estimate based on the method selected.

Example 5.1

Profit and Loss Statement for the Period June–July

	$	$
Income:		
Consulting fee earned		6,060
Expenditure:		
Office salaries	2,280	
Utilities	144	
Insurance	15	
Office stationery	120	
Depreciation: office premises	425	
Depreciation: office equipment	90	
Advertising	630	
Interest	15	
		3,719
Net income		2,341

Statement of Retained Earnings

This is sometimes called statement of owner's capital. It can be directly derived from the retained earnings account after the accounting cycle is completed. Retained earnings is that portion of the owner's equity created by earning and retaining the net income. The statement of retained earnings covers the same time period as the associated profit and loss statement. It shows the sources of increase and decrease in retained earnings for that specific period and what the total owner's equity is composed of. The statement of retained earnings in our example is as shown in example 5.2.

One of the items which normally appears in the retained earnings statement but which is not shown in this example is income tax which a company has to pay to the government on the net income earned. It is treated as 'dividends' to the government rather than an expense item since income tax is not incurred when the company is making a loss. Dividends and income tax are subtracted from the accumulated retained earnings to give the new figure to be carried forward to the next period.

PART TWO FINANCIAL REPORTS AND SPECIFIC ISSUES

Example 5.2

Statement of Retained Earnings for June–July

	$
Retained earnings, 1 June	0
Net income for June–July	2,341
	2,341
less: dividends	1,800
Retained earnings, 31 July	541

Balance Sheet

The balance sheet reports the amount of assets, liabilities and owner's equity of the business entity *at the account-closing day*. It is actually a statement of the accounting equation. Data for the balance sheet can be readily obtained from the balance-sheet columns in the worksheet (except the retained earnings figure which has to be computed separately) or the post-closing trial balance.

A balance sheet is different in nature compared to a profit and loss statement and a statement of retained earnings. It shows the current financial status of the company at a particular date rather than reporting the activities and changes in a certain period. As all values reported are taken at the time assets were acquired and liabilities and owner's equity took place, errors are inherent unless there has been no inflation in the economy. This was a cause of major concern in the high-inflation era of the 1970s.

To a lesser extent, inflation also affects the accuracy of the profit and loss account as the depreciation expense which is based on historical asset values may not be realistic at a current time. Accountants have developed systems for inflation accounting to reflect the effect of price changes but so far these only serve to provide supplementary information to the conventional account statements and are usually not compulsory. This will be discussed further in the next section.

The balance sheet for the example we are working on is shown in example 5.3.

Note that financial statements are reports only, so the convention of debit and credit for the left and right columns is no longer applicable. The figures in separate columns therefore should not be interpreted as such.

Example 5.3

Balance Sheet, 31 July

ASSETS

	$	$
Fixed assets:		
Office premises	51,000	
less: accumulated depreciation	425	
		50,575
Office equipment	5,400	
less: accumulated depreciation	90	
		5,310
Current assets:		
Cash		24,030
Accounts receivable		7,890
Consulting fee receivable		120
Unexpired insurance		525
Office stationery		600
		89,050

LIABILITIES AND OWNER'S EQUITY

	$	$
Liabilities:		
Accounts payable		23,814
Interest payable		15
Office salaries payable		180
Unearned consulting fee		1,500
Loan payable		3,000
		28,509
Owner's equity:		
Capital	60,000	
Retained earnings	541	
		60,541
		89,050

Generally Accepted Accounting Principles

While the primary responsibility of an accountant is to communicate with internal management and interested third parties on the financial performance of a company, there has long been criticism that the means of performing this task by using financial statements prepared by the accountant is far from satisfactory.

In order to ensure uniformity, consistency and prevent deliberate distortion of facts in account statements, accountants have long been establishing a set of fundamental principles which are now generally accepted. Although accounting bodies of different countries publish these principles in the names of their own country standards, they are quite international and can be summarised essentially as follows:

1. **The business entity concept.** The business entity for which the accounting information is prepared and used must be clearly identified. As a general rule, any legal or economic unit which controls economic resources and is accountable for those resources is an accounting entity. For accounting purposes, every business is conceived to be and is treated as a separate entity, separate and distinct from its owners and from every other business.

2. **The going-concern assumption.** It is assumed that a business entity will continue in operation for a period of time sufficient to carry out its existing commitments. Thus the going concern assumption justifies ignoring immediate liquidating values (or market values) in presenting assets and liabilities in the balance sheet since these are not going to be realised in cash immediately.

3. **The time-period principle.** The concept of periodicity refers to the fact that accounting information, by its very nature, involves reporting activities over a relatively short period of time. The data may only be informed estimates as the true worth of some assets and amount of liabilities are unlikely to remain as what have been recorded.

4. **The monetary principle.** Money is used as the basic measuring unit for financial reporting. An implicit assumption made is that the account is only as accurate as the dollar is a stable unit of value. Intangible assets such as the goodwill of the company is also not measured.

5. **The objectivity principle.** This principle means that accounts figures should be unbiased and subject to verification by independent experts. Arising from this are the following principles of valuation:

   (a) *Cost principle of asset valuation.* Assets are initially recorded in accounts at cost and no adjustment is normally made to this valuation in later periods except to allocate a portion of the original cost as an expense as assets depreciate. Such a basis of presentation may result in undue distortion of the account statements in periods of high inflation. Accountants have developed two methods to take into consideration the effects of changing prices:

- *Constant dollar accounting* whereby all historical cost figures are adjusted by a set of price indices to the current year dollar values.
- *Current cost accounting* whereby all historical cost amounts are restated and reported at their current cost based on current replacement values.

Neither of the two systems replaces the historical cost method. They are only used sometimes to provide supplementary information for the normal historical cost account statements.

(b) *The realisation principle of measuring revenue.* According to this principle, revenue is only recognised at the time of sale of goods or the rendering of services. It does not, however, require that cash must be received before revenue is recognised.

(c) *The matching principle of measuring revenue.* Under this principle, costs are matched with revenue such that costs are related to the product sold or services rendered. Similarly, costs are related to the time period during which revenue is earned. This concept is fundamental to the accrual basis of accounting.

(d) *The consistency principle.* The consistency principle implies that a particular accounting method, once adopted, will not be changed from period to period. It does not prohibit a company from changing from one to another acceptable method if this will better reflect the company's activity, but it does prohibit frequent or opportunistic changes.

(e) *The disclosure principle.* Adequate disclosure means that all material and relevant facts concerning the financial position and the results of operation are communicated to users of financial statements. Information need not be presented in great detail but no important fact should be withheld. The accounting policies and accounting methods used as well as any changes the company is making have to be disclosed in notes accompanying financial statements.

(f) *Concept of materiality.* An item is material if there is a reasonable expectation that knowledge of it would influence the decisions of prudent users of financial statements. The extent of importance or significance of a certain item of accounting information is considered in relation to other items of information. Recording procedure and setting up of new accounts are influenced by the concept of materiality.

(g) *Concept of conservatism.* When some doubt exists about the valuation of an asset or the realisation of gain, accountants traditionally select the accounting option which produces a lower net income for the current period and a less favourable financial position.

Practice Problems

5.1 Prepare the financial statements based on the worksheet derived in problem 3.4 in Chapter 3.

5.2 Prepare the financial statements based on the given data and the solutions of problem 4.2 in Chapter 4

5.3 A repair workshop has the following cash receipt and payment records for its first year of operation:

	Receipts, $	Payments, $
Investment in business	15,000	
Equipment		9,000
Materials purchased		4,200
Rent		2,600
Insurance premium		600
Advertising expense		400
Utilities expense		700
Employees' salaries		6,500
Withdrawals by owner		20,000
Revenue collected	41,000	
	56,000	44,000
Cash balance		12,000
	56,000	56,000

The following additional information is given:

1. The supplier of materials is still owed $800.
2. Materials costing $500 are still unused.
3. Shop rent is at $200 per month. Two months' rent was paid at the time the lease agreement was signed and subsequently $200 was paid every month.
4. Insurance was taken out at the beginning of the business. The premium paid covers three years with the first year premium at $250.
5. Unpaid salaries of $100 are still owed to an employee.
6. Customers still owe the shop $300 for repair services they have received.
7. Equipment has an estimated life of ten years with no salvage value. Its value is assumed to decline linearly.

You are required to prepare an income statement on *accrual basis* and a balance sheet for the shop.

Chapter 6

Accounts of Merchandising Firms

The secret of business is to know something that nobody else knows.

Aristotle Onassis

Merchandising firms, or trading companies derive their income from purchasing goods and then selling them at a higher price. The nature of operation of this type of company involves a lot more transactions compared to that of service companies which have been used as examples so far. Although the basic accounting system is the same, the use of special journals including the analytical cash book have been developed to facilitate efficient recording of sales and purchases. Subsidiary ledgers are also required to record information on debtors and creditors.

Special Journals and Analytical Cash Book

The frequency of transactions in a trading company makes the use of a single general journal for all the recording impractical. Special journals are therefore required to enter information on frequently occurring transactions like sales, purchases, cash receipt and cash payment. Instead of a single general journal, the complete journal of a trading firm usually comprises the items listed in Table 6.1.

The cash receipts journal and cash payment journal are usually combined to form an Analytical Cash Book with the left page for cash receipts journal and the right page for cash payment journal. The pages are divided into columns so that recording under different column headings correspond to cash transactions of a different nature.

Sample layout of a sales journal and a cash receipts journal are shown in example 6.1. The formats for purchases journal and cash payment journal are similar.

Table 6.1 Special journals

	Journal	Use	Corresponding double entry
1.	Sales journal	Record sale of goods made on credit	Debit: Accounts receivable A/C Credit: Sales A/C
2.	Purchases journal	Record purchases of goods and other items made on credit	Debit: Purchases A/C Credit: Accounts payable A/C
3.	Cash receipts journal	Record all collection of cash	Debit: Cash A/C Credit: Sales, accounts receivable, capital, loan payable, etc.
4.	Cash payment journal	Record all payment of cash	Debit: Purchases, account payable, expenses, dividends, etc. Credit: Cash A/C
5.	General journal	Record all transactions that will not be accommodated by the other journals, adjustment entries, etc.	–

Example 6.1

SALES JOURNAL

Date	Account debited	Invoice no.	Ref.	Amount
	XYZ Co.	123		500

CASH RECEIPTS JOURNAL

Date	Account credited	Description	Ref.	General ledger (credit)	Accounts receivable (credit)	Sales (credit)	Sales discount (debit)	Cash (debit)
	Capital	Issue share		60,000				60,000
	Loan	90 days at 6%		3,000				3,000
	Sales	Cash sales				1,200	100	1,100
	ABC Co.	Collection			400			400

The columns 'Accounts receivable' and 'Sales' in the cash receipt journal record the credit entries for cash received from debtors and cash sales respectively. These two types of cash transactions are most frequent in a trading firm. The 'Sales discount' column records the discount given to customers, in this case, is mainly for payment in cash (or cash discount). The sales discount account (to which this column total is to be posted) is a contra account to the sales account. In effect it will lower the total sales figure eventually.

Although more columns can be created to accommodate accounts involved in other types of cash receipt transactions, their creation is not justified as they will not be used frequently. Other accounts to be credited are all contained in the ledger so that a 'General ledger' column will suffice for recording purposes.

Note that a journal is just for recording transaction information from a source document and is not an account itself. Note, therefore, that in example 6.1 the order of arrangement of the columns need not follow the rule of debit/credit positions.

It is obvious by now that creating special journals give rise to the following advantages:

1. A special journal is a separate document so that the division of labour and parallel processing by different persons are both possible.
2. Every column of a special journal can be added at the end of a period and only the total figures will be posted to the corresponding accounts rather than posting every transaction regularly.
3. It is much easier to check for mistakes since different types of frequent transaction are segregated during recording

Subsidiary Ledgers

It is not practical to maintain the complete accounts receivable and accounts payable accounts of a trading company in the general ledger. This is due to the normally large number of debtors and creditors as well as the high frequency of transactions in a trading firm. Keeping the necessary details on each debtor and creditor also makes these accounts voluminous and they must therefore be separately filed.

Usually, the general ledger (G/L) of a trading company still necessarily contains all the accounts including the accounts receivable and accounts payable accounts. However, only the total figures for a control period (usually one month) will be entered in these *control accounts*. Detailed and up to date information on individual debtors and creditors are recorded in an *accounts receivable subsidiary ledger* and an *accounts payable subsidiary ledger*. These are actually collections of records detailing the breakdown of the accounts receivable and accounts payable control accounts in the general ledger. An example of a record in an accounts receivable subsidiary ledger is shown in example 6.2.

Example 6.2

Name: XYZ Co.					Credit limit: $1,000	
Address: Tel:					Credit period: 30 days	
Date	Description	Ref.	Dr	Cr	Balance	
					Dr	Cr
June 4	Sales invoice no. 0001	S3	500		500	
July 2	Payment receipt no. 0031	R1		500		0

Posting of Special Journals

The total amounts of various columns corresponding to different special journals are normally posted to the respective accounts in the general ledger at the end of every control period. However, the accounts receivable subsidiary ledger and the accounts payable subsidiary ledger must be updated as soon as possible (say daily) by information recorded in the special journals. This is necessary in order to have effective credit control on customers and also ensure that credit periods and credit limits are not exceeded in paying the company's own suppliers.

Posting from the sales journal can be summarised as follows:

Debit	Credit
Immediately and individual amount: Accounts receivable subsidiary ledger *Monthly* and total amount: Accounts receivable account in general ledger	*Monthly* and total amount: Sales account in general ledger

Similarly, posting from the cash receipts journal is as follows:

Debit	Credit
Monthly and total amount: Cash account in general ledger Sales discount account in general ledger	*Immediately* and individual amount: Accounts receivable subsidiary ledger *Monthly* and total amounts: Sales account in general ledger Accounts receivable account in general ledger Various general ledger accounts

Posting from the cash payment journal follows the same principle of updating the two subsidiary ledgers immediately while control accounts in the general ledger usually have the total figures posted at the end of a control period. In a modern computerised system, recording in subsidiary ledgers is simply achieved by online data entry which updates the subsidiary ledger data files instantly. A house keeping program is executed at the end of every month to update all general ledger files and reinitialise all data entry files.

The Treatment of Opening and Closing Stock

Merchandising firms usually operate a *periodic inventory* system. This means that the stock or inventory account in the general ledger is only updated at the end of an accounting period by a physical stock count. Although the actual level of stock is constantly changing throughout an accounting period, this is not reflected in the inventory account. This is because the sale of goods is recorded in the sales journal (for credit sales), accounts receivable subsidiary ledger (for credit sales), and cash receipts journal (for cash sales). The inventory account is never updated even though sales have resulted in lower inventory level. Similarly, the purchase of goods only involves debiting the purchase journal and crediting the accounts payable subsidiary ledger for purchase on credit. Cash purchases are entered into the cash payment journal. Neither form of recording involves the inventory account. A physical stock check at the end of an accounting period will ascertain the amount of inventory left. In theory the closing stock figure is arrived at as follows:

Closing stock = (Opening stock + Purchase) − Amount of goods sold

Put in another way, the cost of goods sold in that period is:

Cost of goods sold = (Opening stock + Purchase) − Closing stock

The excess of revenue over cost of goods sold is the *gross profit* of that period. Net profit is obtained by subtracting all the expenses from gross profit. This is how it would appear in the format of the profit and loss account:

P & L account

Expenses (except purchases)	Revenue
Inventory (opening) Purchases	Inventory (closing)
	Credit balance (profit)

The three items enclosed in the box give a net debit amount equal to the cost of goods sold. Thus, the opening inventory figure has to be transferred from the inventory account to the P & L account. At the same time, the inventory account has to be updated to the new amount of closing stock. Thus, it should be debited with the closing inventory while the corresponding credit entry is in the P & L account as shown earlier.

The treatment of opening and closing stock at the end of the accounting period as recorded in the general journal is typically as shown in example 6.3.

Example 6.3

Date	Description	Ref.	Debit	Credit
31 July	P & L account		30,000	
	Inventory			30,000
	(To remove the opening inventory)			
31 July	Inventory		34,000	
	P & L account			34,000
	(To set up the closing inventory)			

Opening and closing inventories are dealt with in the worksheet as shown in example 6.4. For clarity, other figures are ignored in the example.

Example 6.4

Accounts	Trial balance		Adjustments		Income statement		Balance sheet	
	Dr	Cr	Dr	Cr	Dr	Cr	Dr	Cr
⋮								
Inventory (1 June)	30,000				30,000			
⋮								
Purchase	128,000				128,000			
⋮								
Inventory (31 July)						34,000	34,000	
					231,000	251,000	152,000	132,000
Net income					20,000			20,000
					251,000	251,000	152,000	152,000

It can be seen from the equation on cost of goods sold that the lower the closing stock, the higher will be the cost of goods sold and therefore the lower will be the profit in any period. The reverse is true so that higher closing stock will result in a higher profit figure. The accountant can therefore apparently alter the profit reported by simply adjusting the closing inventory. This, however, is hampered by the fact that the consistency principle disallows frequent changes in the method of stock evaluation as this will distort the reported profit figure. Further, lower closing stock will result in lower opening stock for the next period. Thus, the effect of lower profit for this period will mean lower cost of goods sold and consequently a higher profit figure for the next period. Using stock evaluation to lower reported profit may be a means of deferring taxation but it is never an effective way to avoid tax.

The nature, justification and effect of any change in cost assignment method must be disclosed by notes accompanying the account statements under the disclosure principle. Basically, four methods are used to evaluate inventory cost flow:

1. Specific invoice price method (or specific identification method). This method assigns costs to goods sold and ending inventory according to the actual cost of purchase of each and every item. It is not practical for companies that sell a large number of identical goods and is therefore seldom used.

2. First-in, first-out (FIFO) method. Under this FIFO method, the cost of the last items received are assigned to the ending inventory. Costs pertaining to the earliest purchase are assigned to the cost of goods sold. Thus the technique of assigning costs to the ending inventory is to work backward on the layers of cost that constitute the cost of goods available for sale in that period.

3. Last-in, first-out (LIFO) method. In the LIFO method, cost of goods sold is assigned cost pertaining to the most recent purchases while ending inventory constitutes assigned costs from the beginning inventory and the earliest purchases. The closing inventory is therefore assumed to be made up from the goods at the start of the period in progressive layers starting from the beginning.

4. Weighted average method. The weighted average cost is determined by dividing the total cost of goods available for sale (i.e., opening inventory plus purchases) by the total number of units available for sale in a specific period. It is a 'weighted' figure because the unit price of a particular purchase will have stronger influence if the volume of that purchase is large compared to the rest. The closing inventory and cost of goods sold are obtained by multiplying their quantities both by the weighted average unit cost.

The weighted average and FIFO methods are commonly used. The weighted average method tends to dampen the effects of changing prices so that profit figures will not be overly affected by fluctuating prices of purchase.

The FIFO method follows the usual pattern of flow of goods in many businesses since most companies try to sell the older goods first. In times of rapidly rising prices the FIFO method will result in higher profit since older stock prices are used in computing the cost of goods sold but current replacement costs are already much higher. The LIFO method, on the other hand, will generally produce a higher cost of goods sold and, thus, lower net income if price levels are rising. The lower ending inventory based on the oldest price, however, does not relate meaningfully to the current replacement cost of closing inventory. The balance sheet figure of inventory is, therefore, distorted.

The Perpetual Inventory System

This system updates the inventory account after each purchase and each sale so that it shows the current amount of inventory on hand whenever all of the entries have been posted. Usually a *subsidiary inventory ledger* (or stock ledger) is kept with detailed records of individual inventory items. This subsidiary ledger is updated immediately when a transaction is recorded. A separate inventory account in the general ledger will be updated only at the end of a control period (usually a month) by the total figures of the subsidiary inventory ledger. The mechanism is the same as that for other subsidiary ledgers. The inventory account in the general ledger is therefore merely a control account.

The account entries in a perpetual inventory system are typically as follows in a general journal recording:

Date		Account titles and explanation	LP	Debit	Credit
June	10	Inventory		200	
		Accounts payable			200
		(Purchase goods on credit)			
June	20	Cash		50	
		Sales			50
		Cost of goods sold		40	
		Inventory			40
		(Cash sales of goods costing $40 for $50)			
July	31	P & L account		40	
		Cost of goods sold			40
		Sales		50	
		P & L account			50
		(Closing entries for sales and cost of goods sold accounts)			

CHAPTER 6 ACCOUNTS OF MERCHANDISING FIRMS

The preceding table is purely illustrative as the inventory subsidiary ledger and the accounts payable subsidiary ledger are usually updated, not the control accounts in the general ledger. Also, cash sales will result in entries in the cash receipts journal. However, the principles involved clearly show:

1. Inventory figures are kept up to date perpetually.
2. Two double entries are required to record a sale. A cost of goods sold account has to be debited every time a sale is made in addition to the normal entry for the sales account. This cost of goods sold account has to be closed to the P & L account at the end of an accounting period.

More and more companies are now switching to a perpetual inventory system with the use of a computerised accounting system. Management can then monitor the status of inventory on hand on a regular basis. Inventory control and planning for future purchase can be improved tremendously. Like the periodic inventory system, a physical stock check is still required at the end of an accounting period to ascertain the closing inventory figures. Financial statements for intermediate periods, however, can now be prepared with much more reliability since inventory figures are being constantly monitored.

The Income Statement

The income statement for a merchandising firm must clearly show the cost of goods sold. A typical format of such a statement is shown in example 6.5.

Example 6.5

Income Statement		
	$	$
Sales		215,000
Cost of goods sold:		
Opening stock (1 June)	30,000	
Purchase of goods	128,000	
Cost of goods available for sale	158,000	
less: closing stock (31 July)	34,000	
		124,000
Gross profit of sales		91,000
Operating expenses:		
Advertising	14,000	
Salaries	38,000	
Utilities	1,100	

Interest	1,900
Depreciation	4,000

	59,000
Net income before income tax	32,000

Practice Problems

6.1 The following are selected transactions of a merchandising firm in a month:

August 2 Sold merchandise to A on credit for $600, invoice no. 801.
        3 Borrowed $6,000 from Bank B to be repaid together with interest in 30 days.
        5 Received $250 from C representing the balance due from a sale made in July without discount.
      10 Sold merchandise to D for $960, invoice no. 802.
      14 Received payment from A pertaining to invoice no. 801.
      15 Cash sales for the first 15 days amounted to $910 with $50 discount given.
      17 Sold merchandise to E for $970, invoice no. 803.
      18 Received payment from D pertaining to invoice no. 802.
      20 Sold surplus equipment costing $10,000 for that amount in cash. (A fixed asset sales account has been kept in the general journal to record such sales.)
      22 Received $460 from F representing the balance due from a sale made in June.
      31 Cash sales for the second half of August totalled $790 with $40 discount given.

You are required to record the above transactions in a cash receipts journal and a sales journal using the formats suggested in example 6.1. Finally, show how the month-end totals are posted to the general ledger by indicating the entries in the relevant T-accounts.

6.2 Fill in the missing amount in the following eight rows representing the performance of a merchandising firm in different periods:

	Sales	Opening inventory	Purchase	Ending inventory	Cost of goods sold	Gross profit	Expenses	Net income or losses
	$	$	$	$	$	$	$	$
1.	160,000	60,000	95,000	_____	105,000	_____	70,000	_____
2.	_____	115,000	220,000	130,000	_____	140,000	_____	50,000

3.	150,000	50,000		30,000		85,000	45,000	40,000
4.	80,000		50,000	35,000		30,000		10,000
5.	110,000	80,000	70,000		95,000		50,000	
6.		75,000	110,000	60,000		100,000	40,000	
7.	185,000	65,000		75,000	80,000		55,000	50,000
8.	50,000	15,000		25,000	30,000			5,000

6.3 A successful small merchandising corporation uses the periodic inventory system. The following trial balance was prepared from the ledger at the end of an accounting period:

	$	$
Cash	12,800	
Accounts receivable	54,400	
Opening inventory	115,200	
Office stationery	4,544	
Unexpired fire insurance	1,728	
Land	64,000	
Buildings	160,000	
Equipment	38,400	
Accounts payable		90,592
Share capital		100,000
Retained earnings		172,000
Dividends	24,000	
Sales		624,800
Sales returns and discount	12,800	
Purchases	371,200	
Purchase returns and discount		9,088
Transportation-in (transportation cost of goods purchased)	15,424	
Selling commissions expense	20,016	
Delivery expense	5,600	
Salaries and wages expense	94,768	
Property taxes expense	1,600	
	$996,480	$996,480

A physical inventory was taken at the end of the period which showed that merchandise on hand amounted to $92,800. Other data given are:

(a) Property taxes accrued but not yet recorded, $2,880.
(b) A physical count showed office stationery remaining amounted to $1,344.

(c) The cost of fire insurance which had expired during the period was $896.
(d) Depreciation rates: 4% on buildings and 10% on equipment.
(e) Income tax for the period was determined to be $22,000.

You are required to prepare an eight-column worksheet (omitting the columns for adjusted trial balance) and, hence, derive the financial statements of the company.

6.4 The abridged balance sheets of a merchandising firm in two consecutive years are as follows:

	Year 2 $	Year 1 $
Cash	8,100	2,500
Accounts receivable	7,300	6,200
Closing inventory	28,500	30,400
Equipment (net after depreciation)	20,600	24,800
Total assets	64,500	63,900
Accounts payable	8,200	9,300
Accrued salaries payable	500	300
Capital	55,800	54,300
Total liabilities and owner's equity	64,500	63,900

Cash receipts and disbursements in year 2 are:

	$	$
Collection of accounts receivable	268,400	
Payment for:		
Accounts payable		166,200
Employees' salaries		48,100
Other operating expenses		18,500
Owner's withdrawals		30,000

The company made all purchases and sales on credit. You are required to:

1. determine the sales, purchases and salaries expenses in year 2 on an accrual basis,
2. prepare the income statement of the company in year 2.

Chapter 7

Statement of Sources and Application of Funds

If all sources of capital investment are dried up, the flow of all income may eventually cease.

Andrew Mellon

Working Capital

A profitable business may not be a viable business if the amount of cash in the company is insufficient to meet the daily demand to discharge current liabilities. The company must be able to pay all current creditors regularly. If payment is overdue for too long, creditors will lose their confidence on the ability of the company to pay its debt and consequently may institute legal actions against the company. A domino effect will result which may eventually lead to the closure of the firm.

The accountant considers all assets which are easily and regularly converted to cash in the daily operation of the firm as *current assets*. These are the resources which are expected to be used to meet the *current liabilities* of the firm during the *operating cycle*.

An operating cycle (or business cycle) is the average time period between the purchase of merchandise and the conversion of this merchandise back into cash. In a broader sense, it is the time to complete a normal cycle of activities in a company. Current assets are, therefore, those assets which are convertible to cash within a business cycle. The following is a list of current assets in descending order in terms of ease of conversion into cash:

1. Cash
2. Marketable securities (shares of public companies)
3. Accounts receivable (debtors)
4. Merchandise inventory
5. Prepayment (prepaid expenses)

Current liabilities, on the other hand are obligations that must be met within an operating cycle. It is a measure of the portion of a firm's total assets in which short-term creditors have an interest or equity. The following are typical current liabilities of a firm:

1. Accounts payable (trade creditors)
2. Expenses payable
3. Taxes payable
4. Short-term loan
5. Currently maturing portions of long-term obligation

Since not all current assets are immediately convertible to cash, they should be more than current liabilities in order to ensure that a sufficient safety margin is available to meet all current obligations at short notice. Consequently, the term *working capital* is defined as follows:

$$\text{Working capital} = \text{Current assets} - \text{Current liabilities}$$

It is a measure of the net amount of current assets at the disposal of a company. Working capital is also simply called *funds*. Another related term is *current ratio* which is defined as:

$$\text{Current ratio} = \frac{\text{Current assets}}{\text{Current liabilities}}$$

Current ratio is a measure of short-term solvency of a firm, that is, its ability to pay its debt to short-term creditors. Usually it has a value greater than two. This concept is discussed further in Chapter 13 on financial ratios.

Flow of Funds

Current assets and current liabilities are usually separated from long-term assets and liabilities in the balance sheet statement.

Let CA = current assets
     CL = current liabilities
     NCA = non-current assets (long-term or fixed assets)
     NCL = non-current liabilities (long-term liabilities)
     OE = owner's equity

The accounting equation can be written as follows:

$$(CA + NCA) = (CL + NCL) + OE$$

or

$$(CA - CL) = NCL + OE - NCA$$

i.e. Working capital
   = Non-current liabilities + Owner's equity − Non-current assets

This formula is an alternative definition of working capital. The same equation can also be written with all positive terms as follows:

Working capital + Fixed assets = Long-term liabilities + Owner's equity

The diagrammatic representation of this equation is shown in Figure 7.1. The double vertical line is for demarcation of terms on different sides of the last equation. It can be readily seen that working capital can be increased at the expense of fixed assets. The reverse is true with working capital reduced by converting it to fixed assets. The sources and uses of working capital are indicated in the diagram also for changes involving long-term liabilities and owner's equity. Since these two items are on the other side of the equation, any increase/decrease will be matched by exactly the same increase/decrease in working capital.

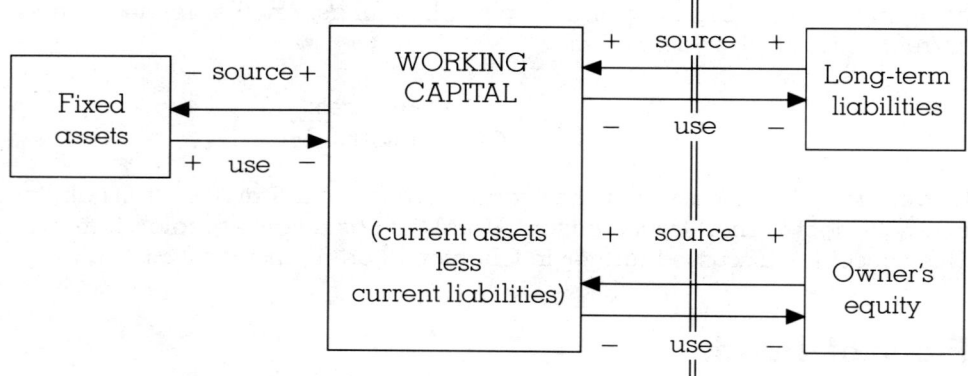

Figure 7.1

Another way to look at the causes and effects of changes in working capital is by analysing the alternative definition of working capital derived at the beginning of this section. It can be written in the format of incremental terms as follows:

$$\Delta(CA - CL) = \Delta NCL + \Delta OE - \Delta NCA$$
$$= \Delta NCL + \Delta OE + (-\Delta NCA)$$

The incremental operators in the equation may be interpreted as causing an increase in the terms. Thus, increase in working capital equals to increase in long-term liabilities plus increase in owner's equity and reduction in fixed assets. The equation naturally also holds true if the incremental operator is interpreted as resulting in a reduction of the terms operated upon.

The diagram and the incremental equation both demonstrate that working capital may be changed in many different ways. Accountants call such changes in working capital *flow of fund*. It is a transfer of economic value from one asset to another, from one equity to another or from an asset to an equity or vice versa. Another related term is *liquidation* which is the conversion of assets to cash.

In the normal course of the operation of a business, working capital grows when a current asset (usually merchandise inventory) is converted by sale to another form (debtors or cash) since gross profit is made in the process. In a service company, working capital increases in the form of more cash and debtors result from services provided to clients. Such increases in current assets eventually translate to an increase in retained earnings. Thus, growth in working capital resulting from net profit made is essentially an increase in owner's equity. This belongs to one of the three main sources of increase of working capital as shown in Figure 7.1.

In practice, the sources and use of funds can be summarised in Table 7.1. The nature of change in each case is also indicated.

Table 7.1 The sources and uses of funds

	Sources of funds	Type		Uses of funds	Type
1.	Net income earned from current operation	ΔOE	1.	Losses in current operation	$-\Delta OE$
2.	Capital invested (shares issued)	ΔOE	2.	Payment of dividends and income tax	$-\Delta OE$
3.	Long-term loan	ΔNCL	3.	Repay long-term loan	$-\Delta NCL$
4.	Sales of fixed assets	$-\Delta NCA$	4.	Purchase fixed assets	ΔNCA

Statement of Sources and Application of Funds

This is also called *statement of changes in financial position* which describes both the sources and uses of working capital and shows how working capital changes from the amount available at the beginning of the period to the amount available at the end of the period. It summarises a company's long-term financing and investing activities as these are the two main types of transactions that cause significant changes in a company's working capital. Specifically, it shows how much working capital was provided by financing activities and how much working capital was used by investing activities of the company. The difference between the amount of working capital provided and the amount used is presented in a schedule showing the changes in all its components.

The statement of sources and application of funds can be based on either cash or working capital. There are many alternative ways of presentation. The discussion below follows the popular format suggested in the Statement of Standard Accounting Practice, SSAP 10 by British accounting bodies. Note that such a statement is not compulsory in many countries for small companies whose annual turnover falls below a certain figure. However, it is essential for management use regardless of the size of a company in view of the vital role of working capital to the operation of all businesses.

The format of the statement of sources and application of funds proposed in SSAP 10 is as follows:

SOURCES OF FUNDS
Net income for 19__ (note 1)
Adjustment for items not involving funds:
   plus: depreciation
   less: profit on sales of fixed assets or investment   _____

Total generated from operation
Funds from other sources:
   Increase in owner's capital
   Increase in long-term loan
   Income on sale of fixed assets or investment   _____

Total sources of funds   _____

APPLICATION OF FUNDS
Dividends paid (actual)
Income tax paid (actual)
Purchase of fixed assets
Repayment of loans   _____

Total use of funds   _____

INCREASE IN WORKING CAPITAL
Increase in stock (merchandise inventory)
Increase in debtors
Decrease in creditors (excluding income tax
   payable and dividends payable)   _____

Movement in net liquid funds:
   Increase in cash balance
   Increase in short-term investment   _____

   _____

Note 1: In cases where profit and loss statements are not given and only retained earnings figures are available from balance sheets, net income has to be derived from the retained earnings figures at the beginning and end of a period as follows:

> Net income (from normal operation)
>   = Increase in retained earnings + Income tax for that period
>   + Dividend declared in that period

Example 7.1 illustrates how the statement of sources and application of funds is derived from the balance sheets of the current and last accounting periods based on the SSAP 10 format.

Example 7.1

Balance sheet figures of a company at the end of the current period and the previous period are as follows:

	Current period $'000	Previous period $'000	Changes $'000
LIABILITIES AND OWNER'S EQUITY			
Share capital	2,200	2,000	+200
Retained earnings	1,600	1,500	+100
Long-term loan	595	680	−85
Creditors	100	300	−200
Dividends payable	160	150	+10
Income tax payable	230	140	+90
Short-term loan	550	100	+450
	5,435	4,870	+565
ASSETS			
Freehold property	1,600	1,500	+100
Plant and machinery	1,400	900	+500
less: depreciation	(300)	–	−300
Investments:			
Long-term (shares in associated company)	1,000	1,000	0
Short-term (shares of public companies)	740	750	−10
Stock	485	350	+135
Debtors	500	300	+200
Cash	10	70	−60
	5,435	4,870	+565

Notes:
1. Dividends for the current period are $155,000.
2. Income tax for the current period is $250,000.
3. New plant and machinery were purchased during the current period at a cost of $500,000.
4. No sale of fixed assets took place during the current period.
5. There is no depreciation charge for freehold property.

The following workings are required to derive the net income, as well as dividends and income tax paid from the balance sheet figures:

1. Net income
 = Increase in retained earnings + Dividends + Income tax
 = $100,000 + $155,000 + $250,000
 = $505,000

2. Dividends paid
 = (Dividends payable at the end of the previous period
    + Dividends for the current period)
    − Dividends payable at the end of the current period
 = ($150,000 + $155,000) − $160,000
 = $145,000

3. Income tax paid
 = (Tax payable at the end of the previous period
    + Tax for the current period)
    − Tax payable at the end of the current period
 = ($140,000 + $250,000) − $230,000
 = $160,000

The following is the statement of sources and application of funds for the current period:

	$'000	$'000
SOURCES OF FUNDS		
Net income		505
Adjustment for item not involving funds:		
add: depreciation		300
Total generated from operation		805
Funds from other sources:		
Increase in capital		200
Total sources of funds		1,005

APPLICATION OF FUNDS
Dividends paid	145	
Income tax paid	160	
Purchase of freehold property	100	
Purchase of plant and machinery	500	
Repayment of long-term loan	85	
Total use of funds		990
Increase in funds		15

INCREASE IN WORKING CAPITAL
Increase in stock		135
Increase in debtors		200
Decrease in creditors		200
Decrease in short-term loan		(450)
Movement in net liquid funds:		
Increase in cash	(60)	
Increase in short-term investment	(10)	
		(70)
		15

The following points on the preparation of statement of sources and application of funds have to be highlighted:

1. Net income is derived from retained earnings figures only if balance sheets are available. Otherwise, it may also be read from the income statement directly.

2. Funds generated from operation under the 'sources of funds' refers to net profit (before dividends and income tax) from normal operation of the company. Extraordinary gains from sale of fixed assets are, therefore, excluded from the total profit derived from increase in retained earnings. Such gains from the sale of fixed assets are the difference between sales price and net book value of the assets sold. If there has been a loss, the amount should be added back to obtain the net profit from normal operations. In any case, the total sales proceeds will contribute to 'funds from other sources'. If the above adjustment is not made, the profit (or loss) from sale of fixed assets will be accounted for twice.

3. Depreciation is a 'non-cash' expense realised only by bookkeeping entries. It does not involve an outflow of funds and therefore should be added back to net income to give the total amount of funds generated from operation.

4. Dividends and income tax paid are the actual amounts paid in the

current period. They are derived from the dividends and income tax payable figures in the balance sheets as shown in example 7.1. Alternatively, dividends and income tax for the current period may be put under application of funds. In this case the decrease in dividends payable and decrease in income tax payable must be included as additional items under 'Increase in Working Capital'. An illustration using figures in example 7.1 and only highlighting the relevant portions of the statement is as follows:

Total sources of funds		1,005
APPLICATION OF FUNDS		
Dividends (of current period)	155	
Income tax (of current period)	250	
Purchases of freehold property	100	
Purchase of plant and machinery	500	
Repayment of long-term loan	85	
Total use of funds		1,090
		(85)
INCREASE IN WORKING CAPITAL		
Increase in stock		135
Increase in debtors		200
Decrease in creditors		200
Decrease in dividends payable		(10)
Decrease in income tax payable		(90)
Decrease in short-term loan		(450)
Increase in net liquid funds		(70)
		(85)

This format however is not shown in the SSAP 10.

5. Figures under 'sources of funds' and 'application of funds' are generally positive in value. This is because the negative-value items can always be placed under the other category so that they become positive figures. Thus, the decrease in the long-term loan in this example has been interpreted as a repayment of a loan and is an application of funds rather than a negative source of funds.

6. Since subtracting the total application of funds from total sources of funds should always be the increase in working capital, all the components of working capital must be defined in terms of an increase in working capital in the statement. This implies that all current liabilities (e.g., creditors and accounts payable) must be stated as reduction in their

values in the standard format. If the actual current liabilities have increased in that period, they must be treated as a negative reduction as is the case of short-term loan in example 7.1.

7. All items in the statement are related to the various types of sources and uses of funds discussed in the section on flow of funds. Tracing all these items and identifying them with the changes in owner's equity, long-term liabilities and fixed assets will give a clearer idea of the working of the statement.

8. There are other formats of presentation depending on the nature of business and the accounting standards adopted. (e.g., the Australian Accounting Standard AAS 12). Some companies also prepare a statement on sources and application of cash for internal control of cash flow. The cash basis statement shows the amount of cash generated by a company's various financing activities, the amount of cash used for its various investing activities, and the resulting increase or decrease in its cash balance. Because all business transactions are recorded on accrual basis, income statement figures must be converted to cash basis to determine the amount of cash received from revenue and the amount of cash paid for expenses. The following formulae using data from the income statement and the balance sheet to derive cash flow are commonly used:

(a) Cash received from customers
= Net sales + Decrease in accounts receivable account
or = Net sales − Increase in accounts receivable account

(b) Cash paid for purchases of goods
= Net purchases + Decrease in accounts payable account
or = Net purchases − Increase in accounts payable account

where Net purchases
= Cost of goods sold + Increase in inventory
or = Cost of goods sold − Decrease in inventory

(c) Cash paid for expenses
= Expenses (other than depreciation) + Increase in prepayments + Decrease in liabilities accrued

Decrease in prepayments and increase in liabilities will instead be subtracted in the equation.

Other sources and uses of cash can also be readily derived from figures in comparative balance sheets.

Practice Problems

7.1 Comparative account balances for a company at the end of year 1 and year 2 are listed below:

	Year 2 $'000	Year 1 $'000
Cash	60	100
Accounts receivable	150	175
Merchandise inventory	325	250
Land	75	–
Plant and equipment	800	625
Patents (net of amortisation)	90	100
	1,500	1,250
Accumulated depreciation (plant and equipment)	263	200
Accounts payable	152	75
Dividends payable	10	–
Long-term loan payable	25	–
Share capital (at $10 par per share)	1,000	875
Retained earnings	50	100
	1,500	1,250

The following additional information is available:

1. The net loss for year 2 amounted to $40,000.
2. Dividends of $10,000 were declared.
3. Land for future expansion has been acquired.
4. Equipment costing $175,000 was purchased. A loan of $25,000 was obtained to pay for the equipment.
5. Additional share capital has been raised at par value.

You are required to prepare a statement of sources and application of funds for year 2.

7.2 The summarised account balances of a company for year 1 and year 2 are as follows:

	Year 2 $'000	Year 1 $'000
Cash	7	10
Short-term investment	80	60
Debtors	370	310
Inventory	650	700
Long-term investment	200	400
Building and equipment	950	800
less: accumulated depreciation	(300)	(380)
	1,957	1,900
Share capital	700	600
Retained earnings	180	110
Long-term loan	350	575
Creditors	500	450
Income tax payable	107	75
Dividend payable	120	90
	1,957	1,900

The following information is given:

1. Equipment costing $150,000 with accumulated depreciation of $125,000 was sold in the early part of year 2 with a profit of $25,000.
2. Income tax for year 2 was $85,000.
3. Dividend of $92,000 has been declared in year 2.

You are required to compute the differences in the account balances and then prepare a statement of sources and application of funds for year 2.

7.3 The summarised account balances of a company for year 1 and year 2 are as follows:

	Year 2 $'000	Year 1 $'000
Cash	7	6
Short-term investment	90	80
Debtors	450	380
Inventory	500	560
Long-term investment	280	330
Building and equipment	800	650
less: accumulated depreciation	(200)	(180)
	1,927	1,826

Share capital	900	780
Retained earnings	100	70
Long-term loan	350	430
Creditors	485	446
Income tax payable	50	40
Dividend payable	42	60
	1,927	1,826

The following information is given:

1. Equipment costing $80,000 with accumulated depreciation of $64,000 was sold in the early part of year 2 with a loss of $6,000.
2. Income tax for year 2 was $38,000.
3. Total dividends declared in year 2 was $85,000.

You are required to compute the differences in the account balances and then prepare a statement of sources and application of funds for year 2.

PART THREE

COST ACCOUNTING AND COST CONTROL

Chapter 8

Classification and Control of Costs

There is no such thing as profit. There are only costs. Costs of doing business and costs of staying in business, costs of labour and raw materials, costs of capital, as well as the costs of today's job, and costs of tomorrow's jobs and tomorrow's pensions.

Peter Drucker

A merchandising company sells to its customers the same goods that it buys from its supplier. A manufacturing company, on the other hand, buys raw materials and incurs expenditures to convert these raw materials into products before selling the latter to retail merchandising companies. Cost accounting is the phase of accounting that has to do with collecting, determining, and controlling the costs of producing a given product or service. It is of particular relevance to manufacturing companies as the knowledge and control of production costs are vital to the good management of such establishments. Many companies use accounting systems that are based on perpetual inventories of raw materials and finished goods. Systems of accounting for manufacturing operations that incorporate perpetual inventory monitoring are called *cost accounting systems*.

Cost Centre and Cost Classification

A *cost unit* is a quantitative unit of a product or service in relation to which costs are ascertained. In other words, it is a unit of output from a *cost centre* which is a location, person or item of equipment (or group of these) in respect of which costs may be ascertained and related. A cost centre is very commonly a location in the sense of a department or section of the business engaged in a particular set of activities. Dividing an organisation into various cost centres makes management control much easier as every cost centre has to be responsible for its own performance.

Costs are generally classified into *direct costs* and *indirect costs*. Direct costs are sometimes also called *prime costs* and are made up of the following:

1. Direct material cost: The cost of material enter into and become constituent elements of a product or service.
2. Direct wages: The cost of renumeration for efforts applied directly to a product.
3. Direct expenses: Other costs which are incurred for a specific product.

Indirect costs are sometimes called *overheads*. They are costs that are not directly related to a cost unit. Indirect costs are usually classified according to the departments where expenditure are incurred or services are provided to other cost centres. A typical classification of direct and indirect costs are as follows:

Direct costs	**Indirect costs**
• Direct material	• Production or factory overhead
• Direct wages	• Administration overhead
• Direct expenses	• Selling and distribution overhead

The behaviour of direct and indirect costs with respect to changes in the level of activities are distinctly different. Direct costs are *variable costs* that tend to vary in direct proportion to changes in volume of output of the cost centre to which they relate. Indirect costs, on the other hand are *fixed costs* that accrue in relation to the passage of time and within definable limits. They tend to be unaffected by fluctuations in the volume of output. The terms direct cost and variable cost, and also indirect cost and fixed cost, are sometimes used interchangeably.

Inventory Control and Economic Reorder Quantity

One of the most important direct costs is raw material. Every company usually has a standard procedure for purchase and a system for inventory control of materials. Typically, on receipt of a *purchase requisition* from the manufacturing department, the purchase department will obtain *quotations* or, for major items, invite *tenders* from suppliers of materials required. Considerations have to be given to price, specifications, conditions of delivery, various charges, time of delivery, terms of payment and discount for cash payment or bulk purchase before a supplier is selected. After the purchaser has decided which quotation to accept, a *purchase order* is prepared with copies for:

- the supplier
- the receiving department (store)
- the accounting department
- the department which initiated the purchase
- retained in the purchasing department

When materials are received, they are kept in individual receptacles and separate records are kept on a *bin card* showing in details all receipts and issues. The bin cards only show quantities and are kept in the store. A *store ledger* is kept in a cost department indicating also the monetary value of each item. The store ledger is actually a subsidiary ledger with the control account 'Raw Material' in the general ledger. Each account in the store ledger represents an item of material in store. When the factory needs material, a source document, the *material requisition form*, is issued to the store. Typical examples of bin card, store ledger card and material requisition form are shown in Figure 8.1.

Bin card

Description:
Normal quantity to order:
Store ledger no.:

Bin no.:
Code no.:
Max. qty:
Min. qty:
Reorder level:

Receipts			Issued			Balance	Remarks
Date	Receipt no.	Qty	Date	Req. no.	Qty	Qty	Goods on order and audit notes

Store ledger card

Stock account no.:
Description:
Location in store:

Reorder level:
Reorder quantity:

Date	Ref.	Receipts			Issued			Balance		
		Qty	Unit cost	Total cost	Qty	Unit cost	Total cost	Qty	Unit cost	Total cost

Figure 8.1

Material requisition form

Requested by: Issued by:	Date:	Material requisition no.: Charge to job no.:		
Stock A/C no.	Description	Qty	Unit cost	Total cost

Figure 8.1 (contd)

Material issued to the production department may be valued by any one of the following methods:

- First-in, first-out (FIFO)
- Last-in, first-out (LIFO)
- Weighted average
- Simple average
- Periodic weighted average
- Periodic simple average
- Standard price

The first three methods of valuation were explained in Chapter 6. The simple average method is based on the average unit cost of the oldest stock to the latest order in the inventory. It is not representative of the true average cost as the quantity of each order is not considered. The periodic weighted average price and simple average price methods both only take into account costs of orders made in a period. These again may not reflect the real cost of inventory in store. The standard price method applies in a company using a system of standard costing. The standard price method is discussed in Chapter 12.

The choice of material evaluation method affects the recorded cost of production which in turn will alter the cost of goods sold and the final net income figure. This was detailed in Chapter 6.

A minimum stock level is usually maintained for material which is continuously used up in the manufacturing process. This is the *buffer stock* which safe-guards against a stock-out situation which will disrupt production and cause unnecessary losses in idle time and factory overheads. Usually the *reorder level* has to be higher than the *minimum stock level* to cover the period before new stock arrives. Figure 8.2 shows the inventory cycles of material in a store. It is sometimes called the *reorder cardiogram*.

Let D = quantity demanded per annum
C_o = cost of ordering (i.e., cost incurred in the purchase process)
p = unit price of material ordered
C_s = unit holding cost per annum (i.e., interest on capital tied down, storage cost, insurance, deterioration and obsolescence cost, etc.)

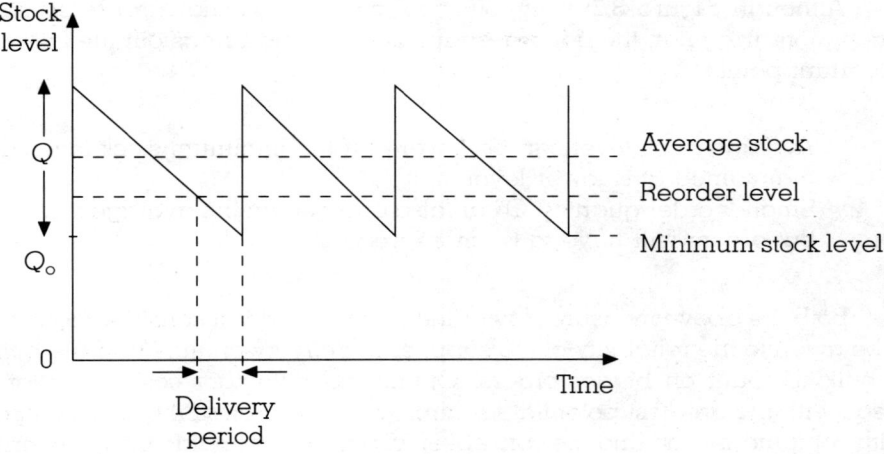

Figure 8.2 Inventory cycles

Q_o = minimum stock level
Q = reorder quantity

Then

$$\text{Number of order per annum} = \frac{D}{Q}$$

$$\text{Average stock level} = Q_o + \frac{Q}{2}$$

$$\text{Annual cost of purchase} = Dp + \left(\frac{D}{Q}\right)C_o$$

$$\text{Annual holding cost} = \left(Q_o + \frac{Q}{2}\right)C_s$$

$$\text{Total cost per annum} = Dp + \left(\frac{D}{Q}\right)C_o + \left(Q_o + \frac{Q}{2}\right)C_s$$

Differentiating the total cost with respect to Q and equating to zero:

$$-\frac{DC_o}{Q^2} + \frac{C_s}{2} = 0$$

Thus, the reorder quantity required in order to minimise overall cost is:

$$\text{Economic reorder quantity} = \sqrt{2D\left(\frac{C_o}{C_s}\right)}$$

Although Figure 8.2 is hypothetical since the actual graph is usually much more irregular, the general shape is valid and brings out the following important points:

1. Average stock level can be lowered if the minimum stock level, Q_o is maintained at a lower level.
2. Smaller order quantity, Q can also bring down the average stock level but orders will have to be more frequent.

Both the above measures lower the holding cost but considerations have to be given to the reliability of the supplier in delivery on time and the benefit of bulk discount on bigger orders. Optimising inventory cost is one of the areas with the greatest potential for improving the profitability of a company. With computerisation and the concept of *just-in-time* manufacturing, inventory level has already been pushed to the lowest limit in many modern production-line factories. Those who ignore the necessity of inventory control are losing out in terms of competitiveness.

Example 8.1 explains the terminology used in a standard inventory control system.

Example 8.1

The following data are applicable to an inventory item:

(a) Budgeted consumption: maximum 300 units/month
minimum 50 units/month
average 150 units/month
annual 1,800 units/year
(b) Lead time for delivery from supplier is a maximum of four months, a minimum of two months and an average of three months.
(c) Storage cost is 10% of stock value per annum.
(d) Ordering cost is $2 per order.
(e) Price per unit is $0.2.

Based on this information, the following is derived:

1. Reorder level
    = Minimum stock level to reorder such that stock will not run out even in the worst situation
    = Maximum consumption rate × Maximum delivery time
    = 300/month × 4 months = 1,200

2. Economic reorder quantity

$$= \sqrt{2 \times \text{Annual consumption} \times \left(\frac{\text{Ordering cost}}{\text{Holding cost per annum}}\right)}$$

$$= \sqrt{2 \times 1{,}800 \times \left(\frac{2}{0.2 \times 0.1}\right)} = \underline{600}$$

3. Minimum stock level Q_o
    = Buffer stock *in normal situation*
    = Reorder level − (Normal consumption rate × Normal delivery time)
    = 1,200 − (150 × 3) = $\underline{750}$

4. Maximum stock level (in normal situation)
    = $Q_o + Q$ = Minimum stock level + Reorder quantity
    = 750 + 600 = $\underline{1{,}350}$

    Maximum possible stock level
    = Reorder level − (Minimum consumption rate × Minimum delivery time) + Reorder quantity
    = 1,200 − (50 × 2) + 600 = $\underline{1{,}700}$

5. Average stock level (in normal situation)
    = Minimum stock level + $\dfrac{\text{Reorder quantity}}{2}$

    = $750 + \dfrac{600}{2} = \underline{1{,}050}$

6. Stock turnover

    $= \dfrac{\text{Average annual consumption}}{\text{Average stock level}}$

    $= \dfrac{1{,}800}{1{,}050} = \underline{1.71}$ times/year

Direct Wages and Direct Expenses

The labour effort applied by workers to transform raw materials into finished products is direct labour. In a production factory, workers usually clock their time of arrival and departure on *time cards*. In addition, they may also be required to fill in weekly or daily *time sheets* with a breakdown of the time spent on each separate job each day so that wages can be apportioned among work in progress of various departmental accounts. Other than the normal salary or *basic rate*, the following items may also constitute direct labour cost:

1. Shift premium (for night shift) is considered direct wages if shift work is regular. It is a direct cost of a customer's order if it is requested by the customer. If the shift work is due to disorganisation in the factory, it will be treated as general factory overhead cost. The same bases also apply to items 2 to 4.
2. Overtime premium.
3. Bonus payment.
4. Holiday pay.

Another factor to consider in assigning direct labour cost is the cost of *idle time*. It is usually attributable to:

1. production causes (e.g., machine breakdown, waiting for tools, materials);
2. administration causes (e.g., surplus capacity, unpredicted drop in demand);
3. economic causes (e.g., seasonal fluctuation in demand).

Controllable idle time should be charged as an overhead or indirect cost of a department if it is caused by factors within the control of that department. Uncontrollable idle time should be charged as direct expenses.

Direct expenses refer to expenditure other than direct material and direct labour incurred directly in the production process. They cannot be associated with a specific cost unit but are nevertheless used to make production possible. Direct expenses are, for example, hire of special equipment for production, the maintenance cost of such special equipment, cost of special layout, and design and drawings.

Absorption and Apportionment of Indirect Costs

Indirect costs are labour wages, material cost and expenses which are not directly associated with finished products. They are usually fixed costs or period costs related to the period of time in which they are incurred and are independent of the level of manufacturing output within certain limits. They are usually classified as follows:

1. Production overhead:
   - Cost of supervision (wages of foremen and supervisors)
   - Internal transportation (annual cost of fork lift and crane, operator's wages)
   - General supplies (lubricant, work-clothes, machine tools, maintenance equipment)
   - Factory premises (depreciation, insurances, utilities charges)

2. Administrative overhead:
   - Salaries (of administrative staff)
   - Rent of office
   - Public utilities charges of office
   - Printing and stationery
3. Selling and distribution overhead:
   - Salaries (of sales staff)
   - Commissions
   - Printing of catalogues and price lists
   - Advertising expenses

Example 8.2 shows how the various items of indirect cost are classified and presented in a manufacturing company.

Example 8.2

The monthly expenditures of a factory producing 10,000 units of transistor clock radios every month are:

		$
1.	Salaries: Administrative staff	20,000
	Sales staff	10,000
	Engineering and R & D	15,000
	Factory production workers	40,000
2.	Rent of factory	10,000
3.	Utilities charges	3,000
4.	Administrative expenses (postage, transport, stationery, etc.)	2,000
5.	Sales expenses (advertising, catalogues, etc.)	1,000
6.	Direct materials used:	
	Radio chassis	30,000
	Semiconductor components and speakers	90,000
	Printed circuit boards	15,000
	Accessory components (screws, nuts, etc.)	8,000

The following is additional information:

1. The machinery and equipment used in the factory cost a total of $100,000 with an estimated useful life of ten years.
2. Stock of materials and finished product is about $80,000 on the average. Due to change of design and advance in technology, 10% of stock becomes obsolete every year.
3. Financing charge by the bank is at 11%.

A statement on total cost of sales of the company will be as follows:

	$	$
Direct costs:		
Direct material		
Radio chassis	30,000	
Components (semiconductors and speakers)	90,000	
Printed circuit boards	15,000	
Accessory components	8,000	
		143,000
Direct labour		
Salaries of production workers		40,000
		183,000
Indirect costs:		
Factory overhead		
Salaries (engineers and R & D staff)	15,000	
Rent of factory	10,000	
Utilities charges	3,000	
Depreciation (plant and machinery) (note 1)	833	
Stock obsolescent cost (note 2)	667	
Stock holding cost (note 3)	733	
		30,233
Administrative overhead		
Salaries (administrative staff)	20,000	
Administrative expenses	2,000	
		22,000
Sales and distribution overhead		
Salaries (sales staff)	10,000	
Sales expenses	1,000	
		11,000
		246,233

Total costs:

Average unit cost = $\dfrac{\$246{,}233}{10{,}000}$ = $\underline{\underline{\$24.62}}$

Notes:
1. Assuming straight-line depreciation,
   Depreciation per month = $\dfrac{\$10{,}000}{10 \times 12}$ = \$833

2. Stock obsolescent cost per month = $\dfrac{\$80{,}000 \times 10\%}{12}$ = \$667

3. Stock holding cost per month $= \dfrac{\$80{,}000 \times 11\%}{12} = \$733$

In example 8.2, direct and indirect cost are added and divided by the units produced to arrive at the total unit cost. This is only applicable to a company producing a uniform single product. In the more common case with multiple products produced by many departments, indirect costs have to be identified with cost centres that collectively incur the overhead cost. If the services procured and/or material used benefit a number of cost centres, their costs will be *apportioned* among user cost centres on some basis which gives a reasonable representation of the benefit they obtain. Direct costs are naturally *allotted* to the cost units to which they relate. The allotment of a whole item of cost to a cost centre is known as cost *allocation*.

In a *full absorption costing system*, the indirect cost allotted or apportioned to a cost centre is *absorbed* or *recovered* by the cost units produced in that cost centre. Thus unit production cost is dependent on the method of apportionment of indirect cost. Example 8.3 illustrates the various possible bases of apportionment of factory overhead.

Example 8.3

A company estimates that its total factory costs for the coming year will be as follows:

	$'000
Direct material	40
Direct wages	60
Prime cost	100
Factory overhead	30
Total production cost	130

There will be 50,000 direct labour hours and 100,000 machine hours incurred, while 200,000 units of various products will be produced.

The factory overhead may be absorbed on the following bases:

1. Percentage of material cost $= \dfrac{\$30{,}000}{\$40{,}000} = 75\%$

2. Percentage of wages cost $= \dfrac{\$30{,}000}{\$60{,}000} = 50\%$

3. Percentage of prime cost $= \dfrac{\$30{,}000}{\$100{,}000} = 30\%$

4. Rate per machine hour = $\dfrac{\$30,000}{\$100,000}$ = $0.3/machine hour

5. Rate per direct labour hour = $\dfrac{\$30,000}{\$50,000}$ = $0.6/direct labour hour

Thus, if the first basis is used and product 1 uses $4 direct material to produce one unit of output, factory overhead to be absorbed by every unit of product 1 will be ($4 × 75%) or $3. Which of the above bases of absorption to choose depends on how closely factory overhead is related to the parameter chosen. If all units produced are homogeneous, factory overhead cost per unit will simply be $30,000/200,000 or $0.15.

A more complex case of apportionment of indirect costs is *inter-service-department transfers*. This involves more than one service department with the costs of each to be apportioned to production departments and also among themselves since the services they provide are used by all other departments. There are two methods to deal with inter-service-department cost transfers:

1. By solving linear simultaneous equations
2. By the algorithm of repeated distribution

Example 8.4 illustrates these two methods.

Example 8.4

A company has three production departments and two service departments which have the following operating costs in a given period:

		$
Production department	A	800
	B	700
	C	500
Service department	1	234
	2	300
Total		2,534

The operating costs of service departments are decided to be apportioned on a percentage basis to other departments as follows:

	Production department			Service department	
	A	B	C	1	2
Service dept 1	20%	40%	30%	–	10%
Service dept 2	40%	20%	20%	20%	–

Simultaneous equation method

The total operating costs of service departments are higher than the figures given above since each of them is obtaining service from the other service department. The actual operating cost therefore should include cost apportioned from the other service department.

Let x = actual total cost of service department 1
y = actual total cost of service department 2

Then
$$x = 234 + 0.2y$$
$$y = 300 + 0.1x$$

Solving the above linear simultaneous equations gives:

$$x = 300$$
$$y = 330$$

Apportioning these to the production departments on the basis of the percentages given:

	Production department			
	A	B	C	Total
Original operating cost	800	700	500	2,000
Apportioned operating cost:				
from service dept 1	60	120	90	270
from service dept 2	132	66	66	264
	992	886	656	2,534

Repeated distribution method

Departments	A	B	C	1	2
Original operating cost	800	700	500	234	300
Apportionment:					
Service dept 1	47	94	70	(234)	23
Service dept 2	129	65	65	64	(323)
Service dept 1	13	26	19	(64)	6
Service dept 2	2.4	1.2	1.2	1.2	(6)
Service dept 1	0.24	0.48	0.36	(1.2)	0.12
Service dept 2	0.05	0.02	0.02	0.02	(0.12)
	991.69	886.7	655.58	0.02	0
Round-up	992	887	656	0	0

The service department costs are distributed in turn to all other departments. Cost figures in brackets are negative values as they are distributed to other departments according to the given percentages and therefore subtracted from the respective service departments. If the method is applied with more decimal significant figures from the beginning, it should yield exactly the same answer as the method of simultaneous equations. This algorithm has been used also by structural engineers in calculating the distribution of moments in structures. The procedure is easily programmable for iteration by computers. It is a very efficient algorithm especially if the number of service departments with costs to be apportioned is large. In that case, the simultaneous equation method will involve too many unknown variables, making solution by hand much more difficult.

Practice Problems

8.1 A company has just been set up to manufacture and sell three products: A, B and C. The production and sales forecast for the next two years are:

	Year 1			Year 2		
	A	B	C	A	B	C
Production (units)	10,000	20,000	30,000	10,000	20,000	30,000
Sales (units)	7,000	16,000	25,000	8,000	19,000	32,000

The sales price and variable cost per unit over the next two years are:

Product	Sales price $/unit	Variable cost $/unit
A	16	4
B	24	8
C	18	6

The labour and machine hours required to produce one unit are:

Product	Labour hour per unit	Machine hour per unit
A	0.1	0.3
B	0.2	0.2
C	0.1	0.3

Annual fixed production overhead cost is forecasted to be $48,000.

Compute and tabulate the profit and loss statements of the three products for the next two years using:

(a) labour hour as the basis for fixed overhead absorption,
(b) machine hour as the basis for fixed overhead absorption.

8.2 A company has just been set up to manufacture and sell three products: A, B and C. The production and sales forecast for the next two years are:

	Year 1			Year 2		
	A	B	C	A	B	C
Production (units)	30,000	20,000	10,000	30,000	20,000	10,000
Sales (units)	24,000	16,000	4,000	24,000	10,000	12,000

Sales price and variable cost per unit over the next two years are:

Product	Sales price $/unit	Variable cost $/unit
A	8	2
B	12	4
C	12	3

Details of the labour and machine hours required for each unit produced are:

Product	Labour hour per unit	Machine hour per unit
A	2	1
B	3	1
C	2	2

Total fixed production overhead costs will be $280,000 in each year.

(a) Prepare three statements showing the annual profit of the three products over the next two years using:
   (i) labour hour as the basis of fixed overhead absorption;
   (ii) machine hour as the basis of fixed overhead absorption.
(b) Comment on the profitability of each product based on the results in (a).

(c) It is decided to increase the production of the first year by 20% in order to provide additional buffer stocks. Calculate the cost of holding the additional stock for a full year if the cost of financing the additional stock is 12% per annum.

8.3 An electronic factory operates a computerised inventory control system. The following information about an inventory item is given:

(i) Maximum lead time to obtain supply = 3 months
(ii) Average consumption = 5,000 units/month
(iii) Maximum consumption = 7,000 units/month
(iv) Storage cost per annum = 20% stock value
(v) Ordering cost = $50 per order
(vi) Price per unit = $0.3

You are required to:

(a) derive the formula for economic reorder quantity and state the formula for reorder level,
(b) determine the economic reorder quantity and reorder level from the data given.

8.4 A company has three production departments and two service departments. Their operating costs in a given period are:

	$'000
Production department A	70
B	60
C	50
Service department 1	20
2	30
Total	230

The operating cost of each service department is to be apportioned to other departments as follows:

	Production department			Service department	
	A	B	C	1	2
Service dept 1	20%	30%	40%	–	10%
Service dept 2	40%	30%	20%	10%	–

Determine the total operating cost of each of the production departments A, B and C.

Chapter 9

Job Order Cost Accounting and Process Cost Accounting

Production is not the application of tools to materials, but logic to work.

Peter Drucker

Cost Accounts in the General Ledger

There are basically two types of cost accounting systems: job order cost accounting and process cost accounting. Job order costing is a system which controls the costs of companies which produce goods for individual orders or perform individual jobs. In such a system, individual cost records are kept for each job. The records therefore accumulate information on prime costs and overheads for each job. The process cost accounting system, on the other hand, is designed to control the costs of companies which mass produce goods. Emphasis is placed on controlling the operating processes or departments within the plant. Cost records are classified according to departments with cost elements analysed and controlled for each separate department.

The accounts used for both job order and process cost accounting are essentially the same. The following six extra types of account are required in addition to the standard financial accounts of a company:

1. *Raw materials and supplies inventory.* This account is part of the perpetual inventory system recording all purchases and consumption of materials used in the production process. Normally records of other materials not related to production are kept in a separate inventory account.
2. *Factory payroll.* This account records wages of workers engaged in manufacturing activities. It includes direct wages as well as labour costs incurred by factory overhead.

3. *Factory overhead.* Factory overhead records the raw material and labour cost used in factory overhead. This is finally transferred (or absorbed) to the cost of work in process according to a selected basis in an absorption costing system.
4. *Work in process.* Separate work in process accounts are maintained for different jobs in job order accounting system. Similarly, separate departmental accounts are kept for different manufacturing processes in process cost accounting system. They record the costs of raw material, direct labour and factory overhead accumulated for a job order or a process department.
5. *Finished goods inventory.* This asset account records the accumulated cost of manufacturing goods still kept in a store. The account is updated regularly when finished goods are transferred to the store and when goods are delivered when they are sold.
6. *Cost of goods sold.* This is part of the perpetual inventory system recording the manufacturing cost of goods sold. This expense account is closed at the end of an accounting period by transferring the debit balance to the profit and loss account.

Example 9.1 illustrates the recording in these cost accounts of a typical manufacturing department (department A) operating a process cost accounting system. All the double entries are numbered in brackets and explained accordingly.

Example 9.1

Raw materials

Opening inventory	30,000	(2)	65,000
(1)	100,000		

Factory payroll

(3)	120,800	(4)	120,800

Factory overhead

(2)	4,000		
(4)	5,000	(6)	81,060
(5)	72,160	(9)	100
	81,160		81,160

Work in process – Department A

Opening inventory:				
Raw material	5,000			
Direct labour	8,700			
Factory overhead	6,090			
	19,790			
(2) Raw material	61,000			
(4) Direct labour	115,800			
(6) Factory overhead	81,060	(7) Finished goods		252,000
	277,650			

Finished goods inventory

Opening inventory	59,300			
(7) From dept A	252,000	(8)		122,300

Cost of goods sold

(8)	122,300			
(9)	100	(10)		122,400

(1) The company purchased $100,000 worth of raw material. The other accounting entry is to credit either a cash account (if purchase has been paid by cash) or an accounts payable account (if purchase has been made on credit). This was not shown as the illustration does not include these standard accounts.

(2) Material requisitions totalling $65,000 have been processed. These include $61,000 used by department A as raw material (thus charged to the work in process account) and $4,000 used in the factory for general purpose (thus charged to factory overhead).

(3) Factory payroll of $120,800 was accrued. The other entry is credited to a salary payable account (not shown).

(4) The factory payroll was apportioned to department A for direct labour cost ($115,800) and factory overhead for indirect labour cost ($5,000). The factory payroll account is a temporary account and was, therefore, closed.

(5) Additional factory overhead of $72,160 has been incurred. The appropriate account (cash or accounts payable) was credited but was not shown here.

(6) The factory overhead has to be absorbed by production departments using a pre-determined rate of 70% direct labour cost which amounts to $115,800 3 70% or $81,060 for department A in this case.

(7) During this period, 40,000 units of goods were completed and transferred to finished goods inventory. These are valued at $252,000 based on a cost-of-production report which will be explained later in example 9.2.

(8) The company, using the FIFO method to assess the cost of goods sold, has sold the opening stock of finished goods costing $59,300 (as shown in finished goods inventory account) and 10,000 units of goods manufactured in this period. The cost of production of these 10,000 units based on the cost-of-production report is $63,000. The total cost of goods sold is therefore $122,300. As explained in Chapter 6 on perpetual inventory system, sales account is credited and account receivable account is debited at the same time the amount of sales at sales price. These financial account entries, however, are not shown here.

(9) Factory overhead was *under-applied* as the actual overhead was more than the amount absorbed by work in process and eventually transferred to finished goods inventory. The shortfall of $100 is, therefore, transferred to the cost of goods sold account to reflect the real cost of goods. Normally, this is done annually at the end of the accounting cycle. Part of this balance in the factory overhead account has to be transferred to the finished goods inventory account if a significant portion of the goods manufactured in that period are still not sold. Factory overhead may be *over-applied* as the predetermined absorption rate can never be exact. In such a case, it will be a credit entry in the cost of goods sold and/or finished goods inventory account. The factory overhead account is always closed at the end of an accounting period.

(10) The cost of goods sold account is closed at the end of the accounting cycle by transferring the total amount to a profit and loss account as explained in Chapter 6. The debit entry in the P & L account is not shown here.

The above example also highlights the following salient points:

1. The raw material, work in process and finished goods inventory accounts are asset accounts and usually have opening and closing balances. The other three accounts of factory payroll, factory overhead and cost of goods sold are all expense accounts that are closed at the end of every recording period.

2. In a company which has more than one department involved in the manufacturing process, the cost of work in process in the first department will have to be passed on to the work in process of the second department. The second department will incur additional direct costs and transfer the total cost of semi-finished goods to the next process department in succession. Finally, the cost of the completed product will be transferred from the last department to the finished goods inventory. Such transfer pricing is elaborated on in problem 1 of Appendix A.

3. Example 9.1 shows the working of a single department in a given period and is applicable to the case of job order accounting in a

department as well as a process manufacturing company with only one production department.

Cost-of-production Report: Weighted Average Method

The cost-of-production report for a department summarises all activities in that department during a relatively short control period of say, one week. The constituent costs of production are derived in the report so that the cost of goods transferred to finished goods inventory and the value of uncompleted work in process can be determined.

Because of the existence of opening inventory and closing inventory, the unit cost of production cannot be obtained simply by distributing the total cost in the period among the number of finished goods. Semi-completed opening inventory carries costs from the previous period and uncompleted closing inventory carries forward production costs of the current period to the next production period. The method of assessing cost flow in the process, therefore, will affect the result of computation of unit production cost. Normally, either the weighted average method or the first-in, first-out method is used. Example 9.2 illustrates the cost-of-production report based on the weighted average method using cost data of example 9.1. It comprises four sections:

1. Activity in terms of units
2. Equivalent production
3. Statement of costs
4. Statement of evaluation

Example 9.2

The cost of beginning inventory and production costs incurred in the current period are as shown in the work in process account in example 9.1. Additional information based on the assessment of opening and ending units in process are contained in the first section of the cost-of-production report. The number of new units started in production during this period is also given.

1. Activity in terms of units:

Units in process, beginning (100% complete as to materials, 60% complete as to direct labour and overhead)	5,000
New units started in production	50,000
Total units to account for	55,000

Units completed during the period and transferred to finished goods		40,000
Units in process, ending (100% complete as to materials, 10% complete as to direct labour and overhead)		15,000
Total units accounted for		55,000

2. Equivalent production in units:

	Direct material	Direct labour	Factory overhead
Units completed and transferred	40,000	40,000	40,000
Units in ending inventory (note 1)	15,000	1,500	1,500
Equivalent whole units	55,000	41,500	41,500

3. Statement of costs:

	Direct material $	Direct labour $	Factory overhead $	Total $
Work in process, beginning	5,000	8,700	6,090	19,790
This period's costs	61,000	115,800	81,060	257,860
Total cost	66,000	124,500	87,150	277,650
Divided by equivalent whole units	55,000	41,500	41,500	—
Unit cost (note 2)	1.20 +	3.00 +	2.10 =	6.30

4. Statement of evaluation:

	$	$
Units completed and transferred to finished goods (40,000 units at $6.30)		252,000
Work in process at end of period (note 3):		
Raw material (15,000 units at $1.20)	18,000	
Direct labour (1,500 units at $3.00)	4,500	
Factory overhead (1,500 units at $2.10)	3,150	
		25,650
Total cost accounted for		277,650

Notes:
1. The principle of equivalent production is that if a number of units are only fractionally completed, they are treated as equivalent to a

number of completed whole units equal to the total units times the fraction of completion. Thus, the 15,000 units 10% completed as to direct labour and factory overhead are equivalent to 1,500 completed whole units so far as direct labour and factory overhead are concerned.
2. Division at least up to three decimal points is normally required in calculating the constituents of unit costs. This is necessary to minimise rounding errors so that total production cost calculated can be reconciled more accurately to actual cost in the statement of evaluation.
3. Value of work in process at the end of this period will be passed to the next period as opening inventory in the work in process account. The cost of 40,000 completed units transferred to finished goods inventory account at $6.30 is $252,000. This justifies the figure in transaction (7) of example 9.1.

Cost-of-production Report: FIFO Method

The method of weighted average was used in example 9.2 by adding the cost of beginning work in process to costs incurred in the current period when computing unit cost of production. In actual fact, manufacturing costs in a period should not be affected by costs of the previous period although the cost of goods sold may incorporate cost of production of those goods manufactured earlier but sold in the current period. The FIFO method recognises these facts and assumes that units at the beginning of work in process will be completed and sold first in the current period. Example 9.3 illustrates the way a cost-of-production report is prepared based on the FIFO method using the same data of example 9.2:

Example 9.3

1. Activity in terms of units:

Units in process, beginning (100% complete as to materials, 60% complete as to direct labour and overhead)	5,000
New units started in production	50,000
Total units to account for	55,000
Units completed during the period and transferred to finished goods	40,000
Units in process, ending (100% complete as to materials, 10% complete as to direct labour and overhead)	15,000
Total units accounted for	55,000

2. Equivalent production in units:

	Direct material	Direct labour	Factory overhead
Units completed and transferred	40,000	40,000	40,000
Units in ending inventory	15,000	1,500	1,500
Equivalent whole units	55,000	41,500	41,500
less: units in process, beginning	5,000	3,000	3,000
Units completed in this period	50,000	38,500	38,500

3. Statement of costs:

	Direct material $	Direct labour $	Factory overhead $	Total $
This period's costs	61,000	115,800	81,060	257,860
Divided by equivalent units completed in this period	50,000	38,500	38,500	–
Unit cost	1.220	+ 3.008	+ 2.105	= 6.333

4. Statement of evaluation:

	$	$
Units completed and transferred to finished goods (40,000 units):		
Work in process, beginning	19,790	
Raw material (40,000 − 5,000) × $1.220	42,700	
Direct labour (40,000 − 3,000) × $3,008	111,296	
Factory overhead (40,000 − 3,000) × $2.105	77,885	
		251,671
Work in process at end of period:		
Raw material (15,000 × $1.220)	18,300	
Direct labour (1,500 × $3,008)	4,512	
Factory overhead (1,500 × $2.105)	3,157	
		25,969
Total cost accounted for		277,640

The following points should be noted:

1. Part one of the report (activity in terms of units) is identical to the earlier example using the weighted average method.
2. Equivalent units completed in that particular period are derived in part two of the report.

PART THREE COST ACCOUNTING AND COST CONTROL

3. The statement of cost compiles the costs of production per unit in the current period without considering the value of beginning work in process. They reflect the true costs of manufacture in that period.
4. The FIFO method is clearly shown in working out the value of units transferred to finished goods under the statement of evaluation. The equivalent units in beginning work in process has to be subtracted from the total units transferred to finished goods so that they will not be accounted for twice.
5. There is a difference of $10 between the actual total cost and the cost accounted for in the statement of evaluation. This is due to rounding off errors in computing unit costs of direct material, labour and overhead.

Cost of production reports prepared at regular intervals are very effective in monitoring the performance of production departments in a manufacturing company. Unit production costs in terms of raw material, direct labour and factory overhead can be compared to fixed standard values or former performance data of the company. Any significant deviation should be immediately investigated so that corrective actions can be taken if the changes are undesirable.

Although the assessment of beginning and ending work in process is subjective and not expected to be exact, final results will not be drastically affected if a lot more new units are started and completed in a period. Similarly, the choice of weighted average or the FIFO method of evaluation will not present significant differences in the end results as witnessed in examples 9.2 and 9.3. The FIFO method is more in line with the actual operation of a typical production department and the unit costs derived represent true manufacturing costs in that period. On the other hand, the weighted average method is simpler to use and gives sufficiently accurate results so that it is also widely adopted.

Practice Problems

9.1 A company operating a job order costing system has the following uncompleted accounts in the general ledger at the end of a period. This is due to incomplete posting with either the debit or credit of a journal entry appearing in the accounts. Also, the amounts shown represent total postings for the period without date.

	Raw material		Factory payroll	
Balance c/d	41,250	45,000	75,000	
	56,250			

	Work in process		Cost of goods sold
Balance c/d	22,500	180,000	
Direct material	37,500		
Direct labour	60,000		

	Finished goods inventory		Factory overhead
Balance c/d	45,000	187,500	63,750

The following additional information is available:

1. Overhead is charged at the absorption rate of 150% direct labour cost.
2. The $63,750 debit in factory overhead represents the sum of all overhead costs other than indirect material and indirect labour.

You are required to supply the missing debits and credits in the accounts and determine:

(a) the closing balance of finished goods,
(b) the cost of goods sold,
(c) the factory overhead incurred,
(d) the factory overhead absorbed by work in process in the period.

9.2 A processing department has 16,000 units of goods in process inventory at the beginning of a period, each of which was 60% complete. An additional 192,000 units were entered into the production process in that period. Subsequently, a total of 168,000 units were completed and transferred to finished goods. If the equivalent finished units produced in the period amounted to 169,600 units, determine the number of units remaining in process and the average stage of completion at the end of that period.

9.3 The following data are from department A of a manufacturing company in a certain month:

1. The beginning inventory in the department consisted of 11,600 units that were 80% complete as to raw material ($29,696), 40% complete as to direct labour ($9,280) and 40% complete as to overhead ($6,960). During the period, 62,000 new units were started in production. The ending inventory is 70% complete as to raw material, and 30% complete as to direct labour and factory overhead.
2. Raw material of $214,625 has been purchased with cash.
3. Materials were issued as follows:

	$
To department A	190,838
To department B	36,500
For general factory use	696

4. The factory payroll was as follows:

	$
Department A (direct labour)	123,160
Department B (direct labour)	36,955
Supervisory labour	19,500

5. Overhead applied to department A was at the rate of 75% of direct labour cost.
6. Factory insurance of $900 was paid.
7. Units completed in department A and transferred to finished goods were 49,000 in total.
8. All completed units transferred were sold for cash at $10 per unit.

You are required to:

(a) prepare a cost of production report for department A based on the weighted average method,
(b) record the business transactions given above in general journal form.

9.4 Prepare a cost of production report using data in problem 9.3 based on the FIFO method.

9.5 A manufacturing company using a process cost accounting system recorded the following data in a month:

(i) There are 5,000 units in the beginning inventory: 100% complete as to raw materials and 30% complete as to direct labour and factory overhead. These are valued at:

Raw materials	$80,000
Direct labour	16,000
Factory overhead	28,800
	$124,800

(ii) During the month 50,000 new units were started.
(iii) Manufacturing costs in the month are:

Raw materials	$800,000
Direct labour	180,000
Factory overhead	324,000
	$1,304,000

(iv) There are 40,000 units completed and transferred to finished goods, leaving 15,000 units in the ending inventory which were 100% complete as to raw materials and 60% complete as to direct labour and factory overhead.

On the basis of weighted average cost, prepare the cost-of-production report which should comprise four sections:

(a) Activity in terms of units
(b) Equivalent production
(c) Statement of cost
(d) Statement of evaluation

Chapter 10

Break-even Analysis and Marginal Costing

Economic efficiency consists in making things that are worth more than they cost.

John Maurice Clark

Marginal cost of a product is the amount at any given volume of output by which the aggregate cost will be changed if the volume of output is increased or decreased by one unit. In cost accounting, this is also the unit variable cost (or unit direct cost) at a certain level of output. The term *marginal cost* and per unit *variable cost* are therefore interchangeable in their use. For most practical purposes, it is assumed that marginal cost remains unchanged regardless of the volume of production. In practice, economy of scale and discount for bulk purchases, etc. cause the marginal cost of production to vary with the volume of output.

Since net earnings or profit is equal to the difference between revenue from sales and total cost of sales, an equation expressing profit in terms of marginal cost can be derived as follows:

Let v = marginal cost (or variable cost per unit)
 p = sales price per unit
 q = number of units sold
 F = total fixed cost
 P = profit

Then
$$P = p \cdot q - (v \cdot q + F) \quad (10.1)$$
or
$$P = (p - v)q - F \quad (10.2)$$

The term $(p - v)$ or sales price minus marginal cost per unit is also called the *contribution* per unit by the accountant. It contributes to the profit of the company by first offsetting the fixed cost. The remaining contribution will end up as net profit of the company.

Break-even Chart

As can be seen from equations developed earlier, both total sales revenue and variable cost increase linearly with the volume of sales. Fixed cost on the other hand is constant and independent of sales. Total sales revenue and total cost can be plotted in a *break-even chart* as a sales line and a total cost line. Referring back to equation (10.1), the break-even chart is plotted in Figure 10.1. The gradients of the sales line and total cost line are p and v respectively.

The break-even point is the point at which there is no profit or loss for the company. It corresponds to the point of sales when total revenue just equals to total cost. Sales below break-even point will result in a net loss (or negative profit) for the company. The difference between prevailing sales and the break-even point represents the *margin of safety* either in terms of sales revenue or sales quantity before a net loss will appear. Referring to equation

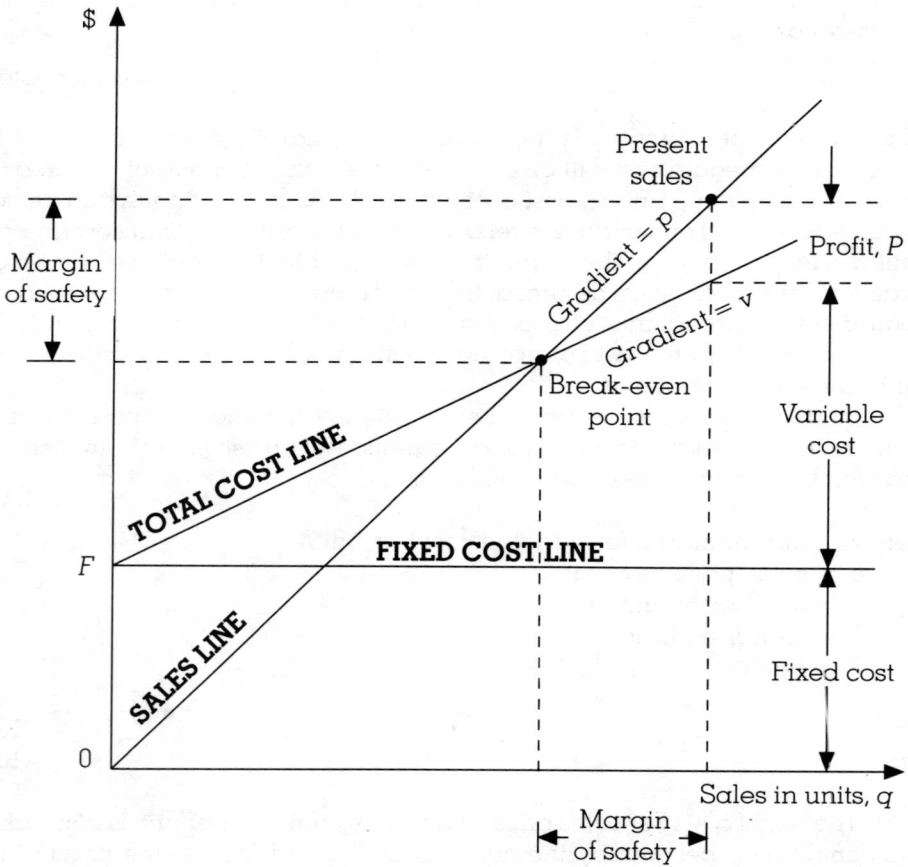

Figure 10.1 Break-even chart

(10.2), break-even occurs when profit is zero. That is:

$$0 = (p - v)q - F$$

or
$$F = (p - v)q \qquad (10.3)$$

Thus, at break-even point, total fixed cost is just offset by total contribution from sales. Equation (10.3) can also be re-written as:

$$q_o = \frac{F}{(p - v)} \qquad (10.4)$$

i.e., $\quad$ Total sales units at break-even $= \dfrac{\text{Total fixed cost}}{\text{Contribution per unit}}$

Revenue at break-even, $S_o = q_o \cdot p = \dfrac{F}{(p - v)} \cdot p \qquad (10.5)$

$$= \frac{\text{Total fixed cost}}{\text{Contribution per unit}} \times \text{Unit sales price}$$

Example 10.1 illustrates this.

Example 10.1

A company is selling a product at $15 per unit. The direct cost of producing one unit is $10 while total fixed overhead of the company is $20,000. The break-even chart of the company is shown in Figure 10.2.

$$\text{Break-even quantity } q_o = \frac{F}{(p - v)}$$

$$= \frac{\$20,000}{(\$15 - \$10)} = \underline{\underline{4,000}}$$

$$\text{Break-even revenue } S_o = p \cdot q_o = \$15 \times 4,000 = \underline{\underline{\$60,000}}$$

Profit/Volume Graph

Graphical representation of equation (10.1) gives rise to the break-even chart whereas equation (10.2) results in the *profit/volume graph*. Equation 10.2 is stated again below:

$$P = (p - v)q - F$$

It is obvious from linear-graph theory that if profit of the company is plotted against volume of sales, a straight line with the gradient equal to

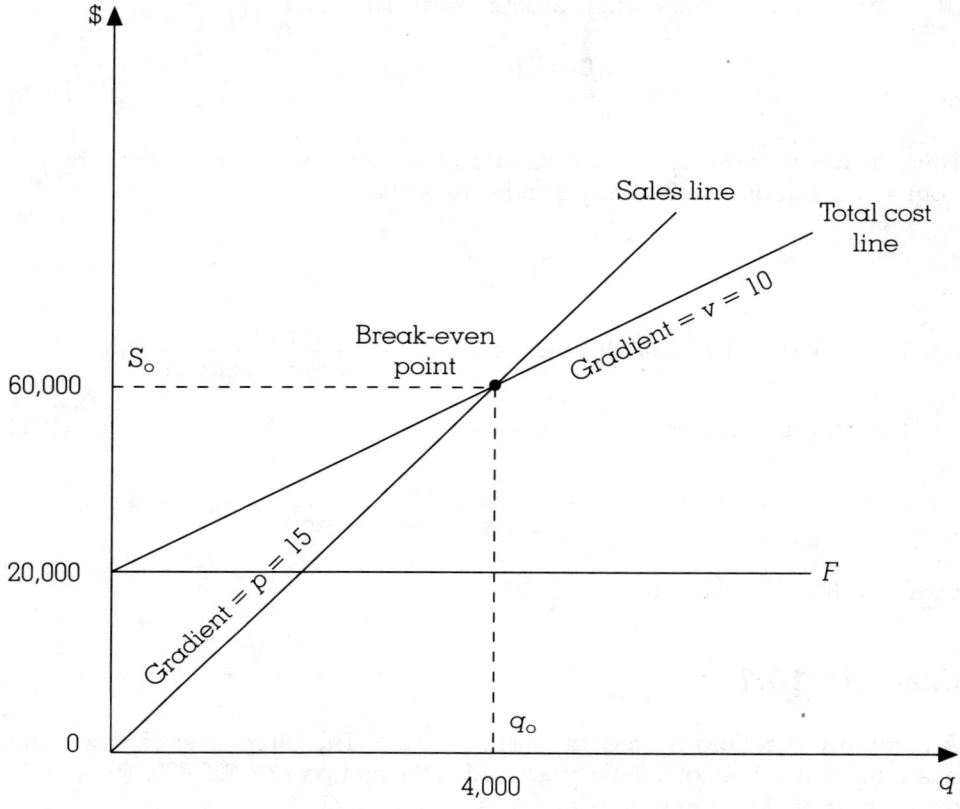

Figure 10.2

contribution per unit will result. The interception of this straight line on the vertical axis will be a negative value represented by the fixed cost of the company.

The accountants, however, prefer to view the profit of a company relative to sales revenues S, in the profit/volume graph which is also commonly called the P/V graph (Figure 10.3). Referring to the same equation again, it can be rewritten as:

$$P = \frac{(p-v)}{p} q \cdot p - F$$

$$= \frac{(p-v)}{p} \cdot S - F \qquad (10.6)$$

Thus, the P/V graph, which shows the profit of a company against sales revenue, will be a straight line with gradient equal to the ratio of contribution

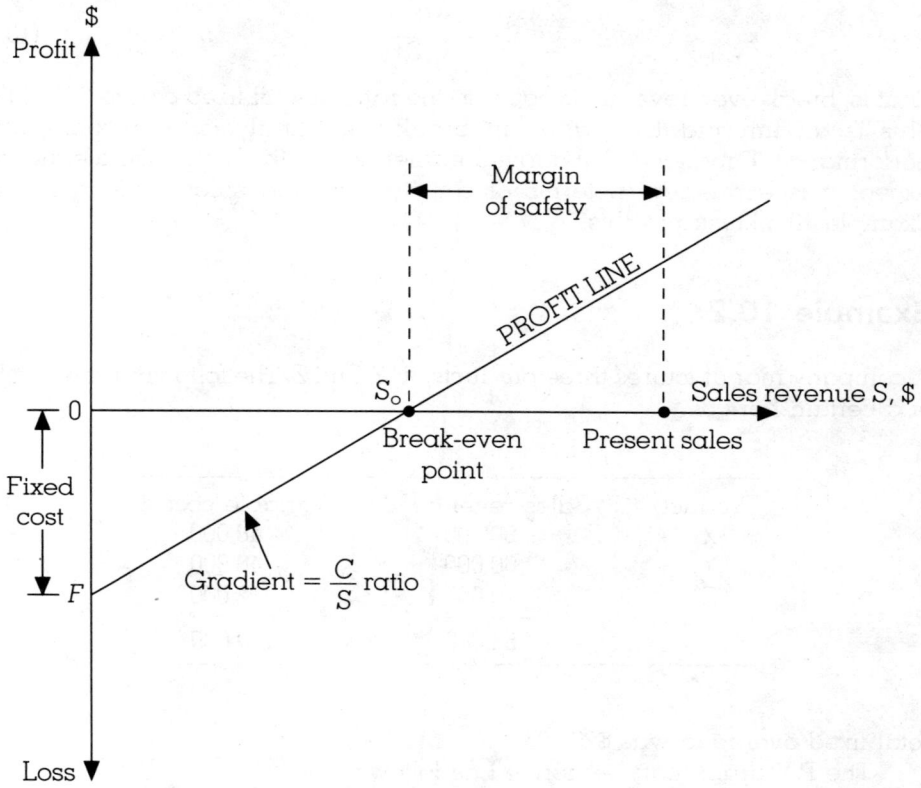

Figure 10.3 Profit/Volume graph

over sales price per unit. The interception of this *P/V* line on the vertical axis is also the negative value of total fixed cost.

The contribution/price ratio can also be expressed in terms of total contribution *C* and total sales revenue *S*:

$$\frac{(p-v)}{p} = \frac{(p-v)q}{p \cdot q} = \frac{C}{S} \quad (10.7)$$

This ratio is therefore commonly called the *C/S ratio*. It is sometimes called the *profit/volume ratio* because it represents the gradient of the *P/V* graph. Equation (10.6) can now be rewritten as:

$$P = \left(\frac{C}{S}\right)S - F \quad (10.8)$$

When the company has zero profit or just breaks even:

$$S_o = \frac{F}{(C/S)} \qquad (10.9)$$

That is, break-even revenue is equal to the ratio of total fixed cost to C/S ratio. This is an important equation in break-even analysis of a company's performance. Equation (10.5) derived earlier is effectively the same equation except it is expressed in terms of contribution and sales price per unit. Example 10.2 illustrates this.

Example 10.2

A company manufactures three products, X, Y and Z. The following are results of a certain period:

Product	Sales revenue, $	Variable cost, $
X	80,000	48,000
Y	60,000	40,000
Z	10,000	12,000
	150,000	100,000

Total fixed overhead was $20,000.
    The P/V graph can be derived as follows:

Product	Sales, $	Contribution, $	C/S ratio
X	80,000	32,000	0.40
Y	60,000	20,000	0.333
Z	10,000	(2,000)	(0.20)
Total	150,000	50,000	0.333

Product Z has negative contribution because its variable cost is higher than sales price. Its P/V graph, therefore, will have a negative slope. See Figure 10.4.
    In practice, plotting of a composite P/V graph comprising more than one product always starts off with the portion having the highest gradient. Other portions will be drawn in sequence of reducing gradients. The resulting graph will be a convex polygon. This practice is conventional rather than necessary since the ending point is the same no matter what the order of plotting the constituent parts. The overall profit line for the whole company is consequently the same. The company profit line can also be derived directly based on total contribution and sales.

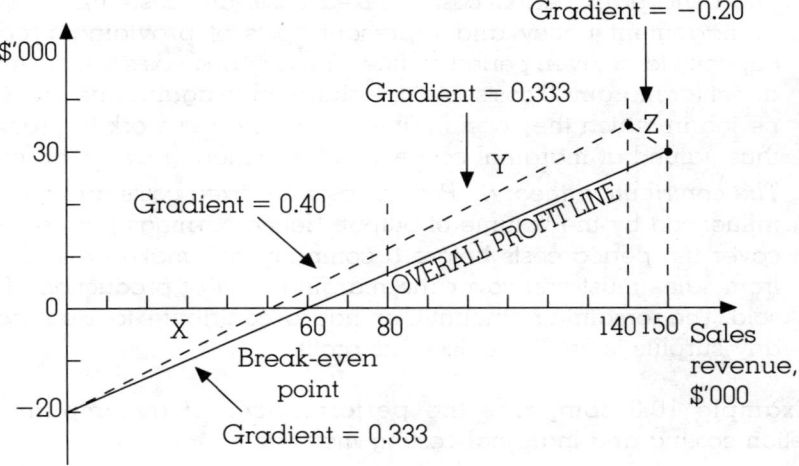

Figure 10.4 P/V graph of products X, Y and Z

Note that the P/V graph of each product covers a horizontal portion equal to its sales revenue. Consequently, the horizontal-axis coordinate of the final ending point is the overall sales of the company.

The overall profit line is based on the implicit assumption that the ratios of sales of the three products are maintained throughout. The break-even sales of the company can also be readily derived using the overall C/S ratio.

$$\text{Break-even sales} = \frac{\text{Fixed cost}}{\text{C/S ratio}} = \frac{\$20,000}{0.333} = \underline{\underline{\$60,000}}$$

Finally, it may seem surprising that product Z is sold at below direct cost in this example. This may be necessary either to corner a market or to market a product at a low price and sell its accessories at high prices so that overall a profit can be made. The strategy of 'crowd pulling' by selling an item below cost in order to attract customers who may end up buying other profit-making items is also commonly practised by retail companies such as departmental stores.

Principles and Application of Marginal Costing

The term *marginal costing* tends to be applied to any accounting system which at one stage or another differentiates between fixed costs and variable costs and measures contribution from sales. Strictly speaking, a marginal costing system must incorporate the following principles in deriving contribution and profit of a company:

1. *The concept of period costs.* Fixed costs are costs that stem from management policy and represent costs of providing production capacity for a given period of time. These *period costs* are distinct from direct (or marginal) costs and are chargeable against the profit of that period in which they occur. Finished goods and work in process are thus valued at marginal cost without considering overhead cost.
2. *The contribution theory.* Period costs are fixed costs and will not be influenced by the volume of output. Hence earnings from sales must cover the period costs before a company can make profit. Revenue from sales must first cover the marginal cost of production of goods sold. The remaining amount then has to 'contribute' to fixed costs and any surplus is finally realised as profit.

Example 10.3 compares the performances of a company using absorption costing and marginal costing methods.

Example 10.3

The following are the recorded data of a manufacturing company for an operating period:

Sales: 5,000 units at $5 per unit
Production: 6,000 units (variable cost $2/unit, fixed cost $1.50/unit based on 6,000 units output capacity)
Administration and selling expenses: $2,500

1. Cost of sales using absorption costing = ($2 + $1.5) × 5,000
   = $17,500
   Marginal cost of sales = $2 × 5,000 = $10,000
   Total period cost = $1.5 × 6,000 + $2,500 = $11,500

2. The income statements will be:

Absorption costing method		Marginal costing method	
	$		$
Sales revenue	25,000	Sales revenue	25,000
Cost of sales	17,500	Marginal cost	10,000
Gross profit	7,500	Contribution	15,000
Adminstrative and selling expenses	2,500	Fixed costs	11,500
Net profit	5,000	Net profit	3,500

3. If sales are increased to 7,000 units while production remains at 6,000 units (1,000 units from finished goods inventory manufactured in the previous period are sold), the income statements will be:

Absorption costing method		Marginal costing method	
	$		$
Sales revenue	35,000	Sales revenue	35,000
Cost of sales	24,500	Marginal cost	14,000
Gross profit	10,500	Contribution	21,000
Adminstrative and selling expenses	2,500	Fixed costs	11,500
Net profit	8,000	Net profit	9,500

The cost of sales and marginal cost are increased proportionally to the units sold while fixed costs remain the same.

In the original case where sales are less than production, net profit by the absorption costing method is $1,500 more than net profit by the marginal costing method. This is because 1,000 units of goods produced were not sold but transferred to stock. The full cost absorption method valued these stock at $3.50 per unit but marginal costing method only valued them at $2.00 per unit. In the absorption costing method, $1,500 of the period cost has been carried forward to the next period. In the marginal costing method, all fixed costs are treated as expenses in the period; thus reducing the net profit of that period.

In the second case where sales exceed production, the reverse occurs. One thousand units of finished goods were drawn from the earlier period as production lagged behind sales. These units are valued at $2 instead of $3.50 by the marginal costing method. Profit is, therefore, higher by $1,500 compared to the profit of absorption costing method since overhead cost of these 1,000 units are not reflected in the fixed cost of that period.

It can be seen that change in profit with respect to sales is much more drastic using the marginal costing method. Comparing the two cases above, the change in profit computed is only $3,000 (from $5,000 to $8,000) with absorption costing but is $6,000 (from $3,500 to $9,500) with marginal costing.

The following are the salient features of the marginal costing method:

1. *Profit sensitivity.* The variation of profit computed using the marginal costing method is equal to the variation of contribution. It is much more sensitive to sales volume compared to using the absorption costing method. This is due to the absence of buffering effect of the fixed cost component.
2. *Profit margin variation.* Once sufficient contribution has been

received to cover period expenses, all further contribution in that period will be profit. Thus, profit margin (i.e., net profit over sales revenue) will change much faster than the change in sales volume generating it if the marginal costing method is used.

The above features of marginal costing tend to emphasise the importance of sales volume. This fact combined with the concept that any price set above marginal cost represents contribution to cover fixed cost and profit, the tendency is for a company to be aggressive in sales by setting low sales prices. This, in some cases, may lead to selling at a price below actual total cost while still yielding some contribution. The fixed costs, however, cannot be fully recovered due to the low contribution from each unit sold.

Practice Problems

10.1 A company manufactures and sells three products, A, B and C. The performance last year was:

	A	B	C
Sales price	$60	$50	$45
C/S ratio	20%	30%	40%
Sales mix	5 :	1 :	4

The combined sales of all products were 9,000 units and total fixed overhead incurred was $72,600.

The company expects sales in the current year to remain at 9,000 total units. However, by dedicating more effort to promote products B and C, the sales mix can be changed to 2 : 3 : 5.

You are required to:

(a) plot the P/V graphs of the company for last year and the forecasted P/V graph for the current year with changed sales mix;
(b) calculate the C/S ratios and break-even sales of the company as a whole in both cases and, hence, advise whether the company should change its sales mix by promoting products B and C.

10.2 The following data are from a manufacturing company for a certain period:

	$'000
Sales	150
Variable selling expense	15
Variable administrative expense	12
Fixed selling expense	20
Fixed factory overhead	10

	$
Variable factory overhead	5
Direct labour	20
Direct material used	50
Fixed administrative expense	5

(a) Assume that there are no beginning and ending inventories, prepare income statements based on marginal costing and absorption costing methods.
(b) Sketch the P/V graph and determine the break-even sales.

10.3 A company is manufacturing near its production capacity. Its abridged income statement for last year is:

	$	$
Sales (120,000 units)		252,000
Cost of goods sold:		
Variable cost	108,000	
Fixed cost	40,000	
		148,000
Gross profit		104,000
Selling and administration expenses:		
Variable overhead	18,000	
Fixed overhead	38,000	
		56,000
Net profit		48,000

The company was approached by a customer to sign a two-year contract to supply 90,000 units of its product at $1.60 per unit for export. The contract would not affect present selling and administrative fixed overhead. However, a new plant has to be added which would double the fixed manufacturing cost. Variable manufacturing cost and selling and administrative overhead per unit would be the same in both the old and new plants.

You are required to derive the following and advise management whether the company should sign the contract:

(a) an income statement for the first year after adding a new plant, assuming no change in domestic sales;
(b) an income statement for the year after the contract has expired with sales and expenses other than fixed manufacturing cost back to the levels before signing the contract;

(c) the P/V graphs and break-even charts for the two years stated above. Also calculate the break-even sales in both cases.

10.4 A manufacturing company has the following performance record in a certain period for product X:

Production – 5,000 units
Fixed cost – $25,000
Variable cost – $10 per unit for the first 2,000 units and $6 per unit for subsequent units
Selling price – $20 per unit for the first 2,500 units and $15 per units for subsequent units

(a) Draw the break-even chart and profit/volume (P/V) graph and calculate the break-even revenue.
(b) If sales is 4,000 units, derive the income statements based on the absorption costing method and the marginal costing method.

10.5 The following are sales and expenditure data of a manufacturing company for the last month:

	$'000
Sales	300
Salary:	
1. Administrative staff	30
2. Sales staff	40
3. Engineering and R & D	20
4. Production workers	60
Rent and utilities charges:	
1. Office	5
2. Factory	15
Administrative expenses	3
Sales expenses	7
Direct material used in production	60
Depreciation of production machinery	10

Altogether 10,000 units of product were manufactured and sold.

(a) Calculate the unit costs based on the absorption costing and the marginal costing methods.
(b) Prepare the income statements based on the absorption costing method and the marginal costing method.
(c) Comment on the pros and cons of the marginal costing method.

10.6 A company manufactures a single product X with the following performance record for a certain period:

Production – 3,000 units
Fixed cost – $50,000
Variable cost – $50 per unit
Selling price – $70 per unit
Sales – 2,500 units

The company is considering producing two products instead, Y and Z, which complement each other. The performance is expected to be:

Production – 1,500 units each of Y and Z
Fixed cost – $50,000
Variable cost – $60 per unit of Y
　　　　　　　$40 per unit of Z
Selling price – $100 per unit of Y
　　　　　　　$50 per unit of Z

You are required to:

(a) derive the income statements for product X based on the absorption costing method and the marginal costing method;
(b) draw a profit/volume graph for X and another for Y and Z. Indicate their gradients and break-even points respectively;
(c) determine the selling price of Z if the profit is the same for both cases and all the units produced are sold.

PART FOUR

MANAGEMENT ACCOUNTING

Chapter 11

Budgeting and Business Forecast

The only thing that we can predict with certainty is change.

Jayne Spain

While financial accounting involves recording historic events in money terms and cost accounting provides information about costs, management accounting uses these information to plan, control and provide problem-solving analysis in order to help the management run a business efficiently. Among the three categories of accounting, management accounting is the most challenging because unlike the other two, there is no standard procedure to follow which will provide a solution with any amount of certainty.

Various tools are used by management accountants to analyse accounting data, control the operation and plan for future direction of a company. One of the most important tasks of management is to set targets and monitor future performance according to the targets set. This is achieved through the use of budgeting and business forecasting.

Budget Centres and Master Budget

A budget is a plan of action expressed in quantitative terms. Normally *budget centres* are various departments in a company. Budgets prepared by these budget centres are combined to build up a *master budget* which usually comprises the following:

1. The budgeted profit and loss account derived from:
    (a) sales budget (based on sales forecast)
    (b) finished goods inventory budget (to determine the opening and closing stock)

(c) production budget (derived from the first two budgets) which in turn produces the various cost budgets below
(d) raw material purchase budget
(e) raw material inventory budget (to determine opening and closing stock)
(f) labour cost budget
(g) various overhead budgets (factory overhead, service department, administration and selling, etc.)
2. Cash budget (based on forecasted cash receipts and payment)
3. Working capital budget (based on forecasted changes in current assets and current liabilities)
4. Fixed assets budget (with information on planned capital expenditure and sales of fixed assets)
5. Concluding budgeted balance sheet (based on all the budgets above)

Budgets are usually prepared to cover a fixed period of time, most commonly a year following the accounting period. They are divided into shorter time periods of usually calender months (known as *control periods*) for purposes of budgetary control. Some companies operate a *continuous budget* which is a process whereby budgets for a year are continuously extended by a month (or a quarter year) as the month (or quarter year) just ended is dropped.

Besides establishing targets for the operating departments to follow, budgeting has the following advantages:

1. Complete planning. It compels management to look ahead for the company as a whole instead of focusing its attention solely on daily problem-solving.
2. Communication and coordination. Managers of different departments are forced to work together in order to integrate their individual plans. This enhances inter-departmental communication, coordination and spirit of team work.
3. Judging actual performance. Budgets can be used as yard-sticks to compare with actual performance in order to highlight the strengths and weaknesses within an organisation.
4. Responsibility accounting. As managers set the budgets for their own department, they will be more aware of the responsibility they bear to achieve the goals set.
5. Behavioural scientists have observed that participation in setting a budget makes a person psychologically involved in the company. Often the employee becomes more committed and motivated to achieve the target set.

Flexible Budgets

Budgeted income and expenditure of a company must be based on a level of activity of that company. Usually, budgets are based on the past performance in the last period and adjusted by a percentage according to the judgement of the management. Zero-based budgeting, on the other hand, is to budget from scratch with all figures justified by the expected level of activity without referring to the past.

No matter which of the above methods is adopted, a *static budget* will result if only a single level of activity is assumed. Since the future is never certain and forecast is just an intelligent guess, a *flexible budget* can be prepared to cater for a range of activity so that it can be adjusted readily to cope with the changed situation. Comparison of actual performance with a *flexed budget* is much more meaningful compared to judging actual performance against a static budget. A simple illustration is given in example 11.1.

Example 11.1

A company with budgeted production of 10,000 units of goods has the following budgeted costs:

	$
Material	20,000
Labour	30,000
Variable overhead	40,000
Fixed overhead	50,000
Total costs	140,000

If actual production turns out to be 9,000 units in the budgeted period, the flexed budget should be:

	$
Material	18,000
Labour	27,000
Variable overhead	36,000
Fixed overhead	50,000
Total costs	131,000

Note that all variable costs have been adjusted proportionately to actual units of production while the fixed overhead cost remains unchanged.

In comparing actual to budgeted figures, the statement should be:

	Actual cost, $	Flexed budget, $	Differences, $
Material	17,000	18,000	(1,000)
Labour	33,000	27,000	6,000
Variable overhead	34,000	36,000	(2,000)
Fixed overhead	52,000	50,000	2,000
Total cost	136,000	131,000	5,000

Actual total cost was $5,000 above what it should have been, even though it was $4,000 below the original static budget.

Comparing the actual performance with the flexed budget is more equitable than comparing it with the original static budget. The comparison shows where the performance deviates significantly from what it should be and therefore highlights areas which require management's attention. This is the principle of *management by exception* and is developed to a high level of sophistication in the system of analysis of variances. The use of a flexed budget as the reference for comparing actual performance will be evident in Chapter 12 on variance analysis.

Methodology of Business Forecasting

The budget of a company normally hinges on a *principal budget factor* which is also called the *key budget factor* or *limiting budget factor*. It is the factor which imposes a limitation or ceiling on the level of activity of the company.

Sales is often the principal budget factor of a company, hence preparation of the master budget usually begins with sales forecast. Following are some methods of forecasting commonly used:

1. Opinion of the sales force

Though this method may seem primitive and unscientific in its approach, it can turn out a remarkably good forecast. This is because sales staff are in constant contact with customers and clients and, therefore, can sense any change in the market with first hand information. It is similar to the *Delphi Method* whereby the opinion of selected experts are consulted. However, since the feedback of sales staff is usually qualitative and may be biased, it is more useful as input to moderate the forecast derived by other methods.

2. Group management decision

If management is well informed of the market and its future trend, a good forecast can be derived by considering also all other factors applicable to the company. The drawbacks of this method are that there may be a diverse number of views and the compromise budget will not be an impartial decision.

3. Statistical techniques

There are numerous statistical models that can be used for sales forecasting. Two of the simpler and more often used techniques are described here:

(a) *Linear regression* based on historical sales data using the *least square method* to relate sales to time. The linear equation used to extrapolate values of future sales is:

$$\text{Sales} = a + b \times \text{Time}$$

where a and b are constants obtained by the least square method and 'time' refers to the period number corresponding to future sales. This method is essentially trend analysis based simply on historical sales. It does not take into consideration causal factors that influence sales. Example 11.2 illustrates the application of this equation.

(b) *Multiple regression* method can be used to relate sales to several variables. The resulting linear equation is also obtained by the least square method:

$$\text{Sales} = a_0 + a_1 x_1 + a_2 x_2 + \cdots + a_n x_n$$

where a_0, a_1, etc., are constants and x_1, x_2, etc., are factors believed to affect sales. These factors can include time, disposable personal income, gross domestic product (GDP), domestic export to overseas markets, etc.

Advocates of this method believe that this *causal model* is more logical since it incorporates the significant factors that influence sales. The major disadvantage is that forecast for future sales will depend on the forecasts of many factors which may not be reliable.

Regardless of the statistical model adopted for sales forecast, historical sales data have to be used to derive the various parametric constants in the modelling equation. Statistical data, however, are usually plagued by both random and cyclical deviations from a normal trend. Techniques are available to get rid of these deviations before applying the statistical data to a model. The *method of moving average* to eliminate regular cyclic variations is demonstrated in example 11.2. Its application to sales data is particularly useful since sales usually experience seasonal variations with a repetitive cycle of twelve months.

The steps for a forecast using linear regression and incorporating the method of moving average are as follows:

1. Determine the period of cyclic variation in the historical data. Usually the period is twelve months for sales data.
2. Derive the *moving average* to smooth out the time series sales data.

3. Use linear regression to derive the parametric constants of the linear equation with the best fit for historical sales data.
4. Substitute forecasted values of the various factors in the equation to arrive at the forecasted sales.

Example 11.2

Monthly sales of a company in the past two years have been as follows:

	Year before last $'000	Last year $'000
January	180	294
February	135	254
March	168	198
April	273	187
May	167	282
June	192	295
July	286	299
August	197	187
September	181	217
October	206	265
November	195	304
December	196	299
	2,376	3,081

The moving average monthly sales for the twelve-month period are first computed. The derivation can be systematically presented as follows:

Monthly sales $'000	Twelve-month average	Average of two consecutive data, y	Period number, x	$x \cdot y$	x^2
180					
135					
168					
273					
167					
192					
286	198	203	1	203	1
197	208	213	2	426	4
181	217	219	3	657	9
206	220	217	4	868	16
195	213	218	5	1,090	25
196	222	227	6	1,362	36
	231				

294		232	7	1,624	49
254	232	232	8	1,856	64
198	231	233	9	2,097	81
187	234	237	10	2,370	100
282	239	244	11	2,684	121
295	248	253	12	3,036	144
299	257	2,728	78	18,273	650
187					
217					
265					
304					
299					

Note that since the cyclic variation is having a twelve-month period, the average of twelve data falls between the sixth and seventh data. Thus, another averaging for every two consecutive numbers is required to bring the result in line with a designated month. This latter step would not be needed if the moving average has been applied to a time sequence with cyclic variation in odd number of data.

Monthly sales = $a + b \times$ time period number

or $y = a + b \cdot x$

where $a = \bar{y} - b \cdot \bar{x}$

and $\bar{y}, \bar{x}$ are averages of y and x respectively.

Also
$$b = \frac{\sum x \cdot y - \frac{\sum x \cdot \sum y}{n}}{\sum x \cdot x - \frac{\sum x \cdot \sum x}{n}}$$

Thus
$$b = \frac{18{,}273 - \frac{78 \times 2{,}728}{12}}{650 - \frac{78 \times 78}{12}} = 3.78$$

$$a = \frac{2{,}728}{12} - 3.78 \times \frac{78}{12} = 203$$

Monthly sales in thousand dollars = $203 + 3.78 \times$ time period number.

Following the period number assigned in the time series above, it will be 19 for the first month to be forecasted (i.e., January in the year following the last historical data). The resulting forecast for the whole year will be:

	Period number	$'000
January	19	275
February	20	279
March	21	282
April	22	286
May	23	290
June	24	294
July	25	298
August	26	301
September	27	305
October	28	309
November	29	313
December	30	316
		3,548

This represents the trend in growth of sales without incorporating the seasonal variations. Adjustments can be made based on historical records to arrive at a more realistic monthly forecast. Such adjustments are usually done by multiplying the monthly forecast by a percentage which accounts for the monthly deviation from the normal trend.

Practice Problems

11.1 A company has the following budgeted income statement based on a sales volume of 6,800 units:

	$	$
Sales		244,800
Cost of goods sold:		
Direct material	39,440	
Direct labour	31,280	
Direct expenses	3,060	
Depreciation of plant	6,000	
Utilities expenses ($4,500 is fixed cost)	8,920	
Salary of factory manager	28,000	
		(116,700)
Gross profit		128,100
Selling expenses:		
Packaging	18,020	
Sales commissions	18,700	
Shipping	10,600	

Salary of sales staff	28,000	
Variable promotion expense	8,500	
		(83,820)
General and administrative expenses:		
Depreciation	5,500	
Consultant's fees (fixed)	4,600	
Administrative salaries	26,000	
		(36,100)
Income from operation		8,180

You are required to prepare a flexible budget for the company, based on sales and production volumes of 6,000 units and 7,600 units. Compare the two net income figures with the original budgeted profit.

11.2 An electrical appliance manufacturer operating a marginal costing system currently produces two models. The budgeted sales for year 1 are:

> Model 1   40,000 units at $90
> Model 2   80,000 units at $50

Estimated total costs are:

> Direct labour $1,500,000
> Direct material $2,000,000
> Variable overhead $1,800,000
> Fixed overhead $1,700,000

Model 1 requires three times as much labour input and two times as much material as model 2. Variable overhead is absorbed in proportion to direct labour cost. Fixed overhead is not apportioned to individual models.

(a) Prepare the budget for year 1 on marginal costing format showing the figures for individual models as well as the combined budget for the company.
(b) A new Model 3 is to be introduced in year 2. It is expected to sell at $170 with estimated direct labour cost of $30 and direct material cost of $40. Production and sales are budgeted at:

> Model 1   20,000 units
> Model 2   80,000 units
> Model 3   20,000 units

You are required to prepare the budget for year 2 in the same format as (a) above.

11.3 Sales of a company are expected to grow following a power law as follows:

$$S = At^B$$

where t is the year number and A, B are constants. Past performance records are as follows:

Year	Sales, $'000
1	165
2	194
3	227
4	278
5	330

By taking the logarithm of the equation, apply linear regression to find the values of A and B. Also, forecast the sales figure in year 10.

Chapter 12

Standard Costing and Analysis of Variances

If standards are not formulated systematically at the top, they will be formulated haphazardly and impulsively in the field.

John C. Biegler

Principles of Standard Costing

The principle of *management by exception* has long been practised by managers of companies in order to focus their attention on areas where management inputs are required. It is an efficient management tool so that time will not be wasted in monitoring routine operations which are at best left to junior staff. One of the most powerful techniques of applying the principle of management by exception is standard costing.

The idea of standard costing evolves from assessing performance basing on the flexed budget. A standard costing system highlights the differences between the actual and budgeted performance of a company. *Standard costs* are carefully predetermined unit costs while budgeted costs are total costs rather than unit costs. In practice, standard costs and budgeted costs are interchangeable in usage by accountants. *Variances* are differences between actual performance data and standard figures adopted. A variance is *favourable* if it causes the profit of the company to exceed the budgeted amount. On the contrary, a variance will be *unfavourable* if it contributes to lower profit compared to the budget.

Standard costing can be applied to any type of company and to both the absorption costing and marginal costing systems. It has been used extensively in cost accounting to investigate the various causes leading to variation of actual costs from budgeted figures.

Since standard costs are usually set by top management based on past performance data and in consultation with managers of operation departments, it has essentially incorporated the idea of *responsibility accounting*. Operational staff are more conscious of the targets they have to meet and seek more efficient ways of carrying out their assignments. At times, standards can be raised to motivate staff to strive for higher goals. However, these goals should be set at attainable, realistic levels rather than ideal levels so as not to discourage staff.

Classification of Sales and Cost Variances

Analysis of variances is the investigation of the deviation of actual data from budgeted figures by tracing such deviations to the changes of component factors from budgeted values. There are two main classes of variances: sales variances and cost variances. Sales and cost are related to the profit of a company by the following equation:

$$\text{Profit} = \text{Sales revenue} - \text{Total cost}$$

Thus, any deviation of profit from the budgeted figures can be explained by analysing the sales and cost variances. The component factors of sales and cost can be expressed in the following diagram:

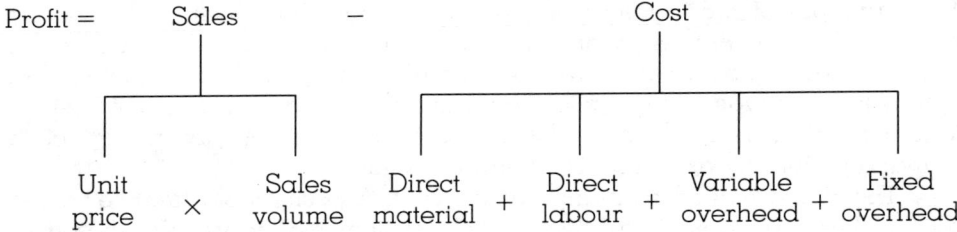

Sales variance is the difference between actual revenue and budgeted revenue. It comprises two component variances:

1. *Price variance* caused by actual selling price being different from budgeted selling price
2. *Volume variance* due to actual sales quantity being different from budgeted sales volume

Component variances of cost are much more complex as there are many factors involved. They can be classified in a tree structure as shown in Figure 12.1.

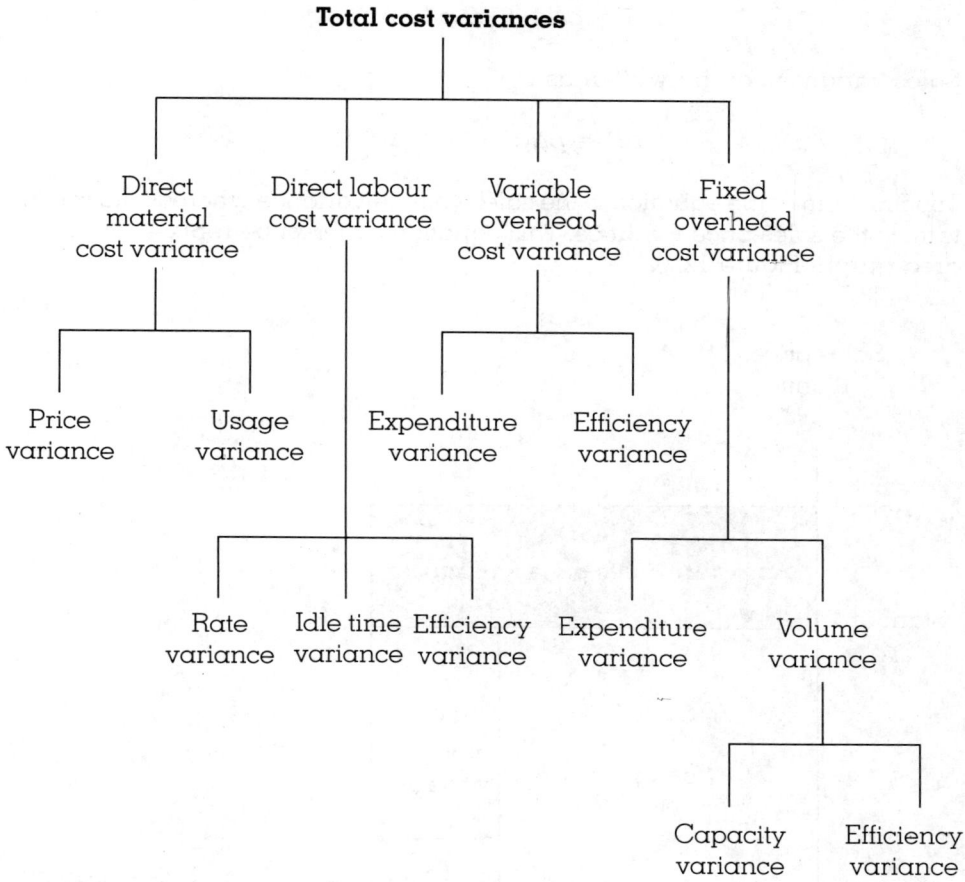

Figure 12.1 Component variances of cost

Mathematical and Graphical Representation of Variances

1. Sales variances

Unit sales price and sales quantity are the two variables involved. Let the standard price be p and standard sales quantity be q. The variations in actual data from standard figures are represented by Δp and Δq. Actual sales revenue will be:

$$(S + \Delta S) = (p + \Delta p)(q + \Delta q)$$

Since standard sales revenue $S = p \cdot q$,

$$\Delta S = p\Delta q + q\Delta p + \Delta p \cdot \Delta q$$

Sales variance can be written as:

$$\Delta S = p\Delta q + (q + \Delta q)\Delta p$$

The first term of the equation is the sales volume variance whereas the second term is the sales price variance. This equation can best be represented by an area graph (Figure 12.2).

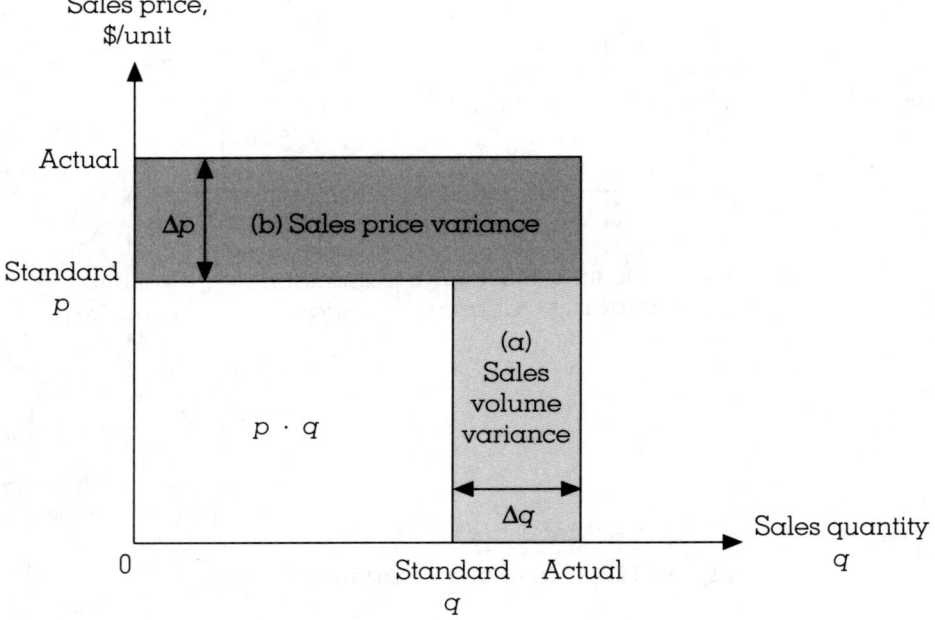

Figure 12.2 Graphical representation of sales variances

From either the equation or the graph, the two component variances of sales can be stated as follows:

(a) Sales volume variance
   = Standard unit price × Volume variance in units
(b) Sales price variance
   = Unit price variance × Actual units sold
   = Actual sales − Standard unit price × Actual units sold

Note that variances are computed using actual values to subtract standard values. Positive sales variances always contribute to higher profit and are, therefore, favourable variances. Negative sales variances are adverse variances.

The graph in Figure 12.2 should only be used to derive sales variance equations before actual data is substituted. It is not to be drawn with actual data because the resulting graph will not be useful. Example 12.1 will demonstrates how sales variances are calculated.

2. Direct material cost variances

Material cost variances are analogous to sales variances. The unit cost of material can be reckoned as unit sales price p, and material used can be treated as the sales quantity q. Thus, the component variances of direct material cost are:

(1) Price variance
 = Unit price variance × Actual quantity
 = Actual material cost − Standard unit price × Actual quantity
(2) Usage variance
 = Quantity variance × Standard unit price
 = [Actual quantity − Standard (flexed) quantity] × Standard unit price

It is obvious that variance equations can be readily derived from the area graph which is also much easier to memorise (Figure 12.3). One more

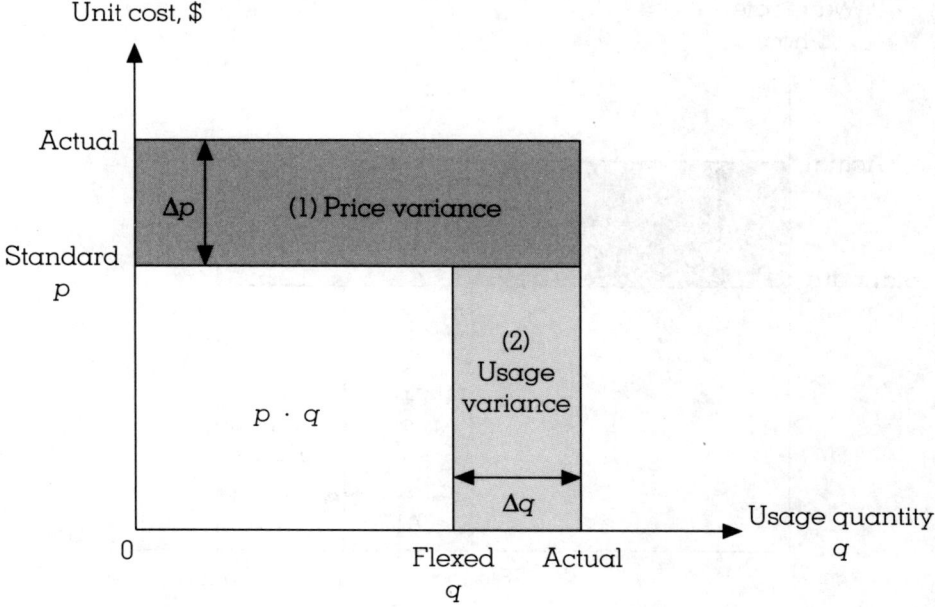

Figure 12.3 Graphical representation of direct material variances

CHAPTER 12 STANDARD COSTING AND ANALYSIS OF VARIANCES

point to note is that contrary to sales variances, all positive cost variances will reduce the profit of a company since actual costs are higher than standard (or flexed) costs. Positive cost variances are adverse variances while negative cost variances are favourable variances.

3. Direct labour cost variances

Standard labour cost, LC is the product of standard hours h, and standard hourly wage rate w. Hence:

$$LC = h \cdot w$$

and
$$(LC + \Delta LC) = (h + \Delta h + t) \cdot (w + \Delta w)$$

where t is the idle time in hours and all the incremental terms are deviations of actual figures from standard values. The standard hours are flexed hours based on actual output. Labour cost variance can then be expressed as follows:

$$LC = w \cdot t + w \cdot \Delta h + (h + \Delta h + t)\Delta w$$

The first term is the idle time variance, the second term represents the efficiency variance and the third term is the rate variance. A graphical representation is shown in Figure 12.4.

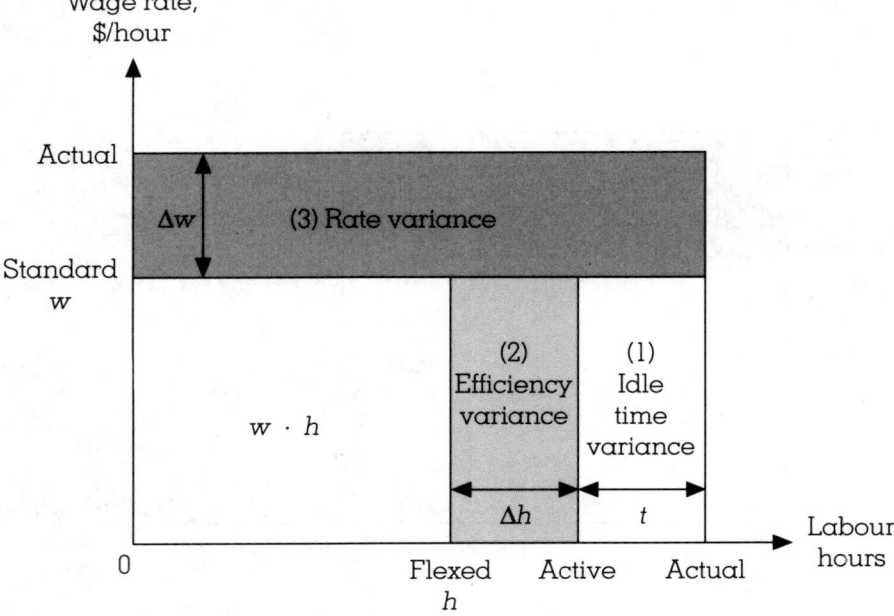

Figure 12.4 Graphical representation of labour cost variances

The components of labour cost variances are:

(1) Idle time variance = Idle time × Standard wage rate
(2) Efficiency variance
   = (Active hours − Flexed hours) × Standard wage rate
(3) Rate variance
   = Wage rate variance × Actual hours
   = Actual labour cost − Standard wage rate × Actual hours

4. Variable overhead variances

Variable overhead variance bears a close resemblance to direct labour cost variance. The mathematical equation defining the variable overhead variance, ΔVO is as follows:

$$(VO + \Delta VO) = (h + \Delta h + t) \cdot (v + \Delta v)$$

where v and Δv are the standard variable overhead rate and the difference of actual rate from v respectively. Since variable overhead $VO = h \cdot v$,

$$\Delta VO = [(h + \Delta h + t)\Delta v + v \cdot t] + v \cdot \Delta h$$

The term in the square bracket is the *expenditure variance* which is equivalent to combining the rate variance and idle time variance in the case of labour cost variances. The other term in the equation above is the *efficiency variance*. These are shown in Figure 12.5.

More specifically, the two variable overhead variances are:

(1) Expenditure variance
   = Actual variable overhead − Active labour hours
     × Standard overhead rate
(2) Efficiency variance
   = (Active hours − Flexed hours) × Standard overhead rate

5. Fixed overhead variances

An analysis of fixed overhead variances is performed to ascertain what factors contribute to the difference between actual fixed overhead and the amount absorbed in an absorption costing system based on the flexed hours and standard absorption rate.

Let the standard labour hours for production of the actual output (i.e., the flexed hours) be h and the differences among standard, active, budgeted and actual labour hours be as shown in Figure 12.6, then:

$$\text{Standard fixed overhead } FO = r \cdot h$$

where r is the standard absorption rate. Fixed overhead variance will be:

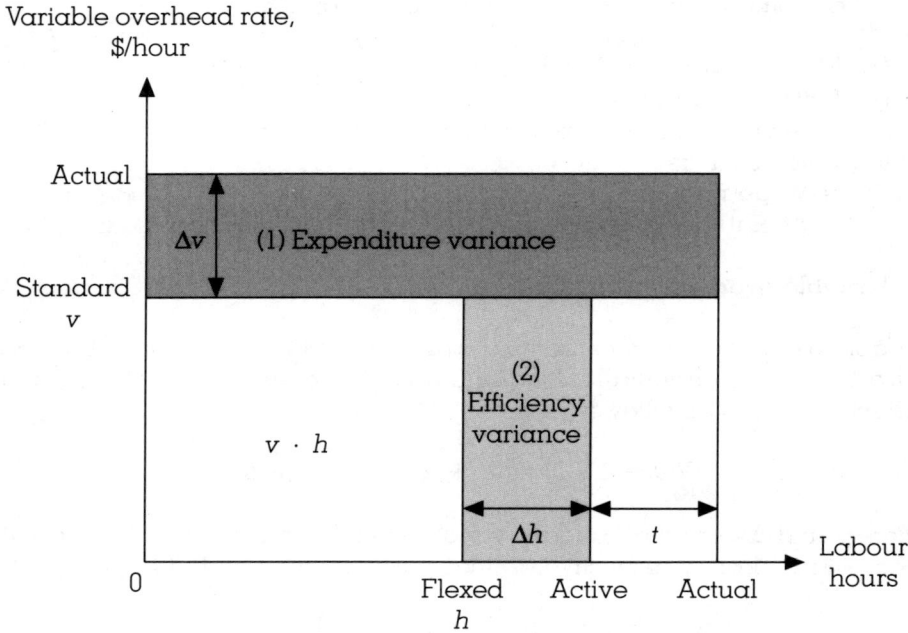

Figure 12.5 Graphical representation of variable overhead variances

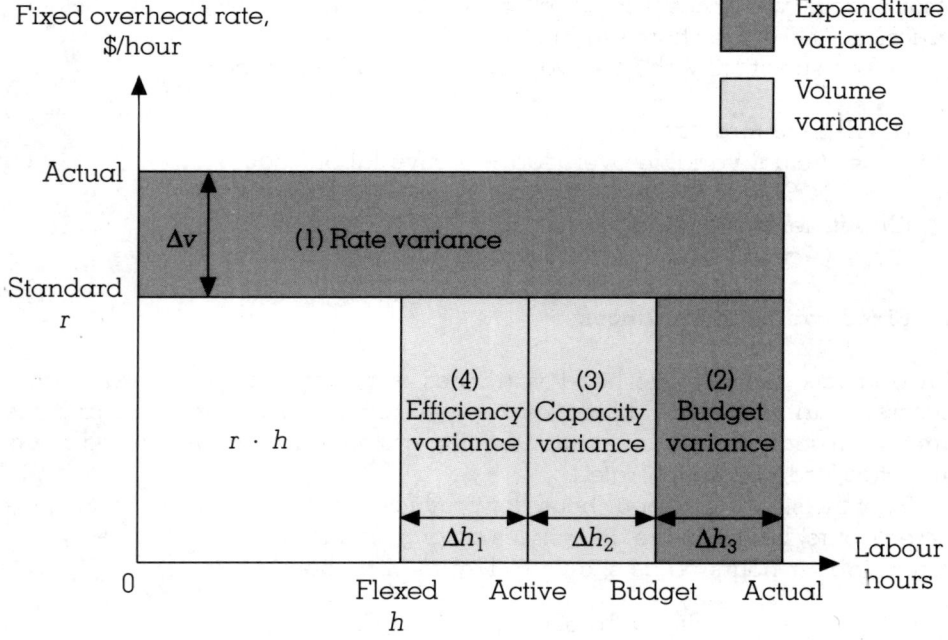

Figure 12.6 Graphical representation of fixed overhead variances

$$\Delta FO = (h + \Delta h_1 + \Delta h_2 + \Delta h_3)(r + \Delta r) - r \cdot h$$
$$= (h + \Delta h_1 + \Delta h_2 + \Delta h_3)\Delta r + \Delta h_3 \cdot r + \Delta h_2 \cdot r + \Delta h_1 \cdot r$$

Each term of the equation for fixed overhead variance is represented by an area in the graph. There are altogether four component variances for fixed overhead:

(1) Rate variance
 = Absorption rate variance × Actual hours
 = Actual fixed overhead − Actual hours × Standard absorption rate
(2) Budget variance
 = (Actual hours − Budgeted hours) × Standard absorption rate
(3) Capacity variance
 = (Budgeted hours − Active hours) × Standard absorption rate
(4) Efficiency variance
 = (Active hours − Flexed hours) × Standard absorption rate

The rate and budget variances are sometimes merged to form the expenditure variance which can be expressed as:

Expenditure variance
 = Actual fixed overhead − Standard absorption rate × Budgeted hours

The capacity variance and efficiency variance are collectively known as the volume variance which can also be defined as follows:

Volume variance
 = (Budgeted hours − Flexed hours) × Standard absorption rate

The applications of all the formulae developed are best illustrated by example 12.1. Note that all variances in the example are numbered in exactly the same manner as in the graphs and equations in this section.

Example 12.1

A company manufactures a single product and operates a standard absorption costing system. The sales price and standard costs per unit of the product are as follows:

	$	$
Sales price		25
less standard costs:		
Direct material (2 litres @ $3/litre)	6	
Direct labour (4 hours @ $2/hour)	8	
Variable overhead (4 hours @ $0.5/hour)	2	

Fixed overhead (4 hours @ $1.5/hour)	6	
		22
Standard profit		3

The fixed overhead absorption rate of $1.50 per direct labour hour has been derived from the budget to produce and sell 100 units of goods. Actual results turned out to be:

	$	$
Sales (110 units)		2,700
less costs to produce the 110 units:		
Direct material (230 litres)	675	
Direct labour (450 hours)	915	
Variable overhead	225	
Fixed overhead	655	
		2,470
Actual total profit		230

It was also found that twenty labour hours were lost due to idle time.

1. The budget, flexed budget and actual performance data are listed before starting the analysis:

	Budget	Flexed budget	Actual
Production and sales (units)	100	110	110
	$	$	$
Sales	2,500	2,750	2,700
less: Direct material	600	660	675
Direct labour	800	880	915
Variable overhead	200	220	225
Fixed overhead	600	660	655
Total costs	2,200	2,420	2,470
Profit	300	330	230

Note that fixed overhead has been adjusted according to the level of activity in the flexed budget. This is contrary to what was stipulated in Chapter 11. The reason is that in the case of fixed overhead variance analysis, comparison is made between actual overhead cost and what has been absorbed and already recorded in cost accounts. Since every unit produced is absorbing fixed overhead at a standard rate, the flexed budget based on actual units produced, therefore, incorporates the actual fixed overhead absorbed.

2. Sales variances:

Total sales variance = Actual sales − Budgeted sales
= $2,700 − $2,500
= $200(F)

where (F) indicates that the variance is favourable. Similarly (A) will imply that a variance is adverse.

(a) Sales volume variance = Standard unit price × Volume variance
= $25 × 10 = $250(F)

(b) Sales price variance
= Unit price variance × Actual units sold
= Actual sales − Standard unit price × Actual units sold
= $2,700 − $25 × 110 = $50(A)

3. Cost variances:

The various direct cost and overhead cost variances are readily obtained by comparing the actual performance and flexed budget:

a. Direct material variance   = $675 − $660 = $15(A)
b. Direct labour variance   = $915 − $880 = $35(A)
c. Variable overhead variance = $225 − $220 = $5(A)
d. Fixed overhead variance   = $655 − $660 = $5(F)
                                              $50(A)

These are analysed in detail as follows:

a. Direct material variances

   (1) Price variance
       = Actual material cost − Standard unit price × Actual quantity
       = $675 − $3 × 230 = $15(F)

CHAPTER 12 STANDARD COSTING AND ANALYSIS OF VARIANCES

(2) Usage variance
= (Actual quantity − Flexed quantity) × Standard unit price
= (230 − 220) × $3 = $30(A)

b. Direct labour variances

(1) Idle time variance
= Idle time × Standard wage rate
= 20 × $2 = $40(A)

(2) Efficiency variance
= (Active hours − Flexed hours) × Standard wage rate
= [(450 − 20) − 440] × $2 = $20(F)

(3) Rate variance
= Actual labour cost − Standard wage rate × Actual hours
= $915 − $2 × 450 = $15(A)

c. Variable overhead variances

(1) Expenditure variance
= Actual variable overhead − Active hours × Standard rate
= $225 − (450 − 20) × $0.5 = $10(A)

(2) Efficiency variance
= (Active hours − Flexed hours) × Standard rate
= (450 − 20 − 440) × $0.5 = $5(F)

d. Fixed overhead variances

(1) Rate variance
= Actual fixed overhead − Standard rate × Actual hours
= $655 − $1.50 × 450 = $20(F)

(2) Budget variance
= (Actual hours − Budgeted hours) × Standard rate
= (450 − 400) × $1.50 = $75(A)

(3) Capacity variance
= (Budgeted hours − Active hours) × Standard rate
= [400 − (450 − 20)] × $1.50 = $45(F)

(4) Efficiency variance
= (Active hours − Flexed hours) × Standard rate
= (450 − 20 − 440) × $1.50 = $15(F)

Combining (1) and (2) gives:
Expenditure variance = $20(F) + $75(A) = $55(A)

Merging (3) and (4) results in:
Volume variance = $45(F) + $15(F) = $60(F)

Expenditure variance is adverse because actual fixed overhead is higher than the budgeted amount by $55. Volume variance is favourable because flexed labour hours based on the increased output is more than the budgeted hours, thus giving rise to overabsorption of overhead. Consequently, actual fixed overhead is viewed favourably compared to the overhead absorbed.

4. Operating statement

The operating statement reconciles the actual profit with the budget profit figures. It is a profit and loss statement of an operating period showing all the sales and cost variances for that period. A typical statement using data derived in this example is as follows:

		$(F)	$(A)	$
Budgeted sales				2,500
less: standard cost of budgeted sales				2,200
Budgeted profit				300
Sales variances		$(F)	$(A)	
1.	Sales volume variance	250		
	Standard cost of sales of volume variance	220		
	Sales volume profit variance	30		
2.	Sales price variance		50	
		30	50	
				20(A)
				280
Profit on actual sales before considering cost variances				
Cost variances:		$(F)	$(A)	
Direct material price		15		
Direct material usage			30	
Direct labour idle time			40	
Direct labour efficiency		20		
Direct labour wage rate			15	
Variable overhead expenditure			10	
Variable overhead efficiency		5		
Fixed overhead rate		20		
Fixed overhead budget			75	
Fixed overhead capacity		45		
Fixed overhead efficiency		15		
		120	170	
				50(A)
Actual profit:				230

Note that sales volume variance gives the change in sales revenue rather than profit. Thus, the standard cost of sales volume variance has to be subtracted in this case to obtain the profit variance of $30(F). If the sales volume variance is adverse, the standard cost of that sales volume variance should be added back because profit is not reduced by as much as the reduction in sales.

Accounting Entries of Variances

All sales and cost accounts in a standard costing system are credited or debited with standard values. In addition. each variance has its own account. Entries in the sales variance as well as cost variance accounts follow the same rule: a favourable variance is a credit entry and an adverse variance is a debit entry.

Sales or cost variance	
Adverse variance	Favourable variance

To illustrate, a credit sales will be accorded as follows:

Debtors		Sales		Sales price variance	
Actual sales revenue			Standard sales revenue	Adverse variance	Favourable variance

Entries of the sales account and sales price variance account should add up to the actual sales revenue. It is readily seen that in effect, a favourable variance will add to the credit balance of the standard sales revenue recorded in the sales account. On the other hand, an adverse variance will reduce the credit balance in the sales account.

Recording in cost accounts is illustrated by the following entries accounting for raw material transferred to work in process.

Raw material		Work in process		Direct material variance	
	Actual cost	Standard material cost		Adverse variance	Favourable variance

PART FOUR MANAGEMENT ACCOUNTING

It can be seen that a favourable variance will reduce the debit balance of the work in process account while an adverse variance will add on to the standard cost recorded in the work in process account.

Variance accounts are similar in nature to contra accounts in the case of fixed assets and accumulated depreciation. Sales or cost accounts which are entered with standard values have to be read in conjunction with their respective variance accounts in order to obtain the actual values. All variance accounts are closed by transferring their balances to the profit and loss account at the end of an accounting cycle.

Practice Problems

12.1 The following information is for a certain period in a manufacturing department:

1. Material usage: 55 kg of materials were issued from the store at $96 per kg. 4,000 units were produced. The standard for this product is 80 kg per unit at $100 per kg.
2. Direct labour: 280 hours were used and wage paid were $1820. Standard time for the work is 5.1 minutes per unit at $6 per hour.
3. Overhead: Actual expenditure for this period amounted to $3,700. The budgeted expenditure was $3500 for an output of 3,500 units (basing on $1 per unit).

You are required to analyse the various variances and summarise them in an operation statement of the department.

12.2 The standard cost of production of a product is as follows:

	$
Direct material (4 kg @ $4/kg)	16
Direct labour (2 hrs @ $3/hr)	6
Variable overhead (2 hrs @ $1/hr)	2
Fixed overhead (2 hrs @ $2/hr)	4
Standard cost per unit	28

The fixed overhead absorption rate is based on direct labour hours and budgeted production of 1,000 units. The actual results turned out to be:

	$
Direct material (3,900 kg)	15,800
Direct labour (1,950 hr)	5,460
Variable overhead	2,100
Fixed overhead	4,500
	27,860

Production was 980 units and 50 labour hours were lost due to unforeseen circumstances.

You are required to prepare:

(a) a cost of production budget based on the planned production volume and a flexed budget based on the actual production,
(b) variance analysis of the various cost components.

12.3 The standard cost of production of a product is as follows:

	$
Direct material (5 kg @ $3/kg)	15
Direct labour (1 hr @ $3/hr)	3
Variable overhead (1 hr @ $1/hr)	1
Fixed overhead (1 hr @ $2/hr)	2
Standard cost per unit	21

The fixed overhead absorption rate is based on direct labour hours and budgeted production of 2,000 units. The actual results turned out to be:

	$
Direct material (9,800 kg)	28,910
Direct labour (2,100 hr)	6,090
Variable overhead	2,200
Fixed overhead	4,000
	41,200

Production was 2,100 units and 100 labour hours were lost due to unforeseen circumstances.

You are required to:

(a) prepare a cost of production budget based on the planned production volume and a flexed budget based on actual production,
(b) prepare a variance analysis of the various cost components,
(c) reconcile the actual and budgeted profit figures by an operating statement.

Chapter 13

Analysis of Financial Statement by Ratios

Next to knowing all about your own business, the best thing to know is all about the other fellow's business.

John D. Rockefeller

When the financial statements of a company are analysed, individual items and absolute amounts are in themselves generally not very informative. It is the relationships among items and their relative magnitude as well as changes that have occurred that are important. Thus, analysis of financial statements are usually based on comparative techniques listed below:

1. *Horizontal analysis.* Comparative financial statements over two or more years are placed side by side. Changes in corresponding items are computed in dollar amounts and/or percentage between each pair of items horizontally.
2. *Trend analysis.* The horizontal analysis is extended for a number of years to establish the trends for items in financial statements.
3. *Vertical analysis.* The dollar amount of each item in a financial statement is expressed as a percentage of a relevant total in the same statement. Usually items in profit and loss statements are divided by net sales and items in balance sheets are divided by total assets. Such *normalisation* of financial data allows more equitable comparison with past performance and with other companies since all items are scaled to get rid of the problem of different sizes of operation. The resulting financial statements in percentage terms are therefore called *common-size financial statements.*
4. *Ratio analysis.* The dollar amounts of two items in a financial statement are compared and expressed in terms of a ratio. Many different ratios can be computed depending on the information needed. Financial ratios at different time periods are subjected to

horizontal and trend analyses. They can also be compared with ratios of other companies operating in the same industry.

The first three types of analysis are easily understood and will not be discussed further. Ratio analysis will be explained with financial ratios classified into four categories under:

1. profitability analysis
2. liquidity analysis
3. finance ratio analysis
4. stock market ratio analysis

Profitability Ratios

This is a class of ratios to measure a company's operating performance in term of its ability to generate profit (net income). Profit and net income are sometimes called *earnings*. Profitability of a company is determined by two factors: profit margin and speed of turnover. Good profit per unit sold and high volume of sales both contribute to good earnings of a company.

The most important ratio to measure profitability is *return on capital employed* or ROCE in short. It measures the efficiency with which a company is utilising its assets. *Return* is the net income from operation of a company which is defined as *earnings before interest and tax*. Accountants commonly call it EBIT in short. Interest is excluded in computing return because financing charge on borrowings is due to capital structure rather than operating efficiency of the company. Tax is also not within the control of the manager and therefore unrelated to measurement of profitability. *Capital employed* refers to the total assets engaged in the company. It is also the owners' capital plus long-term loan as derived from the accounting equation:

(Fixed assets + Current assets)
= (Long-term liabilities + Current liabilities) + Owners' equity

i.e., (Fixed assets + Working capital)
= (Long-term liabilities + Owners' equity)
= Capital employed

In summary:

Return = Earnings before interest and tax (EBIT)

Capital employed = (Fixed assets + Working capital)
= (Long-term liabilities + Owners' equity)

$$\text{Return on capital employed (ROCE)} = \frac{\text{Return}}{\text{Capital employed}}$$

Return on capital employed can be readily expressed in terms of *profit margin* and *asset turnover ratio:*

$$\text{ROCE} = \text{Profit margin} \times \text{Asset turnover}$$
$$= \frac{\text{Return}}{\text{Sales}} \times \frac{\text{Sales}}{\text{Capital employed}}$$

The earlier statement that profitability of a company is determined by profit margin of sales and speed of turnover is readily verified by this equation.

Other ratios measure various factors affecting the profit margin and asset utilisation of a company. These two branches of ratios are grouped in Figure 13.1.

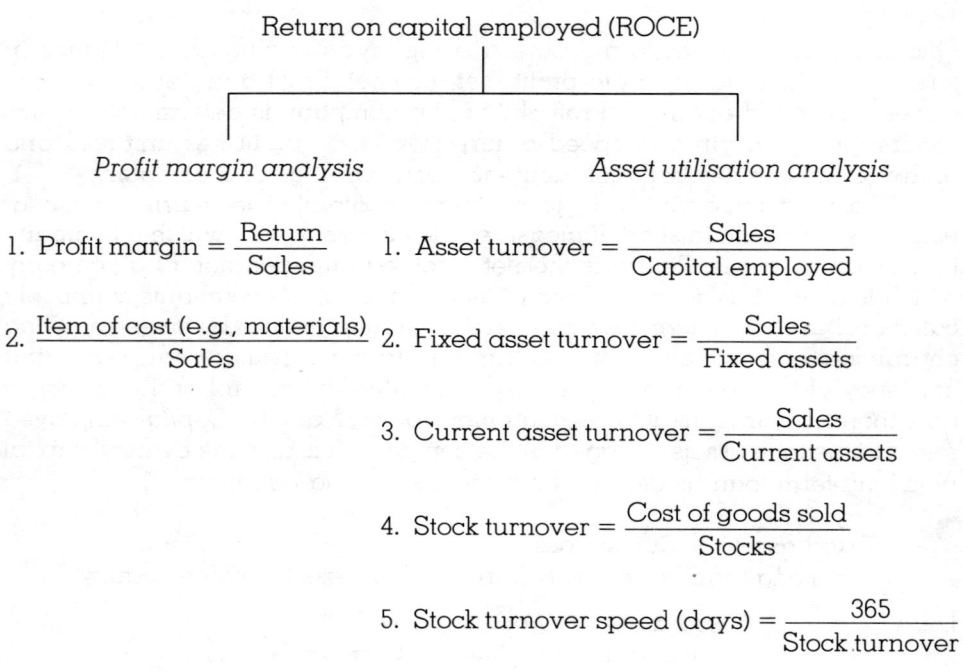

Return on capital employed (ROCE)

Profit margin analysis

1. Profit margin = $\dfrac{\text{Return}}{\text{Sales}}$

2. $\dfrac{\text{Item of cost (e.g., materials)}}{\text{Sales}}$

Asset utilisation analysis

1. Asset turnover = $\dfrac{\text{Sales}}{\text{Capital employed}}$

2. Fixed asset turnover = $\dfrac{\text{Sales}}{\text{Fixed assets}}$

3. Current asset turnover = $\dfrac{\text{Sales}}{\text{Current assets}}$

4. Stock turnover = $\dfrac{\text{Cost of goods sold}}{\text{Stocks}}$

5. Stock turnover speed (days) = $\dfrac{365}{\text{Stock turnover}}$

Figure 13.1

The following points should be noted:

1. Stock turnover is expressed in terms of cost of goods sold. It is sometimes estimated from the ratio of sales revenue to stock if the cost of goods sold figure is unavailable.
2. Working capital turnover can also be computed in addition to current asset turnover.

3. Since all asset values vary from time to time, their average values throughout the year are more representative and should be used if data are available.
4. All profit margin ratios are expressed with sales as denominators while asset utilisation ratios usually have sales as the numerator.

Liquidity Ratios

A company is *liquid* or *solvent* if it can discharge its current liabilities within short notice. As explained in Chapter 7, the ability to pay short-term debt is crucial to the continued viability of a business regardless of whether it is profitable. The liquidity of a company depends on the amount of its working capital. Hence, all the ratios used to measure the liquidity of a company are expressed in terms of current assets and current liabilities. The two most important liquidity ratios are:

1. Current ratio $= \dfrac{\text{Current assets}}{\text{Current liabilities}}$

2. Quick ratio $= \dfrac{\text{Liquid assets}}{\text{Current liabilities}}$

where liquid assets = current assets − (stock + prepayments)

The current ratio is usually taken to be 2 for a stable organisation. However, it is important to consider the type of activity undertaken by the company. Generally a manufacturing firm has a higher current ratio than a merchandising firm.

The quick ratio is also called the *acid-test ratio*. As stock and prepayments are current assets not easily convertible to cash, they are excluded in the computation of this ratio which is a test of the immediate solvency of a business. The quick ratio is generally considered safe if it is greater than one. This, however, depends on the ability of a company to raise further cash from its bank on short notice. Thus, a low ratio may not be dangerous if a company is backed by large institutions with ample financial resources. This ratio may also fall in time of prosperity due to the necessity to keep more stocks to meet sales demand, thus reducing the liquid assets proportionately. Sometimes accumulation of cash without using it to the best advantage will raise the ratio. Therefore, the ratio must be analysed further before asserting if it is satisfactory.

Two of the major current assets which influence and sometimes obscure the current ratio and quick ratio are stocks and debtors. The following two ratios are used to provide more insight to the liquidity of a company:

Stock-to-net-current-assets $= \dfrac{\text{Stock}}{\text{Current assets} - \text{Stock}}$

$$\text{Debtors' ratio} = \frac{\text{Debtors}}{\text{Sales}}$$

High stock-to-net-current-assets ratio may be due to too much stock carried because of bad inventory control. It can also be caused by the presence of obsolete and obsolescent stock. Too low a ratio usually indicates excessive cash balance and/or poor collection of debt. The latter cause can be explored further by analysing the debtors' ratio. A high debtors' ratio implies that customers are not paying the company fast enough. This can be further highlighted by two other ratios similar to stock turnover ratios:

$$\text{Debtors' turnover ratio} = \frac{\text{Sales}}{\text{Debtors}}$$

$$\text{Average debt collection period (days)} = \frac{365}{\text{Debtors' turnover ratio}}$$

For more accurate computation of the above ratios, sales on credit instead of total sales figure should be used if it is available. As most companies give credit periods to customers varying from 30 to 90 days, an average debt collection period of below 60 days may be considered satisfactory. However, this again depends on the type of business a company is engaged in and the profile and size of its customer base.

In combination with stock turnover speed, the average working capital cycle of a company can be derived as follows:

Average working capital cycle
 = Time to convert stock to sale + Time to collect cash from customers
 = Stock turnover speed + Average debt collection period

Short working capital cycle implies that the company is experiencing brisk sales and collecting money quickly to finance further activities. This contributes both to higher profitability and better liquidity of the company.

Finance Ratios

Finance ratios measure the proportion of capital employed raised by fixed interest debt and the ability of the company to repay the debt. Two ratios are commonly used:

1. Debt ratio (also called borrowing ratio, leverage ratio and gearing ratio)

$$= \frac{\text{Fixed interest loan}}{\text{Capital employed}}$$

2. Debt service ratio (also called times interest earned)
$$= \frac{\text{Earnings before interest and tax (EBIT)}}{\text{Interest on fixed interest loan}}$$

Fixed interest loans are usually long-term loans which are employed as part of the funds necessary to finance the operation of a company. Creditors prefer a moderate debt ratio as this increases their security. By contrast, equity owners may seek high leverage (or high gearing) because it magnifies profit increments at the *profit-available-for-shareholders level*. This is because returns on capital employed are usually higher than the rate of interest charged for long-term loans. Obtaining such loans by issuing *debentures* or *loan stocks* is a method of raising additional finance without diluting control of the company.

Debt service ratio measures the ability of a company to pay interest to debenture holders who have priority over shareholders when distributing the profits of the company. A high ratio is desirable to provide a satisfactory margin of safety for debenture holders. Since earnings is used in the computation, it may not directly translate to cash required to pay for fixed interest expenses. Debt service ratio therefore does not reflect directly on the ability of the company to pay a fixed interest and it is not a liquidity ratio.

Stock Market Ratios

Four ratios are commonly published in the share information pages of newspapers together with the share prices of public companies listed in the Stock Exchange of Singapore. These are intended to give the investing public a fair idea of the latest performance of companies in relation to their market prices.

1. Dividend yield $= \dfrac{\text{Gross dividends (before tax deduction) per share}}{\text{Market price per share}}$

2. Earnings per share (EPS) $= \dfrac{\text{Profit after tax}}{\text{Number of shares issued}}$

3. Dividend cover $= \dfrac{\text{Earnings per share}}{\text{Gross dividends per share}}$

4. Price-earnings ratio (P/E ratio) $= \dfrac{\text{Market price per share}}{\text{Earnings per share}}$

Gross dividends and profit after tax used to compute these ratios are based on the latest figures available for the preceding annual period. These ratios are therefore not necessarily the most up-to-date figures as only the market price is current value.

Dividend yield represents the return on money invested before capital gain (or loss) is realised at the time the shares are sold. Earnings per share, on the other hand, gives the amount of entitlement to the latest annual profit, for every share issued. Profit after tax is not necessarily all distributed as dividends to shareholders. Depending on the dividend policy by the board of directors of a company, a bigger or smaller sum may be retained in the company to finance future operation and expansion. This is reflected in the dividend cover ratio.

Finally, the price-earnings ratio is the most important yardstick for assessing the relative worth of a share. It is equal to the number of times of latest annual earnings needed to make up the current market price. The higher the P/E ratio, the greater is the confidence of the investing public in the company's future performance as they are paying a relatively higher price in relation to the latest earnings of the company. It, therefore, reflects the market's appraisal of the future prospect of the shares. Generally, a value of ten has been considered as the norm for publicly listed companies. Numerous factors including the speculative element, expected growth, assets backing per share, etc. usually influence the share price of a company so that no standard P/E ratio can be stipulated.

As P/E ratio is defined in terms of earnings and market price which are also factors in the other ratios, the following relationship can be readily derived:

$$P/E = \frac{\text{Market price per share}}{\text{Gross dividends per share}} \times \frac{\text{Gross dividends per share}}{\text{Earnings per share}}$$

$$= \frac{1}{\text{Dividend yield} \times \text{Dividend cover}}$$

To illustrate the application of all the ratios discussed so far, the abridged profit and loss and retained earnings statement and the balance sheet of a company for two consecutive years are used in Example 13.1.

Example 13.1

Profit and loss and retained earnings statement

	Year 2 $	Year 1 $
Sales revenue	525,000	425,000
Trading profit	54,000	41,000
Interest on: fixed interest loan	(3,000)	(3,000)
bank overdraft	(1,000)	(500)
Profit before income tax	50,000	37,500

Income tax	(20,000)	(15,000)
	30,000	22,500
Dividends	(15,000)	(10,000)
Retained earnings	15,000	12,500

Balance sheet

	Year 2		Year 1	
	$	$	$	$
Share capital		190,000		85,000
Retained earnings		135,000		120,000
		325,000		205,000
Fixed interest loan		50,000		50,000
		375,000		255,000
Fixed assets:				
Premises		125,000		75,000
Machinery		130,000		70,000
		255,000		145,000
Current assets:				
Stock	120,000		100,000	
Debtors	80,000		60,000	
	200,000		160,000	
less: current liabilities:				
Creditors	45,000		30,000	
Bank loan (overdraft)	15,000		5,000	
Tax payable	20,000		15,000	
	80,000		50,000	
		120,000		110,000
Working capital		375,000		255,000

The nominal value of shares issued is $1.00 per share. Market value is $1.50 per share in both year 1 and year 2.

Profitability ratios

	Year 2	Year 1
Return on capital employed	$\dfrac{54,000}{375,000} = 14.4\%$	$\dfrac{41,000}{255,000} = 16.08\%$

CHAPTER 13 ANALYSIS OF FINANCIAL STATEMENT BY RATIOS

Profit margin	$\dfrac{54{,}000}{525{,}000} = 10.29\%$	$\dfrac{41{,}000}{425{,}000} = 9.65\%$
Assets turnover	$\dfrac{525{,}000}{375{,}000} = 1.40$	$\dfrac{425{,}000}{255{,}000} = 1.67$
Stock turnover	$\dfrac{525{,}000}{120{,}000} = 4.37$	$\dfrac{425{,}000}{100{,}000} = 4.25$

Liquidity ratios

Current ratio	$\dfrac{200{,}000}{80{,}000} = 2.50$	$\dfrac{160{,}000}{50{,}000} = 3.20$
Quick ratio	$\dfrac{80{,}000}{80{,}000} = 1.00$	$\dfrac{60{,}000}{50{,}000} = 1.20$
Stock to net current assets	$\dfrac{120{,}000}{200{,}000 - 120{,}000} = 1.50$	$\dfrac{100{,}000}{160{,}000 - 100{,}000} = 1.67$
Debt collection period	$\dfrac{365}{\frac{525{,}000}{80{,}000}} = 56 \text{ days}$	$\dfrac{365}{\frac{425{,}000}{60{,}000}} = 52 \text{ days}$

Finance ratios

Gearing ratio	$\dfrac{50{,}000}{375{,}000} = 13.33\%$	$\dfrac{50{,}000}{255{,}000} = 19.61\%$
Debt service ratio	$\dfrac{54{,}000}{3{,}000} = 18.00$	$\dfrac{41{,}000}{3{,}000} = 13.67$

Stock market ratios

Dividend yield	$\dfrac{\frac{15{,}000}{190{,}000}}{1.50} = 5.26\%$	$\dfrac{\frac{10{,}000}{85{,}000}}{1.50} = 7.84\%$
Earnings per share	$\dfrac{\$30{,}000}{190{,}000} = \$0.16$	$\dfrac{\$22{,}500}{85{,}000} = \$0.26$
Dividend cover	$\dfrac{30{,}000}{15{,}000} = 2.00$	$\dfrac{22{,}500}{10{,}000} = 2.25$
P/E ratio	$\dfrac{1.50}{0.16} = 9.38$	$\dfrac{1.50}{0.26} = 5.77$

Not all the ratios discussed earlier are computed as some of the ratios in the same category provide similar information. For in-depth investigation, specific ratios applicable to the areas to be studied can be further derived and analysed.

Note that return on capital employed has dropped in year 2. This is attributed to lower assets turnover since the profit margin has improved marginally. Stock turnover has increased slightly which implies that inventory control has been consistently managed.

Liquidity of the company is lower in year 2 as reflected by both the current ratio and quick ratio. The drop in quick ratio, however, is not due to over-stocking because the stock to net current assets ratio is lower than in year 1. Other than the disproportionate increase in total liabilities relative to current assets, the longer debt collection period in year 2 also contributes to the deterioration of liquidity of the company.

The capital structure of the company has been strengthened by an increase in paid up share capital. The gearing ratio therefore drops as there is no increase in long-term loan. Debt service ratio also improves in year 2 with an increase in company earnings.

Dividend yield and earnings per share drop in line with the increase in number of shares issued although more dividends have been distributed. The dividend cover has dropped slightly, reflecting the higher proportion of profit distributed to shareholders. The P/E ratio has increased significantly. This indicates that market expectation on the future profitability of the company has been positive so that its shares are in demand. The speculative element may also have contributed to the large increase in P/E ratio.

In conclusion, ratio analysis is a very effective method of appraising the performance of companies. However, note that ratios computed using figures extracted from balance sheets may not be representative as the values are only applicable to a particular point in time. Monthly averages should be used if they are available for all assets and liabilities when computing the financial ratios.

It is the comparative value rather than the exact value that matters in ratio analysis. Thus if a performance ratio suddenly changes, it should be investigated. Similarly, computed ratios should be compared with the averages in similar companies. Such an industry-wide comparison can reveal the company's strengths and weaknesses and force management to take action to enhance the company's operation.

Practice Problems

13.1 The following financial ratios of a company are given for three consecutive years:

	Year 3	Year 2	Year 1
Current ratio	2.4	2.3	1.9
Quick ratio	0.9	1.1	1.2
Stock turnover	8.6 times	9.4 times	10.5 times
Debtors' turnover	7.4 times	7.9 times	8.3 times
ROCE	9.88%	10.35%	10.97%
Fixed asset turnover	4.2	4.1	3.7
Sales trend	128	119	100

You are required to assess the following with reasons:

(a) whether it is becoming easier for the company to meet its current debts on time and to take advantage of cash discounts,
(b) whether the company is collecting its debt more rapidly,
(c) whether the number of debtors is decreasing,
(d) whether the amount of inventory is increasing,
(e) whether the company's investment in fixed assets is increasing,
(f) whether the company is using its fixed assets efficiently,
(g) whether the return on shareholders' investment is becoming more profitable.

13.2 The financial information provided below is for two companies operating in a similar business:

	Company A $'000	Company B $'000
Owners' equity:		
Issued capital	350	470
Retained earnings	250	322
Liabilities:		
Long-term: Long-term loan	55	64
Short-term: Bank overdraft	21	20
Accounts payable	97	132
Other current liabilities	42	48
	815	1,056
Fixed assets:		
Land and buildings	286	381
Plant and equipment	218	342
Motor vehicles	59	62
Current assets:		
Stock	122	97
Accounts receivable	124	166
Cash	6	8
	815	1,056

Profit and loss account (income statement) for one year:

	Company A $'000		Company B $'000	
Sales		747		570
Cost of sales:				
Opening stock	102		92	
Purchase	588		382	
	690		474	
Closing stock	122		97	
		568		377
Gross profit		179		193
Operating expenses:				
Selling and distribution	64		60	
Administration	31		29	
Financial	9		8	
		104		97
Net profit		75		96
Taxation		37		45
		38		51
Dividends		24		37
Retain earnings		14		14

You are required to:

(a) calculate for each company six ratios which you consider most appropriate for indicating the efficiency of operations and short term financial strength of the two firms;
(b) using the financial information provided above and the ratios computed, analyse and compare the efficiency of operation and short-term financial strength of the two companies.

13.3 The summarised financial statements of a company are shown below:

Balance Sheet

	$'000	$'000
Fixed assets:		
Land		800
Building (net book value)		700

Equipment (net book value)		200
		1,700
Current assets:		
Inventory	1,000	
Debtors	900	
Prepayment	10	
Short-term investment	50	
Cash	20	
		1,980
		3,680
Liabilities:		
Creditors		750
Long-term loan		1,200
Tax payable		130
		2,080
Owners' equity:		
Share capital	1,400	
Retained earnings	200	
		1,600
		3,680

Statement of Retained Earnings

Retained earnings brought down		150
Net income (current year)	300	
less: taxation	(130)	
dividends	(120)	
		50
		200

Income Statement

Sales		6,250
less: cost of goods sold		4,700
		1,550
Operating expenses:		
Admin and selling expenses	1,100	
Interest	150	
		1,250
Net income before tax		300

The company has issued 1,400,000 shares at $1 each. Market value per share is $1.30.

You are required to define and compute financial ratios to evaluate the company in the following areas:

(a) Profitability (2 ratios)
(b) Liquidity (3 ratios)
(c) External finance (1 ratio)
(d) Share market appraisal (3 ratios)

Briefly comment on the performance of the company based on the financial ratios computed.

13.4 The following is an abridged balance sheet of a new company which closed its account for the first time at the end of a year:

	$'000	$'000
Fixed assets:		
Plant and machinery	125	
less: accumulated depreciation	10	
		115
Current assets:		
Stock		55
Debtors		40
Cash		5
		215
Owners' equity:		
Share capital	125	
Retained earnings	15	
	140	
less: dividends	30	
		110
Liabilities:		
Trade creditors		75
Owe to bank		30
		215

From the trading accounts for the year, the following information has been extracted:

Sales (cash)	$ 65,000
Sales (on credit)	$105,000
Purchases (on credit)	$150,000

You are required to:

(a) prepare a profit and loss statement showing the cost of goods sold and gross and net profits;
(b) calculate the following financial ratios:
   (i) profit margin
   (ii) debtors' ratio and debtors' collection period
   (iii) creditors' turnover ratio and average credit period allowed by suppliers
   (iv) stock turnover ratio and number of weeks that stock is carried on average
   (v) current ratio and quick ratio
(c) comment on the liquidity position of the firm in the light of the financial ratios derived in (b).

Chapter 14

Capital Budgeting and Discounted Cash Flow Methods

There is nothing so disastrous as a rational investment in an irrational world.

John Maynard Keynes

Capital budgeting is that part of management's long-range planning process that deals with selecting projects or making investments. As financial resources in a company are limited, the proper choice of investment projects is necessary to ensure optimum returns. The company also usually sets a minimum desired rate of return before accepting projects so that projects with expected returns lower than this requirement are immediately rejected. The minimum rate of return should be higher than the cost of finance. It also represents the opportunity cost of forgoing the marginal project.

An essential concept in capital budgeting is the *time value of money*. This concept is important because the investment and return from a project is usually spread over a considerable number of years. The concept of time value of money recognises the fact that a dollar received today is worth more than a dollar to be received sometime in the future. This is always true since money can be invested to earn a return which when added to the original dollar would be greater than the dollar to be received in the future. The discounted cash flow methods to be discussed later are systematic ways to evaluate projects equitably after converting money values at different reference times to a common denominator base.

Capital Budgeting Methods

The first step in project evaluation is to estimate the cost of investment and forecast future revenue or expenditure savings throughout the useful life of the fixed assets purchased. Usually, annual figures are used in such studies. One of the following methods is then applied to evaluate the proposed projects:

1. The return on investment method

Total net revenue or expenditure saved throughout a project life minus the cost of investment is regarded as the return. It is expressed as a percentage of the original investment cost. All figures are taken as they are without considering the time value of money. This ratio is similar to the return-on-capital-employed ratio in Chapter 14 except that it applies to the sum total added throughout the project life of the investment.

2. The pay-back period method

The pay-back period is the number of years it will take for a project to pay for itself out of its earnings. It is the period in the sequence of cash flow of a project when the accumulated revenue (or savings) is just sufficient to offset the total expenses including capital outlay of the investment. Monetary figures arising from different times are simply added without considering the time value of money. This method is comparable in essence to the price-earnings ratio which indicates the number of years required to recoup the initial investment based on the latest annual earnings. It is often used in practice, particularly where quick returns are important to the liquidity of a company.

3. Discounted cash flow methods

These are methods that incorporate the principle of time value of money by converting actual cash payments and receipts at different times to their equivalent values as measured at a common point of time. The methodology for such conversion is discounting. A sum of money F_i in the year i from now is deemed to be equivalent to a present value PW given by:

$$\text{PW} = \frac{F_i}{(1+r)^i}$$

where r is the discount rate which is normally the minimum rate of return on investment decided by the company.

The concept of time value of money and discounting can also be generalised to apply to money received or expended in the past. In that case the period number i will have a negative value so that:

$$\text{PW} = \frac{F_{-i}}{(1+r)^{-i}} = (1+r)^i F_{-i}$$

where F_{-i} represents the amount of money i years in the past. The above formula is obviously the compound interest equation. Therefore, discounting and compounding are analogous to each other except that discounting applies to money in the future while compounding is used to convert money in the past to present value. The following diagram summarises the above theory:

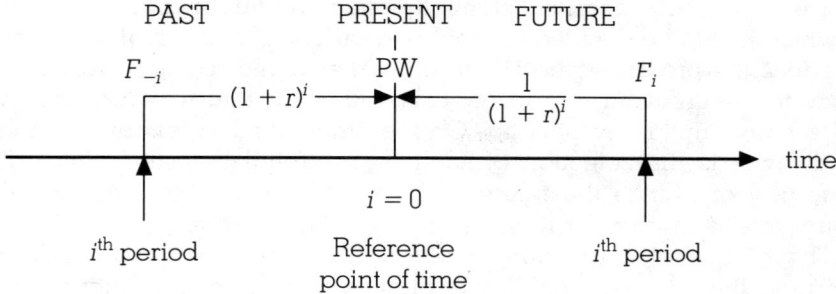

Noted that although the reference point is usually taken as the present time, it may be shifted to any point along the time axis. The discounted (or compounded) values, of course, will then correspond to the reference time chosen. Furthermore, a period may not be one year although the discount rate must necessarily correspond to the duration of period adopted.

Two discounted cash flow methods are commonly used:

1. The net present value method
2. The internal rate of return method

These two methods will be explained in the following sections. Since the return on investment and pay-back period methods do not recognise the time value of money, they are not theoretically correct methods and should only be used as rough estimates for quick assessment of project.

Net Present Value Method

In this method, the stream of cash flow resulting from a capital investment is discounted to a net present value depending on the time of receipt or payment and a pre-determined discounted rate. The project with the highest present value is to be accepted. For a stream of cash flow, the net present value is given by:

$$PW = \sum_{i=0}^{n} \frac{F_i}{(1+r)^i}$$

where F_i is positive for receipt and negative for payment and n is the period of study normally corresponding to the economic life of assets acquired.

The analysis can alternatively consider the cash inflow and outflow separately for a project, in which case the present value of both are calculated and compared. The criterion for acceptance of a project is that its net present value must be positive while the priority of choice among different projects is to rank them according to their net present values.

The factor which can substantially affect the final result is the discount rate which has to be decided on beforehand. The use of a high discount rate will reduce the present value of future payments and receipts. Consequently, it tends to be unfavourable to projects with high future returns but which require heavy initial investments. On the other hand, a low discount rate is biased towards the selection of such high capital investment/high future returns projects. Since the future is always unpredictable, adopting a low discount rate is more risky than using high discount rate.

The choice of a discount rate requires the exercise of judgement concerning the future availability of finance and the opportunity for its use. Usually, it is taken as the prevailing interest rate but it should be more accurately determined as follows:

1. Decided by management to represent the long-term return which ordinary shareholders may reasonably expect based on past performance if a project is financed by internal sources or by raising capital.
2. Adding an additional percentage on the interest rate of an external loan if the project is financed by borrowing.
3. A weighted average of 1 and 2 above if the investment is financed by a mixture of internal and external funds.

Internal Rate of Return Method

This is sometimes called the *investors' method* or *profitability index method*. It has the advantage of avoiding the initial complication of selecting an appropriate discount rate. The discount rate at which the present value of cost and return just break even is deduced instead. It is called the internal rate of return and is obtained by solving the following equation:

$$\sum_{i=0}^{n} \frac{C_i}{(1+r)^i} = \sum_{i=0}^{n} \frac{B_i}{(1+r)^i}$$

where C_i = cost (or cash outflow) in period i, B_i = benefit (or cash inflow) in period i.

The solution of the above equation is tantamount to solving the present value equation in the previous section with PW equated to zero. The present value method and the internal rate of return method, therefore, are only different ways of presenting the same issue.

Since the present value equation is non-linear, a few trial values of r have to be attempted and the internal rate of return is normally obtained by intrapolation from a graph such as Figure 14.1.

The internal rate of return, r_o is a measure of the profitability of an investment. The criterion of choice is that r_o must exceed the required rate of return on capital which is decided on the same basis as the discount rate

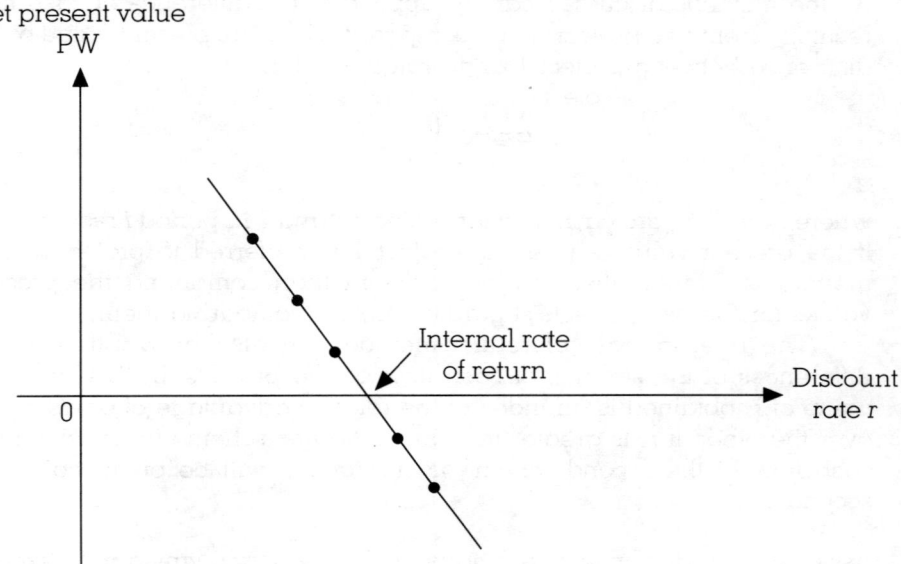

Figure 14.1

discussed in the earlier section. Although this method has avoided the initial fixing of a discount rate, a final decision still has to be made on the acceptable rate of return of investment. The criterion of selection among alternative projects is to choose the one with the highest internal rate of return. This, however, may lead to an erroneous conclusion especially if the patterns of cash flow are substantially different. This is because the internal rate of return may have more than one value when the pattern of cash flow changes direction more than once. The net present value method is, therefore, generally preferred to the internal rate of return method as it is easier to apply and always leads to an equitable solution.

The following additional points on all the capital budgeting methods discussed so far should be noted:

1. Other capital budgeting methods such as *annual equivalent amount method* and *annual cost method* are sometimes used. These are also discounted cash flow methods which usually lead to the same conclusion as the present value method.

2. The discounted cash flow concept can also be incorporated into the return on investment method and the payback period method by first converting all cash flow to a common base year. This refinement will render the results theoretically correct and are useful as an alternative methodology for comparison purposes.

3. All the methods discussed can be applied to the difference of cash flow resulting from two projects to be compared. Thus, the present value of the difference between project 1 and project 2 will be:

$$PW = \sum_{i=0}^{n} \frac{(F_{1i} - F_{2i})}{(1+r)^i}$$

where F_{1i} and F_{2i} are cash flow for projects 1 and 2 in period i respectively. If the present value is positive, project 1 is preferred to project 2. This method is mathematically more efficient than computing the present values for the two projects separately before comparing them.

The internal rate of return method can also be applied to the differences of the streams of cash flow of two projects. In this case, the value of r_o obtained is an index of the relative advantage of one scheme over the other. If r_o is greater than zero, the first scheme (from which the cash flow of the second scheme is subtracted) will be preferred to the second one.

4. Assets acquired in investment have useful life spans which may exceed the study period. In such a case, *salvage values* may be assigned to those assets and are positive values for discounting back to the base year. These salvage values normally reflect the estimated market prices of those assets when they are sold at that time.

5. Inflation is a general rise in price level throughout the years and leads to the purchasing power of money being eroded. Future cash flow, therefore, has higher nominal values compared to the present. A simple quantitative way to allow for inflation is to assume that the rate of inflation remains constant throughout the study period. Thus, a present cost of C_n will have a nominal value at the end of year n given by:

$$C_n(1 + a)^n$$

where a is the annual rate of inflation. The present value on discounting to the present reference time will be:

$$\frac{C_n(1+a)^n}{(1+r)^n} = \frac{C_n}{(1+r-a)^n} \text{ approximately}$$

Thus, inflation effectively lowers the discount rate in favour of 'high capital cost/low future operating cost' type of investment.

6. No matter which method is used for capital budgeting, it involves forecasting into the future. Risk is inherent in all capital investments since there is no guarantee that returns in the future can be the same as those

expected at the time a decision is made. One of the best methods to consider the effect of uncertainty is by means of a sensitivity analysis. The mechanism varies the values of the more important parameters used in the study to yield different sets of results. The importance of certain items are immediately highlighted by investigating the range of changes in the final solution. In one way, the test points out the accuracy required in basic data and in another, it provides a rough idea of the risk inherent in a project due to possible deviation of the situation from what was originally expected.

Example 14.1 illustrates the principles discussed.

Example 14.1

A factory operates a small canteen but its annual operation has consistently shown a loss:

	$	$
Sales		100,000
Cost of food and beverage	50,000	
Salaries	60,000	
		110,000
Net loss		(10,000)

The company is considering buying automatic food and drink vending machines at a cost of $24,000 less $5,000 trade-in on the existing dining room equipment. The estimated useful life of the vending machines is ten years with no scrap value.

The vending machine company would supply the food, drink and services engineers at its own expense. However it would take all sales receipts except 10% of gross receipts to the factory. It is estimated that sales with the vending machines will increase by 50% but price has to be 50% less.

The factory has to employ one attendant in the dining area at an annual cost of $6,300. Termination payments for all other canteen staff are $8,000.

Determine the answers to the following questions:

1. How long is the payback period?
2. What is the net present value of the project assuming cost of capital to be 20%?
3. What is the internal rate of return?
4. Forecast of sales from the vending machine is uncertain. If the factory receives only $2,500 a year for its share of gross receipts, will the project be feasible?

5. What is the minimum annual sales required to justify investment in the vending machine?

Solutions:

1. Net cash outflow in purchasing the machines:

	$	$
Cost of machines	24,000	
less: trade-in equipment	5,000	
		19,000
Redundancy payment to canteen staff		8,000
Total investment		27,000

Annual net cash flow with vending machines will be:

	$	$
Sales		
At current volume and price	100,000	
add: 50% on volume	50,000	
	150,000	
less: 50% on price	75,000	
		75,000
Receipt by the factory (10%)		7,500
less: salaries of attendant		6,300
Net cash inflow		1,200
Current net cash outflow saved (note 1)		10,000
Net annual return		11,200

$$\text{Payback period} = \frac{\$27,000}{\$11,000} = \underline{\underline{3 \text{ years}}}$$

2. Net present value $= \sum_{i=0}^{10} \frac{F_i}{(1 + 0.2)^i}$

$$= -\$27,000 + \$11,200 \times \left[\frac{1}{1.2} + \frac{1}{1.2^2} + \cdots + \frac{1}{1.2^{10}} \right]$$

$$= -\$27,000 + \$11,200 \times \left[\frac{1.2^{10} - 1}{1.2^{10} \times 0.2} \right] \text{ (note 2)}$$

$$= -\$27{,}000 + \$11{,}200 \times 4.192$$
$$= -\$19{,}950$$

3. The internal rate of return is obtained by solving the following equation:

$$27{,}000 = 11{,}200 \times \left[\frac{(1+r)^{10} - 1}{(1+r)^{10} \times r}\right]$$

The following present values are computed using different values of r by trial and error:

r	Net present value, \$
0.30	7,625
0.35	3,408
0.40	32
0.41	−562

The internal rate of return, $r_o = \underline{\underline{40\%}}$

4. If the factory receives \$2,500, net annual return will be reduced by (\$7,500 − \$2,500) = \$5,000.

$$\text{Resulting net annual return} = \$11{,}200 - \$5{,}000$$
$$= \$6{,}200$$

$$\text{Net present value} = -\$27{,}000 + \$6{,}200 \times 4.192$$
$$= -\$1{,}010$$

The project will not be justified as the present value is negative.

5. Net present value of savings must be equal to the present investment cost for break-even:

$$\$27{,}000 = \text{Net annual return} \times 4.192$$

i.e., $\qquad \text{Net annual return} = \dfrac{\$27{,}000}{4.192} = \$6{,}441$

Thus $\quad \$6{,}441 = 10\%$ cash receipt + Savings of current loss − Attendant's salaries

i.e., $\quad 10\%$ cash receipt = \$6,441 − \$10,000 + \$6,300
$$= \$2{,}741$$

Therefore $\quad$ Minimum annual sales $= \dfrac{\$2{,}741}{0.1} = \underline{\underline{\$27{,}410}}$

Notes:
1. It is important, in comparing two different scenarios, to consider the savings as well as cash receipts. In this case, an annual loss of $10,000 will be averted if vending machines are purchased. This represents the main benefit of installing vending machines although no cash flow is involved.
2. The geometric series in the equation has ten terms and a multiplication factor of (1/1.2). The expression inside the bracket can be represented by a simple mathematical proof:

Let
$$S = \frac{1}{(1+i)} + \frac{1}{(1+i)^2} + \cdots + \frac{1}{(1+i)^n}$$

$$\frac{1}{(1+i)} \cdot S = \frac{1}{(1+i)^2} + \cdots + \frac{1}{(1+i)^n} + \frac{1}{(1+i)^{n+1}}$$

Therefore $S\left[1 - \frac{1}{(1+i)}\right] = \frac{1}{(1+i)} - \frac{1}{(1+i)^{n+1}} \rightarrow S = \frac{(1+i)^n - 1}{(1+i)^n \times i}$

This formula is used extensively in compound interest and annuity calculations.

Compound Interest and Annuity Formulae

As explained in the discussion on discounted cash flow method, the idea of compound interest and discounting are both related to the concept of the time value of money. If an amount F is borrowed for n years at $i\%$ interest per annum, the repayment at the end of the nth year from now, including compound interest, will be:

$$F(1+i)^n$$

This is obvious if we consider the time value of money and take the interest rate as the discount rate. Thus, the present value of the future repayment will be the original sum F:

$$\frac{F(1+i)^n}{(1+i)^n} = F$$

If repayment of loan F is by equal year-end instalments of A for n years, the present value of this series of cash flow must necessarily be equal to the amount borrowed.

$$F = \frac{A}{(1+i)} + \frac{A}{(1+i)^2} + \cdots + \frac{A}{(1+i)^n}$$

$$= A \sum_{j=1}^{n} \frac{1}{(1+i)^j} = A \left[\frac{(1+i)^n - 1}{(1+i)^n \times i} \right]$$

Expressing A in terms of F gives the equation for calculating the annual year-end instalment in order to repay a debt in a number of years in the future:

$$A = F \left[\frac{(1+i)^n \times i}{(1+i)^n - 1} \right]$$

Banks usually calculate interest charges on annual rest which means that the periods n and interest rate i are annual values. Monthly payment of $(A/12)$ are normally requested so that borrowers are effectively paying in advance. Example 14.1 illustrates the differences between annual rest and monthly rest methods of repayment of a long-term loan. A non-compounding method used to calculate monthly repayment of loan on hire purchase and leasing terms is also compared.

Example 14.2

A person borrows $35,000 at an interest rate of 6% per annum to be repaid by equal monthly instalments over six years. Calculate the monthly instalment amount based on:

1. annual rest
2. monthly rest
3. hire purchase terms

1. Annual rest method:

$$\text{Annual repayment amount} = \$35,000 \times \left[\frac{1.06^6 \times 0.06}{1.06^6 - 1} \right]$$

$$= \$7,117.70$$

$$\text{Monthly instalment} = \frac{\$7,117.70}{12} = \underline{\underline{\$593}}$$

2. Monthly rest method:

Since interest is calculated on monthly rest basis, repayment will be considered as being divided into $6 \times 12 = 72$ periods.

$$\text{Period interest} = \text{Monthly interest} = \frac{6\%}{12} = 0.5\%$$

Applying the formula to calculate equal instalment of loan:

$$\text{Monthly instalment} = \$35{,}000 \times \left[\frac{1.005^{72} \times 0.005}{1.005^{72} - 1}\right]$$

$$= \$35{,}000 \times 0.01657 = \underline{\underline{\$580}}$$

3. Hire purchase terms:

The hire purchase method of calculating interest considers the whole repayment period as a single period. Interest is added to the principal sum and divided by the number of months to obtain the monthly instalment. Using the same symbols adopted earlier:

$$\text{Total repayment sum} = \text{Principal} + \text{Interest}$$
$$= F + F \times n \times i$$
$$= F(1 + ni)$$

$$\text{Monthly instalment} = \frac{F(1 + ni)}{12n}$$

In this case,

$$\text{Monthly instalment} = \frac{\$35{,}000 \times (1 + 6 \times 0.06)}{12 \times 6}$$

$$= \underline{\underline{\$661}}$$

It is clear that the effective rate of interest depends on the method used in the calculation of instalment payment. This must be considered carefully at the time of taking up a loan.

The two formulae for A and F developed in this section are extremely useful in applications involving series of cash flow in equal amounts. The following applications are particularly relevant based on modifications of the two formulae:

1. If a long-term investment is receiving a return of A every year to perpetuity, the present value of this stream of cash flow will be:

$$F = \lim_{n \to \infty} A \left[\frac{(1 + r)^n - 1}{(1 + r)^n \times r}\right] = \frac{A}{r}$$

Provided there is no intention to sell that investment, its value will be determined by the equation above.

2. An amount of A may be deposited at the end of every year so that the accumulated sum together with interest earned may be realised at the end of the nth year in future for a designated use. The present value of this series of equal instalments of A is given by the formula derived earlier:

$$F = A \left[\frac{(1 + i)^n - 1}{(1 + i)^n \times i}\right]$$

The future value P of this series of cash flow is equivalent to shifting the time of reference to the end of the nth year from now by multiplying F by the factor $(1+i)^n$:

$$P = (1+i)^n \times F = A\left[\frac{(1+i)^n - 1}{i}\right]$$

and

$$A = P\left[\frac{i}{(1+i)^n - 1}\right]$$

Such an annual deposit used to accumulate an amount of money for the future is also called *sinking fund payment*.

3. It is sometimes necessary to calculate the amount still owing in the midst of repayment of a long-term loan. This can be readily derived from the present value formula of F. The amount still owing is the present value at that moment of the series of future annual instalments in the remaining period until the loan is fully paid up:

$$\text{Amount still owing} = A\left[\frac{(1+i)^m - 1}{(1+i)^m \times i}\right]$$

where m is the number of remaining repayment periods.

Practice Problems

14.1 A manufacturing company not only mass-produces a number of consumer products but also is capable of producing special purpose manufacturing equipment to customer specifications. The firm is adding a new product to its product lines and is considering building the special equipment that will be required to produce the new product. The estimated departmental costs for the construction of the special purpose equipment are:

	$
Materials and parts	75,000
Direct labour	60,000
Variable overhead	30,000
Fixed overhead	15,000
	180,000

The market for the new product is expected to last five years. The annual revenue and expenses are estimated to be:

		$	$
Selling price/unit			5.00
Variable cost per unit:			
Material		1.70	
Labour		1.40	
			3.10
Contribution/unit			1.90
Estimated total annual sales			40,000 units
Estimated contribution/year			$76,000
Fixed cost per annum:			
Supervision			$18,000
Insurance			5,000
Maintenance			2,000
			25,000

Salvage value of the special purpose machine at the end of five years will be $10,000.

You are required to evaluate the above plan using net present value method basing on a minimum rate of return of 15%.

14.2 A company is planning to invest in a project with the following cash flow at the end of each year:

Year	Outflow $'000	Inflow $'000
1	500	–
2	300	100
3	200	150
4 to 10	–	180 (each year)

The company has chosen 9% as the minimum rate of return on their investment for accepting a project.

(a) Find the internal rate of return of the project and advise whether it should be accepted.
(b) If the company borrows $500,000 to finance the project, calculate the monthly instalment if the interest rate is 10% for six years on a monthly rest basis.

14.3 A manufacturing company is planning to replace two old machines in a production line with either two new ones or a single automatic machine which integrates their functions. Relevant cost data are given:

	Existing machine	Proposed replacement	
	Operating expenses per year, $	Capital cost, per year, $	Operating expenses per year, $
Machine 1	30,000	80,000	9,000
Machine 2	20,000	55,000	6,000
Automatic machine	–	150,000	10,000

The existing machines have no resale value and the economic life of all new machines is eight years. Discount rate is taken to be 14% by the company.

You are required to:

(a) find the net present values of savings obtainable by replacing the existing machines with:
   (i) two new machines
   (ii) a single automatic machine
(b) give your recommendation and suggest what other factors should be considered.

14.4 A company is considering purchasing either one of two machines each with a useful life of five years:

	Machine A $	Machine B $
Purchase price	50,000	48,000
Annual operating cost:		
Year 1	6,000	6,500
Year 2	5,800	6,600
Year 3	5,600	6,700
Year 4	5,400	6,800
Year 5	5,200	7,000

(a) Assuming a discount rate of 12%, evaluate the two machines and give your proposal.
(b) What are the equivalent annual costs of the two machines considering both purchase and operating costs and at the same discount rate of 12%?

14.5 A company has purchased a factory for $1,200,000 by using $600,000 cash and getting a mortgage loan of $600,000 from a bank. The repayment period of the loan is ten years at an interest rate of 10% with equal monthly instalments calculated on an annual rest basis.

(a) Calculate the amount of monthly instalment.
(b) Calculate the amount still owing to the bank at the end of the fifth year.
(c) Compute the monthly instalment amount if the repayment is calculated on a monthly rest basis.

PART FIVE

COMMERCIAL FINANCE

Chapter 15

Bank Loans and Financial Instruments

Owing money has never concerned me so long as I know where it could be repaid.

Henry Crown

If I owe a million dollars, then I am lost. But if I owe 50 million, then the bankers are lost.

Celso Ming

Banks receive cash from depositors to whom they have to pay interest regularly. Part of what is collected has to be kept in secure financial papers such as government bonds (treasury bonds or T-bonds in the USA) which represent loans to the government at a certain fixed interest rate; part is retained as cash to meet daily transaction needs as is required by law. Banks derive their income by making direct investment in diverse portfolios of current and fixed assets. A major portion of their revenue, however, is from interest received by providing finance to their customers. Lending to business is usually the most important function of the banking sector. Banks also provide personal finance and housing loans. The interest on loans is higher than the rate of interest paid to depositors. They also can lend more money than they have in current assets as long as they remain within the limit set by local regulations. Their gross incomes are, therefore, magnified. Banks are cautious about lending as some customers may default on repayment, and yet their profitability depends on maximising lending in order to increase income.

Practically all businesses obtain external finance from commercial banks. They depend on borrowed money for part of their working capital and long-term loans for investment in fixed assets because of shortages in internal financial resources. This does not necessarily infer that a company is financially unsound. A successful enterprise always seems to be short of funds because of constant growth and the wealth of opportunities for profitable investment. Further, the interest paid to a bank is tax deductible so that the effective interest rate is actually lower. Overall, financing through borrowing from banks is relatively cheap compared to other means. Bank finance is also preferred over increasing paid up capital which may alter the capital structure and in some cases cause loss of control of the company.

There are many forms of bank loans for business borrowing. The most important types are overdraft and term loans. Various financial instruments are also available to enable import and export companies to facilitate their operations. The banks in such instances act as both middlemen as well as financers.

Types of Bank Loan: Overdraft, Term Loan and Mortgage Loan

Overdraft (OD) Facility

This is an agreement by the bank to allow money to be drawn from a *current (or checking) account* by more than the amount deposited in that account. The maximum limit of the overdraft is fixed so that a cheque ('check' in the USA) issued to draw money that results in the overdraft limit being exceeded will be returned or *bounced*. The payer who issues a cheque is called the *drawer*. The payee who receives the cheque (the *drawee*) will present it to his bank which will arrange for it to be honoured by the drawer's bank through a *clearing* system in a *clearing house*. It is at that time that the drawer's bank will check on whether the overdraft limit of the issuer of the cheque has been exceeded. On the other hand, cash may be paid directly on presenting a cheque issued as 'cash' at the branch of the bank where the checking account is kept after the signature and status of the account has been checked on the spot without going through the clearing system.

Banks charge interest on overdraft based on the prevailing market rate in the banking industry. It therefore changes from time to time depending on the availability of funds in the financial market. A bank usually fixes a *prime rate* which is the rate at which the bank will lend to the best customer. The overdraft rate for most customers is normally two to three percentage points above the prime rate depending on the credit standing of the individual customer. Since the amount of overdraft fluctuates according to the transactions of a company, the interest charge is calculated on a daily basis on the amount of overdraft throughout a month. A monthly statement for the preceding month is issued by the bank and sent to the company at the beginning of every month.

Although an overdraft facility is normally secured by fixed assets and/or personal guarantees of the directors of a company, it is considered a short-term loan because the bank usually has the right to recall the facility at short notice.

Term Loan

A term loan has maturity (or borrowing period) for between one to five years. It is therefore a medium-term loan. It is usually secured on fixed assets such as plant, real estate or equipment of the borrower. Interest rates are normally fixed at the time of agreement and are not changed. Two common types of term loans are *leasing* and *hire purchase*.

In leasing, the bank or finance company owns the asset acquired by the borrower who uses the borrowed money to purchase the asset. The lease agreement permits the borrower to use the asset after the basic lease term has expired. Usually, an initial deposit of ten to twenty per cent of the asset is paid by the borrower. For tax purposes, repayment instalments are allowed to be charged out as an expense. On repayment of the loan, the deposit sum may also be charged out as depreciation expense starting from the following year if the asset has not been completely depreciated (or written off). Leasing is frequently used to finance the purchase of plant and machinery inclusive of equipment.

In a hire purchase transaction, legal title of the asset financed belongs to the bank but the borrower will own the asset after full repayment on expiry of the hire-purchase agreement. During the term of hire-purchase agreement, only the interest portion of the instalment can be charged out as expense for tax purposes although the asset value is depreciated annually from the beginning. Motor vehicles can be purchased by hire purchase or through leasing.

Leasing and hire purchase are commonly used to finance the acquisition of plant and equipment because the process of application is fast and simple. The effective interest rates of such loans, however, are relatively high. Due to the ease of obtaining finance to pay for production equipment by this means, most governments encourage companies to turn to leasing to acquire machinery to upgrade their operations and improve productivity.

Mortgage Loan

A mortgage is a contract in which the lender is awarded legal title to certain property of the borrower, with the provision that the title reverts to the borrower when the loan is repaid in full. Mortgage loans are long-term loans with the repayment periods usually exceeding five years. Interest and principal are paid in equal monthly instalments as shown in Chapter 14. The interest rate normally does not fluctuate frequently but the instalment amount is adjusted after the prime lending rate has changed with at least one month's notice being given in advance. The lender (the bank) is called the *mortgagee* and the borrower is the *mortgagor*.

Mortgage loan is a *secured* loan with the mortgaged property as *security* for the loan. It entitles the lender to claim on that asset of the borrower in case of default on repayment. A loan which is unsecured is a *clean facility* which a bank may give to a customer with a good credit history and an established record with the bank.

A mortgage loan is usually obtained to finance the acquisition of major assets such as land and buildings. The effective interest rate is normally lower than that for an overdraft and the lending bank will not recall such a loan if monthly repayment is on schedule. It is a common type of long-term finance for businesses.

Import/Export Transaction by Letter of Credit

An exporter in one country and an importer in another country faces the following problems even if an agreement to sell and buy goods has been reached:

1. The exporter has no guarantee that he will be paid correctly or paid at all after he has sent the goods to the importer. Furthermore, the order may be cancelled after the goods have been manufactured or even shipped. Since the exporter and importer are in different countries, recourse to legal action for compensation in cases of default by the importer is out of the question.
2. The importer is unwilling to pay the exporter before he has received the goods since they may not meet the agreed specifications or may not even have been sent to the importer at all.
3. The importer may not have the financial resource to immediately pay for the imported goods in full. Some means of finance by a bank is necessary to take delivery of the goods.

The first two problems are solved commonly by the use of *letter of credit* or LC in short. A letter of credit is a letter of undertaking by a bank to pay an overseas exporter (the *beneficiary*) against his shipping documents that must be drawn in strict compliance to the terms and conditions of the LC. At least two banks, one in the importer's country and another in the exporter's country are involved as middlemen:

1. The *issuing bank* is the bank in the importer's country which opens the letter of credit.
2. The *advising bank* is the bank in the exporter's country which acts as an agent for transmitting the LC to the beneficiary. It may be the overseas branch of the issuing bank although this is not necessary. Payment to the exporter is made by a *negotiating bank* which is usually the exporter's bank. It may also be the advising bank itself.

The procedure of an import/export transaction by LC is as follows:

1. A sales contract is negotiated and concluded between an importer and an exporter.

2. The importer will approach his bank for facilities to open a letter of credit. It will usually only be granted if assets are pledged as collateral to the bank. The importer then submits an LC application according to the terms of the sales contract. The bank typically charges one-eighth of a per cent of the LC amount as service fee.
3. The issuing bank issues an LC in favour of the exporter and forwards it by airmail, telegraphic transfer or electronic message to the exporter through an advising bank in the exporter's country.
4. The exporter studies the terms of the LC. Request may be made to the importer to amend the LC if found not according to the sales contract. If all terms are in order, the exporter will proceed to ship the goods and prepare all the required *export documents*.
5. The export documents will be submitted by the exporter to the negotiating bank. The negotiating bank will thoroughly check the documents to ensure that they comply strictly with the terms of the LC. The documents will then be forwarded to the issuing bank.
6. On receipt of the documents, the issuing bank will present them to the importer. Upon paying for the amount in the LC, the importer will receive all the documents which can be used to claim the goods.
7. The exporter receives payment from the negotiating bank after the latter has been paid by the issuing bank.

The procedure is illustrated in Figure 15.1.

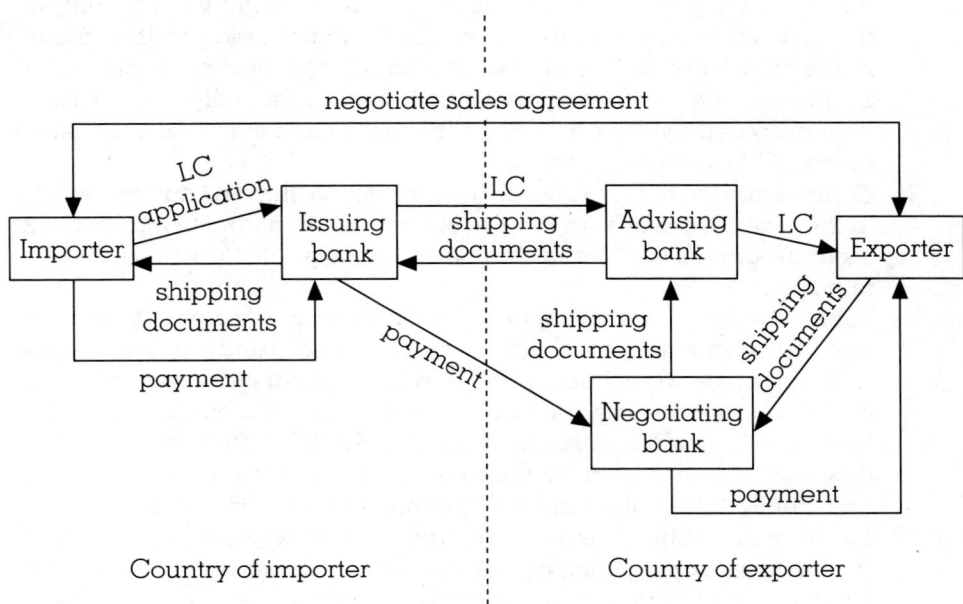

Figure 15.1 The procedure of an import/export transaction by letter of credit

There are many types of letters of credit. Their application depends on the terms in the LC. The following are some common types used:

1. *Irrevocable LC.* The LC cannot be amended or cancelled unless all the parties to the LC consent in writing. This is the most common LC in use.
2. *Confirmed LC.* Upon the request of the exporter, the issuing bank may obtain the confirmation of the advising bank on its irrevocable undertaking so that the LC bears the guarantee of payment by two banks. This is called a confirmed LC. Generally, an LC issued by a reputable bank is seldom confirmed.
3. *LC at sight* or *red-clause LC.* This is to enable the exporter to receive the LC amount in full on presentation of shipping documents. Under this arrangement, the issuing bank is bound to reimburse the negotiating bank, and the importer is ultimately responsible to the issuing bank for advance payment made even if the exporter fails to fulfil his undertaking. For the exporter, this kind of LC is a safe-guard against goods not being taken up on arrival at the importer's country.
4. *Transferable LC.* A letter of credit is said to be transferable when the beneficiary can instruct the paying bank to make payment fully or partially to one or more third parties.

The shipping documents so far mentioned should comprise the following papers:

1. *Bill of exchange* (also called the *draft*). It is a request in writing by the exporter to the importer requesting the importer to pay the amount in the LC to a bank (the negotiating bank) or a third party appointed by the exporter in the exporter's country. It is actually a promissory note prepared by the exporter for the importer to sign when the terms of the LC have been satisfied.
2. *Commercial invoice.* A description of goods shipped corresponding to the letter of credit with the price, contract number, LC number and issuing bank as well as the name of the ship, etc., addressed to the importer.
3. *Insurance certificate.* Prepared by an insurance company to cover risk of damage to goods during storage and transit. If the original agreement between the importer and exporter is a free-on-board (FOB) contract, the importer will be responsible for the insurance and freight. If it is a cost-insurance-and-freight (CIF) contract, insurance cover will be arranged by the exporter. Finally, if it is based on cost and freight (C&F), the importer will need to take up insurance.
4. *Bill of lading* (BL). It is basically an acknowledgement of receipt of goods by a shipping company or its authorised agent and is a contract for delivery of goods. It is generally issued in a set of two or more copies that are all required in order to obtain delivery of goods at the port of destination.

5. *Airway bill.* It is an acknowledgement by an airline company on receipt of goods from the transport agent. It therefore only applies to goods by air freight and is equivalent to the bill of lading for sea freight.
6. *Certificate of origin.* This is a certification of the place where the goods are manufactured. It is prepared and signed by the exporter and sometimes countersigned by local authorities.
7. *Weight list.* Prepared by the exporter or a third party specifying details of the weight of goods shipped.
8. *Packing list.* This is sometimes incorporated together with the weight list signed by the exporter describing the manner in which the goods are packed. The size of the carton may be specified with the number of products in each carton. The total number of cartons may also be included in the packing list.

A set of typical documents used in the process of import/export by letter of credit is included here for illustration. These comprise the following:

- Application for letter of credit by an importer (Figure 15.2)
- Irrevocable letter of credit (Figure 15.3)
- Invoice by the exporter (Figure 15.4)
- Certificate of origin (Figure 15.5)
- Packing list and weight note (Figure 15.6)
- Bill of lading (Figure 15.7)
- Certificate of insurance (Figure 15.8)

Documentary Collections by D/P and D/A

Documentary collections are used mainly to secure payment for goods delivered to importers whom the exporters trust. In these cases, the exporter is prepared to ship goods without requiring payment to be guaranteed in advance unlike in the case of letter of credit. Two banks are involved: the *remitting bank* of the exporter and the *collecting bank* of the importer. The role of the remitting bank is to transmit all the shipping documents to the collecting bank for the importer to clear the goods from the port authority.

The procedure for documentary collection is as follows:

1. The exporter draws a bill of exchange (B/E or b.e.) on his overseas buyer and attaches with it the relevant shipping documents after the goods have been shipped.
2. All the documents are handed by the exporter to the remitting bank specifying the collecting bank and conditions under which the documents may be delivered to the importer.
3. The remitting bank presents all the documents through its overseas branch to the collecting bank in the importer's country.

LETTER OF CREDIT APPLICATION

To: _____ BANK LIMITED   Date: _____

Dear Sirs,

We request you to open an Irrevocable Letter of Credit under the following conditions (tick where applicable):

By	☐ Airmail	☐ Brief preliminary telex advice/with original by Airmail	☐ Full operative telex

Applicant (Name & Address)	Beneficiary (Name & Address)

Advising Bank	Amount (in figures & words)	Terms: C&I/C&F/CIF/FOB

Shipment from to not later than	Partial Shipments: ☐ allowed ☐ not allowed Trans-shipment: ☐ allowed ☐ not allowed Expiry Date in the beneficiary's country.

LIST OF DOCUMENTS MARKED "X" TO BE PRESENTED IN DUPLICATE UNLESS OTHERWISE STATED

☐ Drafts drawn on us at _____ sight for full invoice value of goods specified below.

☐ Signed Commercial Invoices in 4 copies.

☐ Full set of clean ON BOARD Marine Bills of Lading/Airway Bill/Sea or Air Parcel Post Receipt made out to order of _____ BANK LTD notify applicant and marked "Freight prepaid/payable at destination"

☐ Insurance Policy/Certificate endorsed in blank for 110% of invoice value covering Institute Cargo Clauses (WA/FPA/ALL Risks) Institute Strikes Riots and Civil Commotion Clauses Institute War Clauses _____ with claims payable in SINGAPORE.

☐ Insurance Policy/Certificate endorsed in blank for 110% of invoice value covering Institute Cargo Clauses A/B/C/Institute Strikes Clauses (Cargo)/Institute War Clauses (Cargo) _____ with claims payable in SINGAPORE.

☐ Insurance is to be covered by buyer, in which case shipper is to telex details of shipment including quantity, value and name of vessel/flight No. to M/S _____
quoting open policy number/cover note number _____

☐ Certificate of _____ Origin

☐ Packing List and Weight Note

COVERING

SPECIAL INSTRUCTIONS:

All bank charges including reimbursement commission are for account of Applicant/Beneficiary.
Documents to be presented within _____ days after the date of issuance of the shipping document(s) but within the validity of the credit.

IN CONSIDERATION OF YOUR ISSUING THE ABOVE CREDIT WE AGREE:

(1) To make a deposit/to allow your earmarking our current account for Dollars _____ ($ _____)

(2) To all the other conditions governing the issue of the Letter of Credit appearing overleaf.

FOR BRANCH USE	FOR HEAD OFFICE USE			
Particulars verified. Application is approved.	LC No.	P & C		
	Key-In(1)	Key-In(2)	Checked	Authorised
Authorised Signature	Remarks			

Applicant's Authorised Signature(s) & Stamp
Account No:
Telephone No:

Figure 15.2

LETTER OF CREDIT – OPERATIVE TELEX/SWIFT

024718

BANK LTD

Cable address:
Telex number:

Date of Issue: 11 NOV 1992

Irrevocable:

Letter of Credit No.: 72-210448
Expiry Date: 12 DEC 1992
In The Beneficiary's Country: ITALY

Applicant	Beneficiary
KLENCO (S) PTE LTD 7 TUAS AVENUE 1 SINGAPORE 2263	GHIBLI S.P.A. 27020 DORNO (PV) VIA CIRCONVALLAEZIONE 5, ITALY
Advising Bank	Amount
BANCA NAZIONALE DEL LAVORO PAVIA ITALY	ITL****56,827,667 EX-WORKS

Partial Shipments: NOT ALLOWED
Trans-Shipment: NOT ALLOWED

Shipment from: ITALY
TO SINGAPORE
not later than 23 NOV 1992

Credit available with ANY BANK by negotiation against presentation of the documents detailed herein and of your draft(s) at 120 DAYS FROM BL DATE drawn on applicant.

LIST OF DOCUMENTS TO BE PRESENTED IN DUPLICATE UNLESS OTHERWISE STATED

SIGNED COMMERCIAL INVOICES IN 4 COPIES.
FULL SET OF CLEAN ON BOARD MARINE BILLS OF LADING MADE OUT TO ORDER OF OVERSEAS UNION BANK LTD NOTIFY APPLICANT AND MARKED 'FREIGHT PAYABLE AT DESTINATION' AND THIS LC NO. 72-210448.
INSURANCE IS TO BE COVERED BY BUYER, IN WHICH CASE SHIPPER IS TO TELEX OR AIRMAIL DETAILS OF SHIPMENT INCLUDING QUANTITY, VALUE AND NAME OF VESSEL / FLIGHT NO. TO M/S EAST WEST USI INSURANCE PTE LTD 47 SCOTTS ROAD, #03-00 GOLDBELL TOWER SINGAPORE 0922 (TLX: RS 26362 FAX: 7382822) QUOTING OPEN POLICY NUMBER UN 84/29. A CERTIFICATE TO THIS EFFECT IS REQUIRED.
CERTIFICATE OF ITALY ORIGIN.
PACKING LIST AND WEIGHT NOTE.

- 45A COVERING :
  1 X 40FT CONTAINER OF VACUUM CLEANERS, ACCESSORIES, SPARE PARTS AS PER PROFORMA INVOICE DATED 03.11.92 VIA FAX NO. 1998.
- 47A SPECIAL INSTRUCTIONS :
  DISCOUNT CHARGES, IF ANY, ARE FOR BENEFICIARY'S ACCOUNT.
- 47A ALL DRAFTS MUST BEAR OUR LC NUMBER.
- 71B ALL BANK CHARGES OUTSIDE SINGAPORE INCLUDING REIMBURSEMENT COMMISSION ARE FOR ACCOUNT OF BENEFICIARY.
- 48   DOCUMENTS TO BE PRESENTED WITHIN 10 DAYS AFTER THE DATE OF ISSUANCE OF THE SHIPPING DOCUMENT(S) BUT WITHIN THE VALIDITY OF THE CREDIT.
- 49   WITHOUT ADDING YOUR CONFIRMATION.
- 78   AFTER ACCEPTANCE, WE SHALL ADVISE THE NEGOTIATING BANK OF THE MATURITY DATE. ON MATURITY THE NEGOTIATING BANK IS AUTHORISED TO REIMBURSE THE AMOUNT OF THE NEGOTIATIONS BY DRAWING CLEAN SIGHT DRAFTS ON BANCA NAZIONALE DEL LAVORO, ROME
- 78   THE NEGOTIATING BANK IS TO FORWARD ALL DOCUMENTS TO US IN 2 SETS BY CONSECUTIVE REGISTERED AIRMAIL.
  EACH PRESENTATION MUST BE NOTED ON THE REVERSE OF THIS ADVICE BY THE NEGOTIATING BANK WHERE THE CREDIT IS AVAILABLE.

Authorised Signatures

MSG ID	MSG ID	KEYED-IN	CHECKED	RELEASED

Figure 15.3

CHAPTER 15 BANK LOANS AND FINANCIAL INSTRUMENTS

GHIBLI S.p.A.
Capitale Sociale interamente versato L. 1.200.000.000

27020 DORNO (Pv) - Via Circonvallazione, 5
Telefono: 0382/84193 - Telex 340258 GHIBLI

Meccanografico PV 003026
C.C.I.A.A. Pavia n. 144801
Reg. Soc. Trib. Pavia n. 4138
Cod. Fisc. e Part. IVA 00549310183

Spett./Messrs.

KLENCO (S) PTE LTD
7 TUAS   AVENUE 1
SINGAPORE 2263

FATTURA/INVOICE
NUMERO/NUMBER: 949E
DATA/DATE: 13.11.92

CLIENTE	COD. FISC.	PARTITA IVA	CAT. AG. ZON.	CODICE FORNIT.
		XAB0022708/709/710/92 13.11.92		

PORTO/CARRIAGE	SPEDIZIONE/SHIPMENT	PAGAMENTO/PAYMENT
	SERRA & LIESENFELD	LETTERA DI CREDITO N.72-210448

DESCRIZIONE/DESCRIPTION	U.M.	QUANTITÀ/QUANTITY	PREZZO/PRICE	IMPORTO LORDO/GROSS AMOUNT	%	IMPORTO NETTO/NET AMOUNT	IVA
COV ING:1X40 FT.CONTAINER OF VACUUM CLEANERS,							
ACCESSORIES, SPARE PARTS AS PER PROFORMA INVOICE							
DATED 03.11.92. VIA FAX N.1988. EX-WORKS.							
VS/ORDINE N.GB-57 22.10.92.							
ASPIRAPOLVERE MOD.AS10 P A28 COMPLETI		50	104.000	5.200.000	LIT.	5.200.000	
ASPIRAPOLVERE MOD.ASL10 A39 COMPLETI		30	123.000	3.690.000	LIT.	3.690.000	
ASPIRAPOLVERE MOD.AS27 A39 COMPLETI		60	145.000	8.700.000	LIT.	8.700.000	
ASPIRAPOLVERE MOD.AS58/M+SCA COMPLETI		30	258.000	7.740.000	LIT.	7.740.000	
ASPIRAPOLVERE MOD.AS60/M+SCA COMPLETI		20	346.000	6.920.000	LIT.	6.920.000	
ASPIRAPOLVERE MOD.WD400 COMPLETI		50	149.000	7.450.000	LIT.	7.450.000	
CALOTTA S90 GRIGIO WD 2000191		15	4.620	69.300	LIT.	69.300	
CALOTTA WS3 GRIGIO WD 2000286		30	7.175	215.250	LIT.	215.250	
COPERCHIO WS2 GIALLO WD 2000480		10	4.410	44.100	LIT.	44.100	
RONDELLA SEPARATORE WS2 2000910		15	5.880	88.200	LIT.	88.200	
SEPARATORE S90 GIALLO WD 2000930		15	6.300	94.500	LIT.	94.500	
LI LLO GOMMA SPAZZ.50 2010273		6	735	4.410	LIT.	4.410	
CALOTTA PP WD400 GRIGIO 2206600		2	5.530	11.060	LIT.	11.060	
BASAMENTO MOTORE PP WD400 G. 2206700		8	5.880	47.040	LIT.	47.040	
BASAMENTO RUOTE PP WS2/M G. 2207500		4	12.600	50.400	LIT.	50.400	
GANCIO A FILO 2500020		35	189	6.615	LIT.	6.615	
LISTELLO GOMMA PER VENTOSA 2502255		100	735	73.500	LIT.	73.500	
MOTORE A40 V.230 2505100		20	14.450	889.000	LIT.	889.000	
MANIGLIA NYLON WS2 2506350		10	735	7.350	LIT.	7.350	
DADO CIECO M8 2508770		10	161	1.610	LIT.	1.610	
LANCIA PIATTA D.36 2511520		10	595	5.950	LIT.	5.950	

IMPONIBILI IVA	ALIQUOTA	IMPORTI IVA		IMPORTO MERCE/GOODS AMOUNT	ADDEBITI VARI/VARIOUS DEBITS
					./.
TIPO IVA			TOTALE IMPONIBILI	TOTALE IMPOSTA	TOTALE FATTURA/AMOUNT DUE

APPOGGIO BANCARIO

SCADENZA	IMPORTO	SCADENZA	IMPORTO	SCADENZA	IMPORTO	SCADENZA	IMPORTO

CONDIZIONI DI VENDITA / SELLING TERMS
La merce viaggia a rischio e pericolo del committente qualunque sia il modo di spedizione. - Non si accettano reclami 8 giorni dopo il ricevimento della merce. - Qualunque sia il modo di pagamento deve essere fatto al ns. domicilio non essendo riconosciuti i pagamenti fatti a terzi senza ns. autorizzazione. - L'eventuale emissione di tratte da parte ns. o l'accettazione di esse non furmano novazione ne deroga dal pagamento al ns. domicilio. - Con l'accettazione della fattura s'intendono dal Cliente accettate le suddette condizioni. - Per eventuali contestazioni Foro competente è quello di Pavia. - Il destinatario è tenuto a verificare il peso e la buona condizione dei colli. - In caso di ritardato pagamento decorrerà l'interesse nella misura commerciale.

Figure 15.4

1 Speditore - Expéditeur - Consigner - Expeditor	N° 763231 *1369*	D	**ORIGINALE**
GHIBLI SPA V.CIRCONVALLAZIONE 5 DORNO PV	**COMUNITÀ EUROPEA** COMMUNAUTÉ EUROPÉENNE EUROPEAN COMMUNITY COMUNIDAD EUROPEA			
2 Destinatario - Destinataire - Consignee - Destinatario	**CERTIFICATO DI ORIGINE** CERTIFICAT D'ORIGINE CERTIFICATE OF ORIGIN CERTIFICADO DE ORIGEN			
KLENCO (S) PTE LTD 7 TUAS AVENUE 1 SINGAPORE 2263	3 Paese d'origine - Pays d'origine - Country of origin - Pais de origen			
	COMUNITA' EUROPEA ITALIA			
4 Informazioni riguardanti il trasporto (indicazione facoltativa) Informations relatives au transport Transport details - Expedicion	5 Osservazioni - Remarques - Remarks - Observaciones			
CAMION TIR	LETTERA DI CREDITO N.72-210448 TARIFFA DOG.8479/9098000			

6 N. d'ordine; marche, numeri, quantità e natura dei colli; denominazione delle merci N° d'ordre; marques, numéros, nombre et nature des colis; désignation des marchandises Item number; marks, numbers, number and kind of packages; description of goods N° de orden; marcas, numeros, nombre y naturaleza de los bultos; designacion de las mercancias			7 Quantità Quantité Quántity Cantitad
1	SCATOLE	N.308 COLLI TOTALI ASPIRATORI IND.LI+ ACCESSORI VARI Come da fattura allegata KG.5520,7	308 KG.4823,4

8 La sottoscritta Autorità certifica che le merci sopra elencate sono originarie del paese menzionato nel riquadro 3
L'Autorité soussignée certifie que les marchandises désignées ci-dessus sont originaires du pays figurant dans la case N° 3
The undersigned Authority certifies that the goods described above originate in the country shown in box 3
La Autoridad infrascrita certifica que las mercancias designadas son originarias del pais indicado en la casilla N° 3

p. **IL SEGRETARIO GENERALE**
(*Dr. Giorgio Maganzani*)

Geom. **LUIGI CROTTI**

Luogo e data del rilascio; denominazione, firma e timbro dell'autorità competente
Lieu et date de délivrance; désignation, signature et cachet de l'autorité compétente
Place and date of issue; name, signature and stamp of competent authority
Lugar y fecha de expedicion; designacion, firma y sello de la autoridad competente

stampati a cura dell'UNIONCAMERE e distribuiti dalle Camere di Commercio

Figure 15.5

CHAPTER 15 BANK LOANS AND FINANCIAL INSTRUMENTS

GHIBLI S.P.A.

VIA CIRCONVALLAZIONE, 5
27020 DORNO (PAVIA)

```
                              ┌                          ┐
                               SPETT.LE DITTA
                               KLENCO (S) PTE LTD
                               7 TUAS AVENUE 1
                               SINGAPORE 2263
```

INVOICE N. 949E   OF   13.11.92

PACKING LIST – WEIGHT NOTE

PARCELS	MARKS	DESCRIPTION OF GOODS	GROSS WEIGHT KG.	NETT WEIGHT KG.
50	COLLI	CONTRASSEGNATI CON IL N.61 CONTENENTE: N.50 MOD.AS10 P	12	10
30	COLLI	CONTRASSEGNATI CON IL N.62 CONTENENTE:N.30 MOD.ASL10	12.5	10.5
60	COLLI	CONTRASSEGNATI CON IL N.63 CONTENENTE:N.60 MOD.AS27	16	14
30	COLLI	CONTRASSEGNATI CON IL N.64 CONTENENTE:N.30 MOD.AS58/M +SCARICO	28	26
20	COLLI	CONTRASSEGNATI CON IL N.65 CONTENENTE:N.20 MOD.AS60/M +SCARICO	32	29
50	COLLI	CONTRASSEGNATI CON IL N.66 CONTENENTE:N.50 MOD.WD400	20	17
1	COLLO	CONTRASSEGNATO CON IL N.54 CONTENENTE: N.15 CALOTTA S90+N.15 RONDELLA SEP.WS2+N.15 SEPARATORE S90	28	26
2	COLLI	CONTRASSEGNATI CON IL N.53 CONTENENTE: N.30 CALOTTA N.30 GALLEGGIANTE COMPLETO+N.10 COPERCHIO WS2 WS3+N.10 COPERCHIO WS2+N.8 GR.ANELLO WS1 GIALLO	24.5	21.5
1	COLLO	CONTRASSEGNATO CON IL N.51 CONTENENTE/ N.6 LISTELLO GOMMA SPAZZ.50+N.35 GANCIO A FILO+N.100 LISTELLO GOMMA PER VENTOSA+N.20 MOTORE A40+N.10 MANIGLIA IN NYLON WS2+N.10 DADO CIECO M8+N.10 LANCIA PIATTA D.36+ N.40 PENNELLO D.36+N.10 PROLUNGA S D.40+N.10 LANCIA PIATTA D.40+N.30 PROLUNGA VPC D.40 MT.0,50+N.100 SPAZZOLA CARBONE A39+N.30 SPAZZOLA CARBONE A23+N.4 RONDELLA SUGHERO 6X26+N.3 MILLERIGHE CON BUCHI+N.4 BOCCHETTA NYLON COMPLETA+N.1 CARRELLO WS2/M P+N.5 SPAZZOLA SETOLE+N.5 VENTOSA LIQUIDI NYLON+N.20 CHIUSURA COMPLETA WD400+N.2 MOTORE ASP.ES9+N.2 FLESSIBILE ASP.ES+N.1 INNESTO FEMMINA ES9-14 N.5 ATTACCO A T WS2/M+N.50 MOTORE A40	200	185

./.

Figure 15.6

Consignor		
GHIBLI S.P.A. 27020 DORNO (PV) VIA CIRCONVALLAEZIONE 5, ITALY	**FBL** federazione nazionale spedizionieri ITALY No. 1803-41056 IT 380 NEGOTIABLE FIATA COMBINED TRANSPORT BILL OF LADING issued subject to ICC Uniform Rules for a Combined Transport Document (ICC publication 298)	

Consigned to order of
TO ORDER OF OVERSEAS UNICN BANK LTD.

OCEAN BILL OF LADING

Notify address
KLENCO (S) PTE LTD
7 TUAS AVENUE 1
SINGAPORE 2263

SERRA & LIESENFELD
INTERNATIONAL FORWARDERS
GENOA/ITALY

OPERATED BY:
LUIGI SERRA spa
Capitale Sociale lire 1.500.000.000
SPEDIZIONI INTERNAZIONALI
AGENZIA MARITTIMA
fondata nel 1882 sede in Genova
Palazzo Di Negro - Via S. Luca, 2 - 16124 Genova - P.O.B. 378 - 16100 Genova
Tel. 010/55111 - telex 275078 Serrai I
Serrai Genova - Cod. Fisc. e P. IVA 00244070108
C.C.I.A.A. Genova n. 1490 - Trib. Ge n. 7868

Place of receipt		
Ocean vessel FEN HE	Port of loading GENOA	
Port of discharge SINGAPORE	Place of delivery	

Marks and numbers	Number and kind of packages	Description of goods	Gross weight	Measurement
CBHU 115521-0 seal 045294	1 X 40'BX CONTAINER SAID TO CONTAIN : 308 CRTNS VACUUM CLEANERS, ACCESSO- RIES, SPARE PARTS AS PER PROFORMA INVOICE DATED 03.11.92. VIA FAX N. 1988. EX-WORKS. LETTER OF CREDIT LC NO. 72-210448 MARINE BILL OF LADING CLEAN ON BOARD – FREIGHT PAYABLE AT DESTINATION		5520,7 KGS.	

AGENTS :
ROHDE & LIESENFELD PTE. LTD.
450 ALEXANDRA ROAD
* 04-03 INCHCAPE HOUSE
SINGAPORE 0511
FAX 654745746
TEL 654796622

ORIGINAL

CLEAN ON BOARD
2 2 NOV. 1992
SERRA & LIESENFELD
«GOODS ON BOARD»

according to the declaration of the consignor

The goods and instructions are accepted and dealt with subject to the Standard Conditions printed overleaf.

Taken in charge in apparent good order and condition, unless otherwise noted herein, at the place of receipt for transport and delivery as mentioned above.
One of these Combined Transport Bills of Lading must be surrendered duly endorsed in exchange for the goods. In Witness whereof the original Combined Transport Bills of Lading all of this tenor and date have been signed in the number stated below, one of which being accomplished the other(s) to be void.

Freight amount	Freight payable at DESTINATION	Place and date of issue GENOA, NOVEMBER, 22ND 1992
Cargo Insurance through the undersigned ☐ not covered ☐ Covered according to attached Policy	Number of Original FBL's 3/ THREE	Stamp and signature SERRA & LIESENFELD
For delivery of goods please apply to:		

Figure 15.7

CHAPTER 15 BANK LOANS AND FINANCIAL INSTRUMENTS

East West-USI Insurance Pte Ltd

A member of the Sime Darby Group
47 Scotts Road #03-00 Goldbell Towers Singapore 0922 POSTAL ADDRESS Orchard P.O. Box 0037 Singapore 9123
Telephone: 7382818 Telex: RS 26362 UMICO Facsimile: 7382822

THE SCHEDULE

POLICY NO. AS-93-MC-07171	ACCOUNT NUMBER : AS-1302-VQ
DECLARED UNDER OPEN COVER NO :	REPLACING COVER NOTE NO:
THE INSURED:	DATE OF ISSUE : 28/12/92
KLENCO (S) PTE LTD	
	LETTER OF CREDIT REFERENCE
	L/C NO. 72-210448

FINANCIAL INTEREST

CONVEYANCE : FEN HE
DEPARTING (ON/ABOUT) : 22/11/92   ARRIVING (ON/ABOUT) :
VOYAGE : ITALY TO SINGAPORE

SUM INSURED (SO VALUED)SGD   72628.40   PREMIUM: AS ARRANGED   STAMP DUTY: 1.00

DESCRIPTION OF INTEREST	SHIPPING MARKS
1 X 40'BX CONTAINER SAID TO CONTAIN :	CBHU 115521-0
308 CRTNS VACUUM CLEANERS, ACCESSORIES, SPARE PARTS AS	SEAL 045294
PER PROFORMA INVOICE DATED 03.11.92	
GROSS WEIGHT: 5520.7 KGS	

THE FOLLOWING CLAUSES AND CONDITIONS APPLY TO THIS POLICY;
    INSTITUTE CARGO CLAUSES (ALL RISKS) 1.1.63
    INSTITUTE WAR CLAUSES 11.3.80
    INSTITUTE STRIKES RIOTS AND CIVIL COMMOTIONS CLAUSES 1.1.63
    INSTITUTE RADIOACTIVE CONTAMINATION EXCLUSION CLAUSE 1.10.90

SURVEY AGENT	SETTLEMENT AGENT
EAST WEST-USI INSURANCE	EAST WEST-USI INSURANCE
PTE LTD.	PTE LTD

ENTERED BY: THAM

SIGNED FOR AND ON BEHALF OF
THE COMPANY

....
MANAGER

IMPORTANT : THE WORD "UNDERWRITERS" AND "COMPANY" WHERE USED IN THIS POLICY AND CLAUSES ARE SYNONYMOUS WITH "ASSURERS".

Figure 15.8

PART FIVE   COMMERCIAL FINANCE

4. The collecting bank will have to ensure that the exporter's conditions are met before the documents are released to the importer and he is allowed to claim the goods. There are two types of conditions for collection of the documents:
   (a) Deliver documents against payment (D/P).
   Documents are to be delivered to the buyer only after payment. Such payment is usually by a *bank draft* issued by the importer's bank and is essentially a cheque in the exporter's local currency which can be realised for cash in the exporter's country.
   (b) Delivery documents against acceptance (D/A).
   The bill of exchange prepared by the exporter gives a deferred date for payment. It is called a *term bill*. In this case, documents are delivered to the importer upon his acceptance of the bill of exchange by signing it and the collecting bank will only collect payment for remittance to the exporter on the due date of the bill.

The whole process of documentary collection is summarised in Figure 15.9.

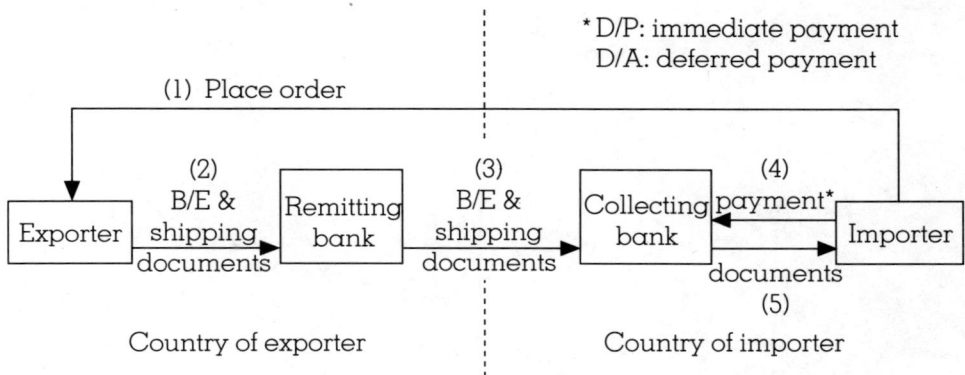

Figure 15.9 The procedure for documentary collection

Import Finance by Trust Receipt and Bank Guarantee

The D/A form of documentary collection is the type of import finance granted by the exporter to the importer allowing the latter to defer payment for the goods. This usually results from the goodwill built up between the parties so that the exporter is willing to give a credit term of either 30 or 60 days. In all other cases, the importer may also obtain financial facilities from his own bank using a trust receipt or T/R in short.

A trust receipt enables the importer to obtain the goods without first paying. Shipping documents are given to the importer so that goods can be released and held in trust for the bank. Such a facilitity allows the importer to take early delivery of the goods in order to sell them. The importer is responsible to the bank for payment plus interest since the bank has already paid the exporter's bank on behalf of the importer. Usually, trust receipts may be granted for duration of 30, 60 or 90 days by the bank.

Sometimes goods may arrive before the importer receives the bill of lading and other shipping documents. In such circumstances, the importer may apply to his bank for a shipping guarantee to be issued to the shipping company to indemnify and guarantee the shipping company for the release of goods without production of the bill of lading. The charge for such a guarantee is normally one-eighth of a per cent of the bill of exchange. Banks normally will not issue a guarantee to clear goods under a letter of credit and D/P. Such an arrangement is actually not a means of import finance but rather enables the importer to circumvent the problem of delay in receiving the bill of lading. The importer must pay for the goods as usual according to the terms of the D/A.

Chapter 16

Business Organisations

Business is more exciting than any game.

Lord Beaverbrook

Business firms can be classified according to their output into two types: those selling services and those selling goods. The latter type may be either merchandising firms or manufacturing firms. The basic accounting systems for these business firms have already been explained in previous chapters.

Most businesses can also be classified by their legal forms of organisation into three groups: the sole proprietorship, the partnership and the corporation or limited company. Each of these three types of firms have their own characteristics and advantages as well as disadvantages.

Sole Proprietorship

A sole proprietorship is a business owned by one person. It is the smallest and simplest kind of organisation. The objectives of the firm depend to a large extent on the goals of the individual owner. Often the owner also acts as the manager. This form of organisation is common for small retail stores and service enterprises including professional practices in law, medicine, engineering and public accounting. The business and its owner are not separate entities from a legal viewpoint.

The advantage of sole proprietorship is the ease of formation. No complicated legal documentation is required. Registration at the Registry of Businesses is simple and cost of formation is low. Another advantage is that although proper accounts have to be kept for the business, there is no legal requirement to appoint a public accountant to audit the accounts. Overhead costs for detailed accounting and auditing are therefore saved. Finally, although the owner and business are separate accounting entities, profit from business is included with other income of the owner for the purpose of calculating income tax. Since the average rate of personal income tax rate is generally lower than the tax rate of corporations, lower tax on profit will be paid. This enables faster accumulation of capital to finance expansion of the business.

The main disadvantage of sole proprietorship is the unlimited liability of the owner to creditors of the firm. This is because the owner and his firm are both the same legal entity so that debt owed by the business has to be borne in full by the owner. Another disadvantage is that there are limited avenues for obtaining finance for a sole proprietorship. Funding for expansion and investment are solely dependent on the limited internal resources of the firm and the owner.

Table 16.1 summarises the advantages and disadvantages of a sole proprietorship.

Table 16.1 Advantages and disadvantages of a sole proprietorship

Advantages	Disadvantages
1. Ease of formation	1. Unlimited liability of owner
2. Low cost of formation	2. Difficult to obtain external finance
3. No requirement for auditing by a public accountant	3. Lack of support by external parties
4. Lower tax on profit	

Partnership

The partnership is a business owned by two or more persons voluntarily associated as partners so that they can combine their efforts to meet common goals. Partnerships are also widely used for small business and professional practices. There is usually a written agreement among the partners which specifies the details of conducting the business. This *articles of partnership* often states the following:

1. Nature and purpose of the business
2. The rights and duties of each of the partners
3. Amount initially invested and how profits or losses will be shared among partners
4. Provision for limitations on the amount of assets each partner is allowed to withdraw
5. Conditions for withdrawal of old partners and admission of new partners
6. Authority of each partner in entering contracts for the firm

7. Procedures to be followed in the event of dispute among partners
8. Procedures to be followed when the partnership is dissolved

Partnerships have the following distinctive characteristics:

1. *Ease of formation.* Like sole proprietorships, no specific legal permission or approvals are required. Registration at the Registry of Businesses is simple once the name chosen for the partnership is approved.
2. *No separate legal entity.* A partnership is not a legal entity in itself. The partners are themselves the entities so that each partner is personally liable for the debts of the partnership. Although the firm is a separate accounting entity, there is no legal requirement to have the accounts audited by a public accountant. As in the case of a sole proprietorship, a partnership is not taxed as a separate entity. Instead its net income or loss is divided among partners as per the articles of partnership and reported in their individual tax returns.
3. *Unlimited liability.* Each partner is personally liable to creditors for all debts incurred by the partnership. This means that if creditors cannot be paid from a partnership's assets, they may seek to have their claim satisfied from the personal assets of the individual partners. A partner's liability for the partnership's debt is therefore not limited to the amount invested in the partnership.
4. *Co-ownership of property and profit.* When a partner invests assets in a partnership, he or she does not retain any personal right to the assets contributed. The assets invested become the property of all partners jointly. Similarly, a partnership's profit or loss belongs to all the partners and is distributed among them according to their agreement in the articles of partnership.
5. *Mutual agency.* Each partner acts as an agent of the partnership, with authority to bind the partnership to contracts with other parties provided the act is within the scope of normal operation. However, activities outside the scope of partnership require authorisation by all partners.
6. *Limited life.* A partnership dissolves with any change in the personnel of its membership. Thus, a partnership may be ended at any time by the withdrawal, bankruptcy, incapacity or death of any member of the firm. The admission of a new partner or the retirement of an existing partner also means an end to the old partnership so that a new partnership must be formed to continue the business. Sometimes a partnership is dissolved when the period specified in the articles of partnership expires or when the objective specified in the agreement has been achieved.

In view of the above characteristics, the advantages and disadvantages of a partnership can be summarised as shown in Table 16.2.

Table 16.2 Advantages and disadvantages of a partnership

Advantages	Disadvantages
1. Ease of formation	1. Limited life
2. Low cost of formation	2. Unlimited liability
3. Combines experience and managerial skills of partners	3. Mutual agency causing concern of personal liability resulting from the acts of other partners
4. Less government regulations such as requirement to engage public accountant	4. Difficult to transfer ownership interest
5. Lower tax burden	5. Difficult to raise funds for expansion and investment
6. More freedom to act compared to limited companies	

Limited Company or Corporation

A limited company or corporation are the same form of business organisation except the latter term is commonly used in the USA. Although there are fewer limited companies than proprietorships and partnerships, their combined size dominates the economy in every aspect.

A corporation has been defined (by Chief Justice of the USA, John Marshall in 1819) as 'an artificial being, invisible, intangible, and existing only in the contemplation of the law'. It is regarded as a legal entity having a continuous existence apart from that of its owners who are shareholders.

The company operates under a framework spelt out in a Memorandum and Articles of Association (the Corporate Charter in the USA) which has to be approved at the time of incorporation. The formation of a limited company requires registration with the Registry of Companies. Usually, the professional services of a lawyer or a public accountant is sought for registration. A Certificate of Incorporation will be issued on successful registration.

To administer the affairs of the company, the shareholders elect a board of directors. The directors in turn select a general manager (the president or chief executive office (CEO) in the USA) and other corporate officers to carry out the management of the business. A typical corporate organisational structure is shown in Figure 16.1.

If the general manager is also a director (who is necessarily a shareholder), he is called the managing director. Similarly other managers may be called directors such as administration director, personnel directors, etc., if they are also in the board of directors. In America, the titles president and vice-president are usually used. The designations chief executive officer and executive officer are also popular there. This organisational structure is by no means the only one. There are many types of corporate structure

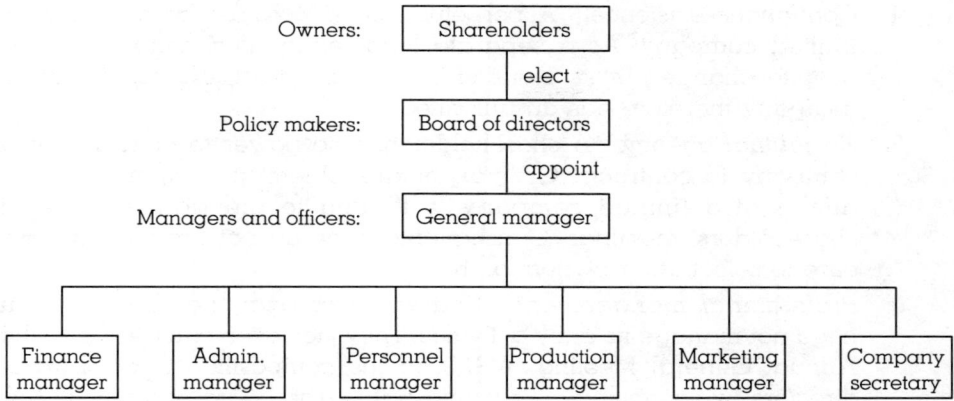

Figure 16.1 Corporate organisational structure

depending on the nature and size of operation of the business.

A limited company whose shares are only transferable by private arrangement is a *private limited company* or Pte Ltd Co. in short. A private limited company which has a good track record and has achieved a certain minimum volume of turnover may 'go public' by applying to the Stock Exchange of Singapore. After an elaborate process to allow the general public to subscribe for shares in the company, its shares will be listed on the stock exchange so that they can be readily bought and sold. Additional funds can also be raised from the general public by various ways such as right issues and loan stocks. A limited company whose shares are listed in the stock exchange is a *public limited company* or *public corporation*.

The main characteristics of a limited company are as follows:

1. *Separate legal entity.* A limited company is a separate legal entity, distinct from its shareholders who are its owners. It can, through its agents, conduct business with the same rights, duties, and responsibilities as a person.
2. *Limited liability for shareholders.* As a separate legal entity, a limited company is responsible for the liabilities incurred in its own name. Thus the creditors of a limited company have a claim against the assets of the company but not against the personal assets of the shareholders. The liability that each shareholder has for company debt is only limited to the amount paid for his or her shares.
3. *Ease of transferring ownership rights.* Ownership rights in a limited company are represented by shares. These can be transferred to other individuals or entities through private sales and brokerage firms in the case of a private limited company and through established stock exchanges for public company. The transfer has no effect on the company and its operations.

4. *Continuous existence.* A perpetual life is possible for a successful limited company. As a separate legal entity, it continues to exist despite changes in its ownership by transfer of shares. A limited company therefore has an unlimited life.
5. *No mutual agency.* A shareholder has no power to bind a limited company to contracts. Ordinary shareholders' participation in the affairs of a limited company is limited to the right to vote at shareholders' meetings. Consequently they do not have to exercise care to select other owners of the business.
6. *Professional management.* Shareholders own the company but need not manage its daily activities. They, however, can decide in the Annual General Meeting (AGM) on the composition of a board of directors by exercising their voting rights. The board of directors has the broad responsibility for administering the company's affairs. They may select a managing director and other directors in charge of other duties among themselves or hire professional managers to take care of the running of the business. For large corporations, ownership and management are normally separated so that the best managerial talent available can be sought out and hired for conducting the activities of the business.
7. *Ease of capital assembly.* Limited shareholders' liability, lack of mutual agency, and the ease with which an ownership interest may be transferred make it possible for a corporation to amass large amounts of capital from the combined investments of many shareholders. In the case of public companies, additional shares for existing shareholders to subscribe (right issues) and borrowing from the general public by issuing loan stocks (or bonds in USA) are commonly used to raise funds.
8. *Tight government regulation.* Limited companies are subjected to much tighter government regulation. Public accountants must be engaged to audit their accounts and a company secretary has to be appointed to file the many reports with the Registry of Companies every year. A report of the board of directors incorporating the audited financial statements has to be prepared. This document has to be sent to all shareholders in the case of public limited company.
9. *Greater tax burden.* Corporate income tax on profit is normally fixed at a flat rate higher than the average effective rate of personal income tax. Depending on the tax law of a country, dividends may be added to other income of shareholders and taxed again. In some countries, a tax rebate derived from the gross dividends and the difference of the corporate tax rate and the highest marginal rate paid by the person receiving the dividends is allowed.

The overall advantages and disadvantages of a limited company are summarised in Table 16.3.

Table 16.3 Advantages and disadvantages of a limited company

Advantages	Disadvantages
1. Limited liability for shareholders	1. High cost of formation
2. Ease of transferring ownership	2. Higher overhead on accounting and secretarial services
3. Continuous existence	3. Tighter government regulation and more extensive public disclosure
4. No mutual agency	4. Separation of ownership and control makes it difficult for shareholders to take concerted action to oust bad management group
5. Professional management	
6. Ease of capital assembly	
7. Private limited companies may become public companies	

Finally, which type of organisation a business should adopt depends on the nature and the size of its operation. Thus, professional practices are usually partnerships because this structure pools the expertise of the associated partners and the working capital requirement for service firms is usually not great. Similarly, for a new business with low capital requirements, a sole proprietorship or partnership is easier and more economical for operation as it is not fettered by too many legal rules and regulations. However, there is usually a limit to the growth of such organisations when further expansion requires the injection of more working capital. At that stage, conversion to a private limited company permits the assembling of more capital by enlarging the ownership base without disrupting the operation of the business. In the ultimate stage of development of a private limited company, getting listed on the stock exchange and thereby permitting general public to subscribe to its shares is the most effective way to enlarge its capital without losing management control of the company. It is also the best way for the existing owners to realise part or all of their equity in the company as cash after having built it up to a successful enterprise.

APPENDICES

APPENDICES

Appendix A

Some Cost and Management Accounting Problems and Solutions

The theories expounded in this book can be employed to solve most of the problems in cost and management accounting. More complex problems closer to real-life situations have not been included in the text to avoid the reader from getting confused before the basic principles have been grasped. Seven problems relating to various areas of cost and management accounting and their suggested solutions are given here. It is hoped that the reader will then appreciate the challenges faced by business managers and will consider accounting as a stimulating and lively subject rather than a dull and stereotyped discipline.

Problem 1. Transfer Pricing Among Cost Centres

A company has three divisions. Division 1 manufactures product A which is sold to division 2 as a component of its product B. Product B is then sold to division 3 which uses it as a component in product C. The finished product C is sold by the company to customers for $28 each.

Products A and B have no external market. A unit of product C uses one unit of product B which in turn uses one unit of product A. Standard costs of production and other data relating to the three divisions in the current year are:

Standard cost per unit:	Product A $	Product B $	Product C $
Material purchased externally	2.00	3.00	1.00
Direct labour	1.00	1.00	2.00
Variable overhead	1.00	1.00	2.00
Fixed overhead	3.00	4.00	1.00

	Division 1	Division 2	Division 3
Standard volume of production	10,000	10,000	10,000
Average inventory and work in progress	$70,000	$15,000	$30,000
Net fixed assets	$30,000	$45,000	$16,000

You are required, as the manager of division 3, to prepare a divisional statement of profit or loss for this year on the basis of 90% of standard volume under each of the following alternative rules for inter-division transfer pricing of product A and B:

1. Total standard cost per unit plus an additional charge per unit based on a 10% per annum return on average inventory and work in progress and net fixed assets.
2. Standard variable cost per unit will be the transfer price. However a lump sum charge will be invoiced by divisions 1 and 2 to division 3 equal to their total fixed overhead costs together with a 10% per annum return on average inventory, work in progress and net fixed assets at the end of the period.

Give your views, with reasons, as to which of the two transfer pricing rules should be preferred by the general manager of the company.

Solution

The first transfer pricing rule is to use the total absorption basis to calculate the transfer price. The second rule is based on marginal costing so that total fixed costs are charged out in lump sums at the end as period cost.

1. Computation using the first rule

The requirement to have 10% return on average inventory and work in progress and net fixed assets increases the unit costs of divisions 1 and 2 by the amounts calculated as follows:

	Division 1	Division 2
Total inventory and fixed assets	$100,000	$60,000
Return of 10%	$10,000	$6,000
Volume of production (units)	9,000	9,000
Additional cost per unit	$1.11	$0.67

The transfer price of division 1 to division 2 will be:

	$	$
Standard cost of product A		
Material purchased externally	2.00	
Direct labour	1.00	
Variable overhead	1.00	
Fixed overhead	3.00	
		7.00
Additional cost		1.11
Transfer price of product A		8.11

The transfer price of division 2 to division 3 will be:

	$	$
Standard cost of product B		
Transfer cost of product A	8.11	
Material purchased externally	3.00	
Direct labour	1.00	
Variable overhead	1.00	
Fixed overhead	4.00	
		17.11
Additional cost		0.67
Transfer price of product B		17.78

Profit and loss statement of division 3:

	$	$	$
Sales ($28 × 9,000)			252,000
1. Transfer cost of product B		160,020	
2. Variable costs:			
Material purchased	9,000		
Direct labour	18,000		
Variable overhead	18,000		
		45,000	
3. Fixed overhead		10,000	
Total cost			215,020
Profit of division 3			36,980

Although not required by the question, the profits of divisions 1 and 2 can be derived as follows:

	$	$	$
Transfer price to division 2 ($8.11 × 9,000)			72,990
1. Variable costs:			
Material purchased	18,000		
Direct labour	9,000		
Variable overhead	9,000		
		36,000	
2. Fixed overhead		30,000	
Total cost			66,000
Profit of division 1			6,990

Profit and loss statement of division 2:

	$	$	$
Transfer price to division 3 ($17.78 × 9,000)			160,020
1. Transfer cost of product A		72,990	
2. Variable costs:			
Material purchased	27,000		
Direct labour	9,000		
Variable overhead	9,000		
		45,000	
3. Fixed overhead		40,000	
Total cost			157,990
Profit of division 2			2,030

The total company profit will therefore be as follows:

	$
Division 1 profit	6,990
Division 2 profit	2,030
Division 3 profit	36,980
Company profit	46,000

Transfer prices are only inter-divisional charges within the same company. They will not affect the overall profit of the company which can also be derived as follows:

	$	$
Sales		252,000
less: variable cost		
Division 1	36,000	
Division 2	45,000	
Division 3	45,000	
		(126,000)
less: fixed overhead		
Division 1	30,000	
Division 2	40,000	
Division 3	10,000	
		(80,000)
		46,000

2. Computation using the second rule:

If transfer prices are the standard variable costs, the price of product A transferred to division 2 will be $4 and the price of product B transferred to division 3 will be ($4 + $5) or $9. The lump sum charges by divisions 1 and 2 to division 3 will be:

	Division 1	Division 2
Fixed overhead	30,000	40,000
10% returns on inventory and fixed assets	10,000	6,000
	40,000	46,000

The profit and loss statement of division 3 will be:

	$	$
Sales		252,000
less: transfer cost of product B	81,000	
Variable costs:		
Material purchased	9,000	
Direct labour	18,000	
Variable overhead	18,000	
Fixed cost	10,000	

		136,000
		116,000
less: charges of division 1	40,000	
charges of division 2	46,000	
		86,000
Profit of division 3		30,000

The variable costs of divisions 1 and 2 have already been charged as transfer price of product B to division 3. Similarly fixed overheads of divisions 1 and 2 have been included in the lump sum charges to division 3. The 10% returns on inventory and fixed assets charged to division 3, therefore, represent the profits of divisions 1 and 2. In summary:

	$
Division 1 profit	10,000
Division 2 profit	6,000
Division 3 profit	30,000
Company profit	46,000

It is clear that company profit will not be affected by the method of calculation of inter-division transfer price. The general manager of the company should prefer the transfer pricing rule which motivates every division to achieve better performance for the benefit of the company as a whole. One division should not be motivated to improve its own result at the expense of the company's overall results.

There are two ways to increase the overall profit of the company:

1. *Cutting costs.* Reduction of both variable and fixed costs will improve the overall performance of the company. By the first method of transfer pricing, divisional profits will increase if either variable cost or fixed cost are reduced. However, by the second method of transfer pricing, profits of divisions 1 and 2 will not improve by cutting fixed costs since their actual costs are charged to division 3 in any case.
2. *Increasing production and sales.* If sales is limited by production, increase in productivity will increase the profits of all three divisions. The first method of transfer pricing will motivate all divisions to increase output. By the second pricing method, the profits of divisions 1 and 2 are fixed at 10% of their inventory and fixed assets values. These two divisions will not be motivated towards greater productivity, to the detriment of the overall profitability of the company.

As can be seen, profits of divisions 1 and 2 are both higher if the second method of transfer pricing is used in this case. Managers of these two divisions are likely to advocate this method which will be objected to by the manager of division 3. The general manager of the company should prefer method 1 instead since it will lead to cost consciousness and improvement of productivity by all divisions.

It is interesting to note that while the marginal cost pricing policy usually encourage sales, it is not suitable for application to transfer pricing if period costs are passed to other divisions as transferred costs.

Problem 2. Buy or Make Decision

A company which manufactures office equipment is preparing its budget for the next year. An initial review shows that it will not be possible to manufacture enough of components A, B, C and D to meet expected sales demand because the normal metal pressing capacity of 20,000 hours will be exceeded.

The company can choose between the following alternative courses of action to obtain the products in excess of normal production capacity:

(a) To buy entirely from outside suppliers.
(b) To buy from outside suppliers and/or use a partial second shift.

The forecasted data for next year are:

1. Standard production cost per unit

Component	A $	B $	C $	D $
Variable costs:				
Direct materials	18.50	13.50	12.50	22.00
Direct wages	5.00	4.00	11.00	20.00
Direct expenses	5.00	10.00	5.00	30.00
Fixed overheads	2.50	2.00	5.50	10.00
	31.00	29.50	34.00	82.00
Requirements in units	2,000	3,500	1,500	2,800

2. Direct expenses are incurred by the metal presses which cost $5 per machine hour to operate. Fixed overhead is absorbed as a percentage of direct wages.
3. Second shift operation would increase direct wages cost by 25% over the

normal shift and fixed overhead by $250 for each 1,000 (or part thereof) second shift hours worked.
4. The delivery-to-factory costs of components from outside suppliers are:

	$
A	30.00
B	29.50
C	26.00
D	84.00

As production manager of the company, you are required to decide:

(a) which components, and in what quantities, should be manufactured in the 20,000 hours of press time available;
(b) whether it would be profitable to make any of the balance of components required on a second shift basis instead of buying them from outside suppliers.

Solution

Since press hour is the resource constrained by availability, the approach is to first work out the advantage per press hour gained by making the components internally. Priority for manufacturing in-house should be graded according to the advantage per press hour gained compared to buying from outside suppliers.

	A	B	C	D
	$	$	$	$
Purchase cost	30.00	29.50	26.00	84.00
Total variable cost to make	28.50	27.50	28.50	72.00
Advantage gained by making	1.50	2.00	(2.50)	12.00
Press hours per unit $\left(=\dfrac{\text{direct expenses}}{\$5}\right)$	1	2	1	6
Advantage gained per hour by making	$1.50	$1.00	($2.50)	$2.00
Order of priority for press capacity	2	3	none	1

(a) Components to be manufactured in the 20,000 hours of press time should be:

Component	Units	Press hours
D	2,800	16,800
A	2,000	2,000
		18,800
B	600	1,200 (balance)
		20,000

(b) Component C is uneconomical to make and would be even more so in a second shift operation. Since the total requirement for component B is 3,500 units, there remains a balance of 2,900 units either to be purchased or made using a second shift operation.

The decision to make by a second shift depends on whether the advantage gained by making in a normal shift (i.e., $2 per unit) is sufficient to cover the additional costs in operating the second shift.

Additional costs to make 2,900 units in a second shift:

Additional wages ($4 × 2,900 × 25%)	$2,900
Additional fixed overhead ($250 × 6)	$1,500
	$4,400

Additional fixed overhead is based on (2,900 × 2) hours rounded to 6,000 hours at $250 per 1,000 hours.

Additional cost per unit of component B is therefore $\frac{\$4,400}{2,900} = \$1.52$

To summarise:

	$
Advantage per unit gained by making component B in normal shift	2.00
Additional cost per unit in second shift	1.52
Advantage of making in second shift	0.48

Since there will still be an advantage of $0.48 per unit to make component B in a second shift operation, the balance of 2,900 units should not be purchased.

Note that fixed overheads are period costs which will be incurred in any case. As shown in this case, the decision to make or buy therefore is not affected by fixed overhead costs. The concept of marginal costing is fundamental in comparing different situations in such analysis.

Problem 3. Production and Sales Strategy

A company is selling two products A and B with market demand far exceeding its production capacity. The company, therefore, is considering concentrating its production on one of the two products only in order to maximise profit.

The standard selling price and standard prime cost of each product manufactured by two processing departments are:

	A		B	
	hours	$	hours	$
Selling price		150		220
Prime cost:				
Department 1:				
Direct materials		9		15
Direct wages ($0.80/hr)	10	8	15	12
Department 2:				
Direct materials		3		4
Direct wages ($1.20/hr)	15	18	20	24

Standard overheads of the company are absorbed based on direct labour hours of the two departments:

	Department 1	Department 2
Fixed overhead per annum	$80,000	$160,000
Variable overhead per direct labour hour	$0.60	$0.80

The labour force of the company is budgeted at 50,000 direct labour hours in department 1 and 80,000 direct labour hours in department 2.

The company has selected the following sub-contractors to supplement the production capacity of departments 1 and 2:

(a) Company X can produce up to a maximum of 2,500 units of product A or 2,000 units of product B in a year in respect of the type of work performed in department 1. Their prices, delivered to the factory, would be $35 and $55 each respectively including raw materials.

(b) Company Y can produce up to a maximum of 1,600 units of product A or 1,000 units of product B in a year in respect of the type of work performed in department 2. Their prices, delivered to the factory, would be $60 and $75 each, respectively, including raw materials.

Market research has concluded that for more than 5,500 units of product A to be sold in the year, the price for all units sold need to be reduced to $135. If more than 4,500 units of product B are to be sold, their price has to be reduced to $190 each.

As the general manager of the company, you are required to:

(a) determine the standard percentage profit on sales of products A and B respectively based on absorption costing;
(b) decide whether the company should concentrate its resources on product A or B if:
   (i) it does not use sub-contractors and the work force in either department can be reduced if it exceeds production requirement;
   (ii) it uses sub-contractors and restricts its sales to the level beyond which the price per product would have to be reduced;
   (iii) it uses sub-contractors to the full extent of its own and the sub-contractors' production capacities.

Solution

(a) Fixed overhead absorption rate:

	Department 1	Department 2
Fixed overhead	$80,000	$160,000
Direct labour hours	50,000	80,000
Fixed overhead absorption rate (per direct labour hour)	$1.60	$2.00

	Department 1	Department 2	Total
Product A:			
Direct labour hours	10	15	—
Fixed overhead absorbed	$16	$30	$46
Product B:			
Direct labour hours	15	20	—
Fixed overhead absorbed	$24	$40	$64

Standard percentage profit on sales for products A and B:

	Product A			Product B		
	$	$	$	$	$	$
Selling price (per unit)			150			220
less variable costs:						

Department 1				
Direct materials	9		15	
Direct wages	8		12	
Variable overhead	6		9	
		23		36
Department 2				
Direct material	3		4	
Direct wages	18		24	
Variable overhead	12		16	
		33		44
Total variable costs		56		80
		94		140
less fixed overhead:				
Department 1		16		24
Department 2		30		40
		46		64
Profit		48		76
Profit as percentage of sales		32.00%		34.55%

(b) Production and sales strategies

The fixed overhead of the company should not be taken into consideration when analysing production and sales strategies. This is because period costs are unaffected by production volume and whether external sub-contractors are engaged. Marginal costing instead of absorption costing principle will therefore be used.

(i) Without using sub-contractors but with maximum in-house production:

It has to be determined first whether labour hours of department 1 or department 2 is the limiting factor constraining the production of products A and B.

	Department 1	Department 2
Budgeted labour hours	50,000	80,000
Product A		
Labour hours per unit	10	15
Maximum production	5,000	5,333
Product B		
Labour hours per unit	15	20
Maximum production	3,333	4,000

Thus, available labour hours in department 1 is the limiting factor in the production of both products A and B. To decide on which product the company should concentrate its manufacturing resources, the contribution per department 1 labour hours for products A and B should be compared.

	Product A $	Product B $
Selling price	150	220
less: total variable cost	56	80
Contribution per unit	94	140
Department 1 labour hours	10	15
Contribution per department 1 hour	$9.40	$9.33

Since product A has higher contribution per department 1 labour hour, production should concentrate on product A alone with 5,000 units to be produced. The resulting profit will be:

	$	$
Contribution ($94 × 5,000)		470,000
less: fixed overhead		
Department 1	80,000	
Department 2	160,000	
		240,000
Profit		230,000

(ii) Use sub-contractors to supplement in-house production and restrict sales to 5,500 of product A or 4,500 of product B:

If the company concentrates on producing and selling 5,500 of product A, the company profit will be:

	$	$
Sales (5,500 @ $150)		825,000
less variable costs:		
Department 1 (5,000 @ $23)	115,000	
Contractor X (500 @ $35)	17,500	
Department 2 (5,333 @ $33)	175,989	
Contractor Y (167 @ $60)	10,020	

		$	$
			318,509
Contribution			506,491
less: total fixed overhead			240,000
Profit			266,491

If the company concentrates on producing and selling 4,500 of product B, the company profit will be:

	$	$
Sales (4,500 @ $220)		990,000
less variable costs:		
Department 1 (3,333 @ $36)	119,988	
Contractor X (1,167 @ $55)	64,185	
Department 2 (4,000 @ $44)	176,000	
Contractor Y (500 @ $75)	37,500	
		397,673
Contribution		592,327
less: total fixed overhead		240,000
Profit		352,327

(iii) Maximum production using both in-house and contractor's manufacturing capacities:

	Department 1	Department 2
Product A		
Own production	5,000	5,333
Contractor X or Y	2,500	1,600
	7,500	6,933
Product B		
Own production	3,333	4,000
Contractor X or Y	2,000	1,000
	5,333	5,000

Thus, labour hours of department 2 type of work is the limiting factor of production.

Based on the results in (ii) above, the new profit figures can be derived for the two cases of concentrating on producing product A (maximum 6,933 units) and on producing product B (maximum 5,000 units). First of all, the contribution per unit of product A and product B made by contractors X and Y and selling at the new selling prices will be:

	Product A	Product B
	$	$
Selling price	135	190
less: contractor X cost	(35)	(55)
contractor Y cost	(60)	(75)
Contribution	40	60

Concentrating on producing 6,933 units of product A:

	$
Contribution as in (ii) above for 5,500 units	506,491
less: reduction due to $15 drop in selling price	82,500
	423,991
Additional contribution (1,433 units @ $40)	57,320
Total contribution	481,311
less: total fixed overhead	240,000
Profit	241,311

Concentrating on producing 5,000 units of product B:

	$
Contribution as in (ii) above for 4,500 units	592,327
less: reduction due to $30 drop in selling price	135,000
	457,327
Additional contribution (500 units @ $60)	30,000
Total contribution	487,327
less: total fixed overhead	240,000
Profit	247,327

The overall conclusion is that the best strategy is to concentrate on the production of product B using both in-house manpower and external contractors and restrict sales to 4,500 units without dropping the sales price.

APPENDIX A SOME COST AND MANAGEMENT ACCOUNTING PROBLEMS AND SOLUTIONS

Problem 4. Cost Reduction by Automation

A company has decided to install semi-automatic machines to replace its existing manual controlled ones now producing long runs of identical products. The following data are given:

	Existing manual machine	New semi-automatic machine
Standard time for one operator to handle one machine to produce one unit:	minutes	minutes
Operation:		
Loading unit on machine	8.5	2.5
Machining	25.0	17.0
Unloading finished unit	2.5	1.5
Inspection	2.5	2.5
Greasing and placing into box	1.5	1.5
Cost per hour:	$	$
Overhead per machine hour	1.68	4.50
Wage of operator	1.50	1.50

The new machines will be so located that the walking time between machines can be ignored.

The management of the company has to determine:

(a) the unit costs for using the existing machines and semi-automatic machines with one operator to each machine;
(b) the maximum number of semi-automatic machines each operator should control to minimise the unit cost of production;
(c) the hourly bonus based on one quarter of the savings obtained against existing cost the operators should receive for undertaking multi-machine control operation.

Solution

(a) In the existing manual operation, the standard time to produce one unit is the total time for all the operations (i.e., 40 minutes). It should be realised that with semi-automatic machines, an operator will be freed during the machining operation so that he can inspect, grease and place the unit machined in the last operation into storage box. The total production time per unit is thus 21 minutes on average comprising 17 minutes machining time and 4 minutes loading and unloading time.

Unit machining costs using one operator to one machine are calculated as follows:

		Existing machine		New machine	
		min	$	min	$
1.	Operator time	40		21	
	Wages @ $1.50/60 = $0.025/min		1.00		0.525
2.	Machining time	25		17	
	Overhead @ $1.68/60 = $0.028/min		0.70		
	Overhead @ $4.50/60 = $0.075/min				1.275
			1.70		1.80

(b) As the semi-automatic machines are assumed to run for 17 minutes without the need for operator intervention and the operator has only 4 minutes worth of other jobs (inspecting, greasing and packing) to do during these 17 minutes, he can be more productively employed by having more machines to operate.

With every semi-automatic machine, 8 minutes of manual work (loading, unloading, inspection, greasing and packing) is required. For two machines per operator, the loading and unloading on each machine can be staggered so that all the 16 minutes of manual work can be done in the 21 minutes that an operator must be on hand for each units operating cycle. Total machining time is 2 x 17 minutes.

With three machines per operator working in parallel, labour becomes a limiting factor because 3 x 8 minutes of manual work will be required. This is more than the labour cycle time of 21 minutes with one or two machines. Subsequently, an extra 8 minutes of labour time will also be required for an additional machine and machining time will increase by 17 minutes per machine.

Unit costs for cases with two, three and four machines per operator are tabulated as follows:

	2 machines $	3 machines $	4 machines $
Wages at $0.025 per minute:			
(17 + 4) minutes	0.525		
3 × 8 minutes		0.600	
4 × 8 minutes			0.800
Overhead at $0.075 per minute of machine time:			
2 × 17 minutes	2.550		
3 × 17 minutes		3.825	
4 × 17 minutes			5.100
	3.075	4.425	5.900
Number of units produced	2	3	4
Cost per unit	1.537	1.475	1.475

APPENDIX A SOME COST AND MANAGEMENT ACCOUNTING PROBLEMS AND SOLUTIONS

Thus, three machines in a group will produce units at a lower unit cost than one or two machines in a group. With three or more machines, labour becomes the limiting factor and unit cost will remain the same because the incremental cost is 8 minutes of wage and 17 minutes of overhead. Machines will stand idle as operators perform their manual tasks.

The preceding calculations and conclusions are based on the assumption that an operator would work for an unbroken 60 minutes per hour.

(c) Computation of operator's bonus:

	$
Unit cost with existing machines (from (a) above)	1.70
Unit cost with 3 new machines	1.475
Savings per unit	0.225
Bonus per unit (25%)	0.056

As three units will be produced in 24 minutes, the bonus per hour

$$= \$0.056 \times \frac{60}{24} \times 3 = \$0.42$$

Problem 5. Cost of Loss of Production

A company manufactures and sells a standard design of small pleasure boat. Business is thriving and the company can sell boats as soon as they are produced. The company's budget for a four-week period, period 8, is:

	$	$
Sales of 400 boats (100 per week) @ $2,500		1,000,000
less costs of production:		
Direct materials	300,000	
Direct labour	300,000	
Depreciation	100,000	
Other overheads	100,000	
		800,000
Budgeted profit		200,000

The managing director is insensitive in his relations with his employees. As a result of a dispute, there was a mass walk-out by all employees engaged in direct labour work, at the beginning of week 3 of period 8. Production came to a complete standstill, and with the strike continuing to the end of the week, the managing director announced that the strike had cost the company $250,000 which was the loss in turnover from the estimated lost production of 100 boats.

Good sense eventually prevailed and the strike was called off. Normal production resumed at the beginning of week 4.

During the stoppage, the company had taken the opportunity to carry out its thorough annual overhaul of plant and machinery. The work was done by maintenance staff using indirect materials costing $10,000, thereby saving the cost of hiring an outside contractor to do the job including materials for $40,000 during period 10.

At the end of period 8, it was agreed that the lost production of 80 boats should be made up in overtime in period 9. Direct labour wage was one and a half times for overtime, but the variable overhead cost per boat would remain the same as in normal hours, which is $25 per boat. Actual results for period 8 were:

	$	$
Sales (320 boats @ $2,500)		800,000
Production (320 boats):		
Direct materials	260,000	
Direct labour	230,000	
Depreciation	100,000	
Other overheads	105,000	
Total cost		695,000
Actual profit for period 8:		105,000

The following additional information is available:

(1) Depreciation is charged on a straight line basis. It has been estimated, however, that the drop in the realisable value of plant and machinery is currently $10,000 per week, whether or not it is used, with an additional fall in value of $100 for every boat produced.

(2) Actual other overheads in period 8 were:

	$
Variable overhead	7,500
Fixed overhead	87,500
Overhaul material	10,000
	105,000

APPENDIX A SOME COST AND MANAGEMENT ACCOUNTING PROBLEMS AND SOLUTIONS

(3) No overtime was worked in period 8, and actual hours worked in weeks 1, 2 and 4 were as budgeted.
(4) Employees on strike received no pay from the company.

You are required to prepare:

(a) a statement reconciling the budgeted and actual profit for period 8, showing the variances in such a way as to be as informative as possible to the management;
(b) an assessment of the cost of the strike, taking into consideration all known factors.

Solution

(a) To begin with, the standard sales price and costs of production per boat have to be derived by dividing the original budget by 400. The given data of 'other overheads' can be analysed into variable and fixed portions by noting that variable cost has been given as $25 per boat. Depreciation is also included in the fixed overhead.

$$\text{Fixed overhead per boat} = \frac{\$100{,}000 + (\$100{,}000 - \$25 \times 400)}{400} = \$475$$

The standard sales price and costs per boat are:

	$	$
Sales price		2,500
less: direct material	750	
direct labour	750	
variable overhead	25	
Total variable cost		1,525
Contribution		975
Fixed overhead		475
Profit		500

1. Sales variances

There was no sales price variance. Sales in period 8 was 320 boats instead of 400 boats. The sales volume variance of 80 boats (adverse) can be explained as follows:

Loss of production due to strike	100 boats (A)
Efficiency variance	20 boats (F)
	80 boats (A)

Sales volume variance in terms of contribution is:

	$
Loss of production due to strike ($975 × 100)	97,500 (A)
Efficiency variance ($975 × 20)	19,500 (F)
Sales volume variance	78,000 (A)

Sales volume variance in terms of profit is:

	$
Loss of production due to strike ($500 × 100)	50,000 (A)
Efficiency variance ($500 × 20)	10,000 (F)
Sales volume variance	40,000 (A)

2. Material cost variances

   Price and usage variances cannot be derived due to lack of information on unit prices. Total material cost variance is:

	$
Actual material cost	260,000
Standard material cost ($750 × 320)	240,000
	20,000 (A)

3. Direct labour cost variances

	$
Actual direct labour cost	230,000
Standard direct labour cost ($750 × 320)	240,000
	10,000 (F)

Because no overtime was worked, actual labour hours in the productive weeks were as budgeted. The production of 320 boats instead of 300 boats in those three weeks may be attributed to a favourable efficiency variance of 20 boats which attributes a favourable direct labour variance of $750 × 20. The labour wage rate variance is, therefore, deduced as follows:

	$
Total direct labour cost variance	10,000 (F)
less: labour efficiency variance	15,000 (F)
Labour wage rate variance:	5,000 (A)

4. Variable overhead variances

	$
Actual variable overhead	7,500
Standard variable overhead ($25 × 320)	8,000
Variable overhead variance	500 (F)

Analysing into efficiency and expenditure variances:

Efficiency variance = $25 × 20 = $500(F)

Therefore, expenditure variance = 0

5. Fixed overhead variances

	$
Actual fixed overhead (including depreciation)	187,500
Standard fixed overhead ($475 × 320)	152,000
	35,500 (A)

Analysing further:

	$
Loss of capacity due to strike of 1 week ($475 × 100)	47,500 (A)
Efficiency variance ($475 × 20)	9,500 (F)
Volume variance	38,000 (A)

Expenditure variance = total variance − volume variance
= $35,500 (A) − $38,000 (A)
= $2,500 (F)

Since contribution less fixed overhead is profit, the fixed overhead volume variance can be reconciled with sales volume variances derived earlier as follows:

	$
Sales volume variance in terms of contribution	78,000 (A)
less: fixed overhead volume variance	38,000 (A)
Sales volume variance in terms of profit	40,000 (A)

Reconciliation of budgeted and actual profits for period 8:

	Favourable variance $	Adverse variance $	Total $
Budgeted profit			200,000
Sales volume efficiency variance	10,000		
Material cost variance		20,000	
Direct labour efficiency variance	15,000		
Direct labour wage rate variance		5,000	
Variable overhead efficiency variance	500		
Variable overhead expenditure variance	0	0	
Fixed overhead efficiency variance	9,500		
Fixed overhead expenditure variance	2,500		
Effects of the strike:			
Loss of standard profit in week 3		50,000	
Fixed overhead capacity variance due to strike		47,500	
Costs of overhaul		10,000	
	37,500	132,500	
			95,000 (A)
Actual profit			105,000

(b) The short-fall of 80 boats is to be made up by production using overtime which will result in direct labour cost increased by 50%. The contribution from each boat made in overtime will be:

	$	$
Sales price		2,500
less: direct materials	750	
direct labour ($750 × 1.5)	1,125	
variable overhead	25	
		1,900
Contribution		600

Since 80 boats instead of the original 100 boats are to be built, there is savings in the realisable value of plant and machinery of $100 × 20. The quantifiable cost of the strike is therefore:

	$	$
Loss of contribution due to strike ($975 × 100)	97,500	
less: contribution from production using overtime ($600 × 80)	48,000	
Net loss in contribution		49,500
Savings in overhaul cost ($40,000 − $10,000)	(30,000)	
Savings in realisable value of plant and machinery ($100 × 20)	(2,000)	
		(32,000)
Net cost of the strike		17,500

Problem 6. Replacement of Obsolescent Equipment

A company making automobile components uses three separate machines to undertake the turning, boring and grinding operations. The present machines are old and unreliable so that the engineering manager has put forward two alternative proposals for their replacement by:

1. three new individual machines
2. a combined multipurpose machine

The following data are given:

	Present machines		Proposed machines	
Type of machine	Original cost $	Annual operating cost $	Capital cost $	Annual operating cost $
Turning	25,000	20,000	50,000	7,000
Boring	35,000	21,000	53,000	8,000
Grinding	20,000	12,000	31,000	6,000
Multipurpose	–	–	147,000	17,000

The economic life of all the new machines is eight years and by that time it is estimated that their salvage value will be equal to their dismantling cost.

The company normally expects new capital investment to provide a 14% discounted-cash-flow return.

You are required to:

(a) evaluate the two proposals, and
(b) write a short appraisal of your analysis making a firm recommendation on the replacement action to be taken.

Solution

(a) Annual savings in operating cost using three new individual machines
 = $(20,000 + 21,000 + 12,000) − $(7,000 + 8,000 + 6,000)
 = $32,000

Annual savings in operating cost using a new multipurpose machine
 = $(20,000 + 21,000 − 12,000) − $17,000
 = $36,000

The present value factor:

$$= \left[\frac{1}{1.14} + \frac{1}{1.14^2} + \cdots \frac{1}{1.14^8}\right] = \frac{1.14^8 - 1}{1.14^8 \times 0.14} = 4.639$$

Therefore, the net present value savings of buying three new individual machines = −$(50,000 + 53,000 + 31,000) + $32,000 × 4.639
 = −$134,000 + $148,448
 = $14,448

The net present value savings of buying a new multipurpose machine
 = −$147,000 + $36,000 × 4.639
 = −$147,000 + $167,004
 = $20,004

APPENDIX A SOME COST AND MANAGEMENT ACCOUNTING PROBLEMS AND SOLUTIONS

Both proposals are acceptable basing on a 14% discounted-cash-flow return.

(b) In comparing the two proposals, the one with higher net present value should be recommended unless the following considerations prove to be more decisive:

1. sensitivity analysis
2. available finance
3. maintenance and machine reliability

First of all, sensitivity of the result is evaluated in terms of discount rate, capital cost and operating cost respectively.

1. The adopted discount rate is compared with the internal rate of return to determine the margin of safety in each case:

At the point of break-even (i.e., where discount rate equals to the internal rate of return):

Capital cost = Annual saving in operating cost × Present value factor

Thus, in the case of replacement with three new machines:

$$\$134,000 = \$32,000 \times \text{Present value factor}$$

or   Present value factor = 4.1875

By trial and error, the present value factor is 4.1875 when the discount rate is between:

17% (present value factor = 4.207)
and   18% (present value factor = 4.078)

By intrapolation, the internal rate of return

$$= 18\% - \left(\frac{4.1875 - 4.078}{4.207 - 4.078}\right) \times 1\% = \underline{\underline{17.15\%}}$$

In the case of replacement with a multipurpose machine:

$$\$147,000 = \$36,000 \times \text{Present value factor}$$

or   Present value factor = 4.0833

This value also falls between the cases with discount rates of 17% and 18% as above. The internal rate of return by intrapolation is therefore:

APPENDICES

$$18\% - \left(\frac{4.0833 - 4.078}{4.207 - 4.078}\right) \times 1\% = \underline{17.96\%}$$

The margin of safety for the second proposal is slightly higher in terms of the discount rate chosen.

2. Sensitivity analysis of capital cost

   Break-even capital cost = Annual savings × Present value factor

   In the case of buying three separate machines,

   Break-even capital cost = $32,000 × 4.639 = $148,448

   Marginal of safety = $148,448 − $134,000 = $14,448

   or 10.8% of the orginal estimate.
   This is also the net present value of the proposed plan. Similarly, the margin of safety for the case of buying a new multipurpose machine is $20,004 or 13.6% of the original estimated capital cost.
   The multipurpose machine project is therefore less sensitive to changes in capital cost.

3. Sensitivity analysis of operating cost

   The sensitivity of each project to difference in the expected annual savings of operating cost is measured as follows:

   The proposal to buy three separate machines will just break even if the present value of savings falls by

   $$\$14{,}448 \text{ or } \left(\frac{\$14{,}448}{\$148{,}448}\right) = 9.7\%$$

   In terms of annual savings, the project will still break-even if the savings in operating cost drops by $32,000 × 0.097 = $3,104.
   In case of the second proposal to buy a single multipurpose machine, the project will break-even if the present value of savings falls by

   $$\$20{,}004 \text{ or } \left(\frac{\$20{,}004}{\$167{,}004}\right) = 11.98\%$$

   This implies that the annual savings will have to drop by $36,000 × 0.1198 = $4,313 to reach the break-even point.
   The project to buy a multipurpose machine is, therefore, less sensitive to changes in the level of annual savings.
   Overall, the proposal to buy a multipurpose machine is recommended because:

1. it has a higher net present value,
2. it is less sensitive to changes in the cost of capital (the discount rate), capital cost and annual operational savings.

This is provided that:

1. sufficient finance is available as the capital cost is higher by $(147,000 − 134,000) or $13,000, and this fund could not be employed more profitably elsewhere;
2. the maintenance considerations and performance reliability of the multipurpose machine are satisfactory. A breakdown of the machine would affect all production, whereas with three machines, a breakdown of one machine might not immediately affect production of the others.

Problem 7. Cost of Acquisition of a Company

In an effort to diversify, company A is contemplating acquiring company B which is presently the market leader in its area. You are required to assess a fair price to pay for the acquisition from the point of view of both shareholders of company A and company B based on the latest profit and loss statement and balance sheet of company B given as follows:

Profit and Loss Statement

	$'000	$'000
Sales		5,263
less: cost of sales		
Opening stock	960	
add: purchase	2,580	
carriage inward (transportation cost)	199	
less: closing stock	(1,100)	
		2,639
Gross profit		2,624
less: expenses	1,605	
accrued expenses	301	
interest	144	
		2,050
Operating profit		574
add: other income (profit from subsidiaries)		283
Total net profit		857

Balance Sheet

	$'000	$'000
Fixed assets		2,537
Long-term investment		150
Interest in subsidiaries		1,028
		3,715
Current assets:		
Inventory	1,100	
Trade debtors	1,023	
Other debtors and prepayment	36	
Fixed deposit	23	
Cash	1	
	2,183	
less: current liabilities		
Trade creditors	710	
Hire purchase creditors	34	
Other creditors and accruals	68	
Sundry loan	144	
	788	
	1,744	
Working capital		439
		4,154
Financed by:		
Share capital	1,000	
Capital reserve	358	
Retained earnings	1,050	
Current year earnings	857	
Total shareholders' equities		3,265
Long-term loan		889
		4,154

Solution

Three main factors have to be considered in the acquisition of a company:

1. Return on investment derived from the profit of operation
2. Prospect for future growth in earnings
3. Net assets including goodwill of the company

1. Return on investment

   Return in this context is not merely the dividends shareholders receive. It should rightfully be the net profit after interest and tax as this belongs to the shareholders even though it is not all distributed as dividends.

   In order to simplify the analysis in this case, net profit before tax is taken as earnings which is different from the stock market ratio defined in Chapter 13. From data in the balance sheet:

   $$\text{Return on investment} = \frac{\text{current year earnings}}{\text{total shareholders' equities}}$$

   $$= \frac{\$857,000}{\$3,265,000} = 26.24\%$$

   The maximum amount company A is willing to pay for shares in company B depends on the minimum return on investment its shareholders expect. If that is say 15%, the purchase price should be:

   $$\frac{\$857,000}{0.15} = \$5,713,333$$

   On the other hand, from the point of view of shareholders of company B, shareholders' equities of \$3,265,000 is the minimum amount they expect to realise if they relinquish their shares. It is, however, not beneficial for them to sell unless the money they receive can be reinvested to obtain similar or better return.

   In the extreme case, the safest investment is by way of a fixed deposit in banks which pay interest of say 7%. Shareholders of company B will be able to realise the same return if they sell their shares for the amount below and place the money in fixed deposit:

   $$\frac{\$857,000}{0.07} = \$12,242,857$$

   By doing so, they can avert future business risk and still receive the same return. However, they also will not benefit from whatever future growth of the company.

   A more common way to measure return on investment is the price-earnings ratio. References can be based on values quoted for public companies in local stock exchange. It is recognised that P/E ratio of 10 is common for companies in developed countries. Most public companies in developing countries are having P/E ratios higher than that. This is attributed to the high growth potential and speculative nature of those share markets.

   Based on the data given and considering earnings as profit before tax, the worth of company B with P/E ratio equals to 10 is:

$$\$857,000 \times 10 = \$8,570,000$$

From the investor's point of view, paying a P/E ratio of 10 means that the immediate return on investment is 10% since:

$$\frac{\text{Earnings}}{\text{Price paid}} = \frac{1}{10} = 10\%$$

The final price for company B is likely to be between the extremes of $5,713,333 and $12,242,857 depending on the P/E ratio agreed by both parties.

2. The growth potential

If an investment is long term and there is no intention to sell in the near future, the price to pay, P, should be the present value of annual earnings, E, in future years:

$$P = \frac{E}{1+r} + \frac{E}{(1+r)^2} + \cdots$$

where r is the required rate of return on investment. If earnings is growing at a rate of g per year, the present value

$$P = E\frac{(1+g)}{(1+r)} + E\frac{(1+g)^2}{(1+r)^2} + \cdots$$

$$= E\frac{(1+g)}{(r-g)}\left[1 - \left(\frac{(1+g)}{(1+r)}\right)^n\right]$$

$$= E\frac{(1+g)}{(r-g)} \quad \text{if } r \text{ is greater than } g \text{ and } n \text{ is large}$$

Thus, if a company has high growth potential, its worth should not be based on the previous year's performance alone. Considering company A has a target return on investment of 15% and the earnings of company B is anticipated to grow at 5% a year, the present worth of company B will be:

$$\frac{\$857,000 \times 1.05}{0.15 - 0.05} = \$8,998,500$$

3. Net asset basis of evaluation

An evaluation based on net tangible asset is a conservative way to assess the net worth of a company. Based on data in the balance sheet:

	$'000	$'000
Fixed assets		2,537
Current assets		2,183
		4,720
less: current liabilities		(1,744)
Net assets employed in operation		2,976
add: long-term investment	150	
investment in subsidiaries	1,028	
		1,178
Total tangible assets		4,154
less: long-term loan		889
Net tangible assets		3,265

A company's value should be more than its net tangible assets since it has also accumulated an intangible asset of goodwill. The value of goodwill can be evaluated basing on earnings of the company compared to the fair average return of companies in the same business. If the average return is 12% on tangible assets employed, the value of goodwill of company B can be computed as follows:

	$'000
Net profit	857
less: fair return on tangible assets employed ($4,154,000 × 12%)	498
'Super profit' due to goodwill	359
Value of goodwill by capitalising super profit at 12% ($359,000/0.12)	2,992

The above evaluation gives a market value of $6,257,000 for company B comprising $3,265,000 of net tangible assets and $2,992,000 of goodwill.

4. Other factors

As can be seen from the above analysis, there is no definite way of putting a value to a company. The final agreed price depends on negotiation between the buyer and the vendor. Other factors that may affect the price include:

(a) Accepting new shareholders in order to inject additional capital to finance an impending expansion by a company. This step is usually taken if the company is highly geared so that bank finance is not forthcoming and existing shareholders are unable to put up more capital.

(b) An investing company will usually be willing to pay a higher price to acquire ownership of a company in order to:
 (i) establish an inroad to a new and unfamiliar market,
 (ii) achieve synergy benefit by complementing its existing operation,
 (iii) establish monopoly by acquiring the competitors.

(c) Usually, a higher price is paid for controlling shareholdings if full ownership is not allowed or intended.

Appendix B

Answers to Practice Problems

Chapter 1

1.1 End-of-period balances:

Cash	6,000	Office equipment	2,000
Accounts receivable	5,000	Creditors	11,000
Land and building	44,000	Long-term loan	15,000
Machine	10,000	Capital	41,000

1.2 Total debit balance = total credit balance = 67,000

1.3 Debit total = credit total = 378,000

Chapter 2

2.1 End-of-period balances:

Cash	43,800	Rent expense	900
Accounts receivable	1,000	Advertising expense	200
Equipment	6,000	Salaries expense	3,600
Office stationery	500	Capital	50,000
Accounts payable	3,000	Owner's withdrawal	2,000
Service fee	5,000		

2.2 Total debit balance = total credit balance = 58,000

2.3 Account balances:

Cash	2,370(Dr)	Accounts payable	700(Cr)
Accounts receivable	600 (Dr)	Capital	6,000(Cr)
Prepaid rent	2,000(Dr)	Withdrawals	50(Dr)
Unexpired insurance	480(Dr)	Legal fee earned	2,000(Cr)

Office stationery	100(Dr)	Salaries expense	1,200(Dr)
Law library	1,800(Dr)	Telephone expense	100(Dr)

2.4 Account balances:

Cash	7,650(Dr)	Service fee earned	3,500(Cr)
Motor vehicles	8,000(Dr)	Office stationery	150(Dr)
Capital	23,000(Cr)	Accounts receivable	1,500(Dr)
Prepaid rent	1,000(Dr)	Utilities expense	350(Dr)
Advertising expense	200(Dr)	Travel expense	550(Dr)
Office equipment	5,400(Dr)	Withdrawals	1,500(Dr)
Accounts payable	1,400(Cr)	Salaries expense	1,600(Dr)

2.5 No key figure

Chapter 3

3.1 Capital = 26,000
Trial balance total = 477,000

3.2 Account balances:

Office stationery expense	50(Dr)	Prepaid rent	1,000(Dr)
Office stationery	50(Dr)	Insurance expense	40(Dr)
Office rental expense	1,000(Dr)	Unexpired insurance	440(Dr)

Trial balance total = 8,700

3.3 Straight-line method annual depreciation = 16,000

Unit-of-production method annual depreciation:
 11,111, 16,667, 20,000, 17,778, 14,444
Sum-of-the-years'-digits method annual depreciation:
 26,667, 21,333, 16,000, 10,667, 5,333
Double-declining-balance method:
 51,000, 30,600, 18,360, 11,016, 5,000

3.4 Totals of columns in worksheet:

Trial balance	247,980
Adjustment	163,836
Adjusted trial balance	288,816
Income statement	127,920
Balance sheet	164,040

Net income = 3,144

Chapter 4

4.1 Account balances:
Capital   15,000 (Cr)
Retained earnings   8,650 (Cr)

4.2 Trial balance total = 141,125
Post-closing trial balance total = 73,245

Chapter 5

5.1 Retained earnings = 34,564
Total assets = Total liability + owners' equity
            = 160,740

5.2 Net income = 9,630
Retained earnings = 1,630
Balance sheet total = 64,345

5.3 Net income = 25,550
Balance sheet total = 21,450

Chapter 6

6.1 Month-end totals in cash receipts journal:

Accounts receivable	2,270	Sales discount	90
Sales	1,700	Cash	19,880

Account balances:

Cash	19,880(Dr)	Sales	4,230(Cr)
Sales discount	90(Dr)	Accounts receivable	260(Dr)
Bank B	6,000(Cr)	Fixed asset sales	10,000(Cr)

6.2 1. 50,000, 55,000, (15,000)
     2. 345,000, 205,000, 90,000
     3. 45,000, 65,000
     4. 35,000, 50,000, 20,000
     5. 55,000, 15,000, (35,000)
     6. 225,000, 125,000, 60,000
     7. 90,000, 105,000
     8. 40,000, 20,000, 15,000

6.3 Totals of columns in worksheet:
Adjustment 39,216
Income statement 726,688
Balance sheet 470,576

Net income = 50,864
Retained earnings = 198,864
Balance sheet total = 414,336

6.4 Sales = 269,500
Purchases = 165,100
Salaries = 48,300
Net income = 31,500

Chapter 7

7.1 Total sources of funds = 183,000
Application of funds = 250,000

7.2 Total sources of funds = 617,000
Application of funds = 640,000

7.3 Total sources of funds = 423,000
Application of funds = 441,000

Chapter 8

8.1 (a) Year 1 profit:
A 79,800   B 236,800   C 285,000
Year 2 profit:
A 91,200   B 281,200   C 364,800

(b) Year 1 profit:
A 77,700   B 246,400   C 277,500
Year 2 profit:
A 88,800   B 292,600   C 355,200

8.2 (a) (i) Year 1 profit:
A 48,000   B 32,000   C 20,000
Year 2 profit:
A 48,000   B 20,000   C 60,000

(ii) Year 1 profit:
A 48,000   B 64,000   C 4,000
Year 2 profit:
A 48,000   B 40,000   C 12,000

(c) 4,080

8.3 (b) Economic reorder quantity = 10,000
Reorder level = 21,000

8.4 A 87,575   B 76,667   C 65,758

Chapter 9

9.1 (a) Closing balance of finished goods = 37,500
(b) Cost of goods sold = 183,750
(c) Factory overhead incurred = 86,250
(d) Factory overhead absorbed = 90,000

9.2 Number of units remaining in process = 40,000
Average stage of completion = 28%

9.3 Total units accounted for = 73,600

	Equivalent production	Unit cost
Raw material	66,220	3.3303
Direct labour	56,380	2.3491
Factory overhead	56,380	1.7618
		7.4412

9.4

	Equivalent production	Unit cost
Raw material	56,940	3.3516
Direct labour	51,740	2.3804
Factory overhead	51,740	1.7853
		7.5173

9.5

	Equivalent production	Unit cost
Raw material	55,000	16.00
Direct labour	49,000	4.00
Factory overhead	49,000	7.20
		27.20

Chapter 10

10.1 (b)

	C/S ratio	Break-even sales
Last year	27.736%	261,754
Forecasted	32.121%	226,020

Net income will increase from 59,700 to 70,500 with changed sales mix.

10.2 (a) Contribution (marginal costing) = 48,000
Gross profit (absorption costing) = 65,000
Net income for both cases = 13,000

(b) Gradient of P/V graph = 0.32
Break-even sales = 109,375

10.3 (a) Net profit = 57,500

(b) Net profit = 8,000

(c) First year:

Gradient of P/V graph = 0.34375 (export sales portion)
= 0.5 (domestic sales portion)

Break-even sales = 281,000

The year after export contract expires:
Gradient of P/V graph = 0.5
Break-even sales = 236,000

It is not advisable to accept the order.

10.4 (a)

	Gradient of P/V graph
First 2000 units	0.5
2001–2500 units	0.7
2501–5000 units	0.6

Break-even revenue = 47,140

(b) Profit (absorption costing) = 20,500
Profit (marginal costing) = 15,500

10.5 (a) Unit cost (absorption costing) = 25
Unit cost (marginal costing) = 12

APPENDIX B ANSWERS TO PRACTICE PROBLEMS

(b) Gross profit (absorption costing) = 135,000
Contribution (marginal costing) = 180,000
Net profit for both cases = 50,000

10.6 (a) Profit (absorption costing) = 8,333
Profit (marginal costing) = 0

(b) Gradients of P/V graphs:
X: $\frac{2}{7}$ Y: $\frac{2}{5}$ Z: $\frac{1}{5}$

Break-even sales:

X   175,000 (2,500 units)
Y and Z   150,000 (1,000 units each)

Chapter 11

11.1 Net income (6,000 units) = (4,853)
Net income (7,600 units) = 21,213

11.2 (a) Year 1 budgeted profit = 600,000
(b) Year 2 budgeted profit = 1,570,000

11.3 A = 128,528
B = 0.61505
Forecasted sales in year 10 = 529,722

Chapter 12

12.1 Direct material variances:
   Price 220(F)   Usage 500(A)
Direct labour variances:
   Rate 140(A)   Efficiency 360(F)
Fixed overhead variances:
   Volume 500(F)   Expenditure 200(A)
Variance between original and flexed budgets
   = production volume variance = 1,380(A)

12.2 Direct material variances:
   Price 200(A)   Usage 80(F)
Direct labour variances:
   Idle time 159(A)   Efficiency 180(F)   Rate 390(F)
Variable overhead:
   Expenditure 200(A)   Efficiency 60(F)

Fixed overhead:
   Expenditure 500(A)   Volume 80(A)
   Efficiency 120(F)   Capacity 200(A)

12.3 Direct material variances:
   Price 490(F)   Usage 2,100(F)
   Direct labour variances:
      Idle time 300(A)   Efficiency 300(F)   Rate 210(F)
   Variable overhead variances:
      Expenditure 200(A) Efficiency 100(F)
   Fixed overhead:
      Expenditure 0   Volume 200(F)
      Efficiency 200(F) Capacity 0

Chapter 13

13.1 (a) No   (e) Yes
     (b) No   (f) Yes
     (c) No   (g) No
     (d) Yes

13.2 (a)

	A	B
ROCE	11.45%	11.21%
Profit margin	10.04%	16.84%
Asset turnover	1.14	0.67
Stock turnover	5.07	3.99
Gross profit to sales	23.96%	33.86%
Expenses to sales	13.92%	17.02%
Fixed asset turnover	1.33	0.73
Current asset turnover	2.96	2.10
Current ratio	1.58	1.36
Quick ratio	0.81	0.87
Stock to net current asset	0.94	0.56
Debtor ratio	0.17	0.29
Debtor collection period	61 days	106 days

13.3 (a) ROCE   16.07%
         Profit margin 7.2%
         Asset turnover 2.23
         Stock turnover 6.25 times/year

APPENDIX B ANSWERS TO PRACTICE PROBLEMS

(b) Current ratio   2.25
    Quick ratio   1.10
    Stock to net current assets   1.02
    Debtor collection period   52.56 days
    Debtors' turnover   6.94 times/year

(c) Gearing ratio   0.75

(d) Dividend yield   6.59%
    Earnings per share   0.1214
    P/E ratio   10.71
    Dividend cover   1.4166

13.4 (a) Net profit = 45,000

(b) Profit margin   26.47%
    Debtors' ratio   38.1%
    Debtors' collection period   139 days
    Creditors' turnover ratio   2 times
    Average credit period   182.5 days
    Stock turnover ratio   1.727 times
    Average stock period   30.11 weeks
    Current ratio   0.95
    Quick ratio   0.43

Chapter 14

14.1 Net present value = 10,932

14.2 (a) 10%
     (b) 9,263

14.3 (a) 27,365, 35,560

14.4 (a) Present value: A 70,350   B 72,128
     (b) Annual cost: A 19,516   B 20,008

14.5 (a) 8,137.27
     (b) 370,160
     (c) 7,929

Bibliography

There are numerous books published on principles of accounting. The following list is only a cross sample of books used in fundamental accounting courses and/or referred to during the writing of this book.

Bell, A. (ed.), *Introductory Accounting & Finance*, Thomas Nelson, Melbourne, 1990.
Cerepak J.R. and Taylor D.H., *Principles of Accounting*, Prentice Hall, Englewood Cliffs, NJ, 1987.
Droms W.G., *Finance and Accounting for Nonfinancial Managers*, Addison-Wesley, Reading, MA, 1983.
Dyson J.R., *Accounting for Non-accounting Students*, Pitman, London, 1987.
Flamholtz E.G., Flamholtz D.T. and Diamond M.A., *Principles of Accounting*, Macmillan, New York, NY, 1987.
Helmkamp J.G., Imdieke L.F. and Smith R.E., *Principles of Accounting*, John Wiley, New York, NY, 1983.
Horngren C.T., *Cost Accounting* (5th edition), Prentice Hall, Englewood Cliffs, NJ, 1982.
Horngren C.T. and Harrison W.T., *Accounting*, Prentice Hall, Englewood Cliffs, NJ, 1989.
Larson K.D. and Pyle W.W., *Fundamental Accounting Principles* (11th edition), Irwin, Homewood, IL, 1987.
Marriott N. and Simon J., *Financial Accounting, a Spreadsheet Approach*, Prentice Hall, Hemel Hempstead, Herts, UK, 1990.
Maxwell R.J., *Introductory Accounting: Principles and Practice*, Prentice Hall, Sydney, 1987.
Meigs R.F. and Meigs W.B., *Accounting: The Basis for Business Decisions* (8th edition), McGraw-Hill, Singapore, 1990.
Nikolai L.A., Bazley J.D. and Stallman J.C., *Principles of Accounting* (2nd edition), Kent, Boston, MA, 1986.

Reynolds I.N., Sanders A.B. and Hillman A.D., *Principles of Accounting* (3rd edition), Holt-Saunders, New York, NY, 1984.

Schroeder R.G. and Zlatkovich C.P., *A Survey of Accounting*, Irwin, Homewood, IL, 1991.

Solomon L.M., Vargo R.J. and Schroeder R.G., *Accounting Principles*, Harper, New York, NY, 1983.

Stickney C.P., Weil R.L. and Davidson S., *Financial Accounting* (6th edition), Harcourt Brace Jovanovich, Orlando, FL, 1991.

Thacker R.J., *Accounting Principles* (2nd edition), Prentice Hall, Englewood Cliffs, NJ, 1979.

Weygandt J.J., Kieso D.E. and Kell W.G., *Accounting Principles*, John Wiley, New York, NY, 1987.

Index

Absorption costing, 89, 114–5
Accounting cycle, 19
Accounting equation, 3, 47, 65
Accounts payable subsidiary ledger, 54
Accounts receivable subsidiary ledger, 54, 55
Accrual concept, 24
Advising bank, 186
Airway bill, 189
Analytical cash book, 52
Annuity, 174
Assets, 4
    Asset turnover, 152
    Asset valuation, 49
    Current assets, 8, 65
    Fixed assets, 8
    Liquid assets, 153

Balance sheet, 47
Bill, 12
Bill of exchange, 188
Bill of lading, 188, 195
Bin card, 81
Borrowing ratio, see Debt ratio
Break-even chart, 108
Budgeting, 123
    Budget centre, 123
    Continuous budget, 124
    Flexible budget, 124
    Master budget, 123
    Principal budget factor, 126
    Static budget, 125
    Zero-based budget, 125
Business cycle, see Operating cycle
Business entity concept, 49

Capital, 4, 11
Capital budgeting, 165
Cash flow, 73
Cash payment journal, 52
Cash receipt journal, 52, 53
Certificate of origin, 189, 193
Collecting bank, 189
Compound interest, 174
Conservatism, concept of, 50
Consistency principle, 50
Constant dollar accounting, 50
Contribution, 107
Contribution/price ratio, 111
Contribution theory, 114
Control accounts, 54
Control period, 54
Corporation, see Limited company
Cost, 79
    Cost apportionment, 25, 26–7
    Cost centre, 79
    Cost of goods sold, 56, 96
    Cost principle (of asset valuation), 49
    Cost unit, 79
    Cost variances, 135

Direct cost, 80
Fixed cost, 80
Indirect cost, 80, 86
Marginal cost, 107, 113
Prime cost, 80
Variable cost, 80, 107
Cost-of-production report, 99, 101
Credit, 6
Credit control, 55
Creditor, 4
C/S ratio, see Contribution/price ratio
Current account, 184
Current cost accounting, 50
Current ratio, 65, 153

Debit, 6
Debt ratio, 154
Depreciation, 28–9
  Declining-balance method, 29
  Double-declining-balance method, 29
  Straight-line method, 28
  Sum-of-the-years'-digits method, 29
  Units-of-production method, 29
Disclosure principle, 50
Discount rate, 166
Discounted cash flow methods, 166–7
Dividend cover, 155
Dividend yield, 155
Dividends, 9, 37
Documentary collections, 189
Double-entry, 7
Draft, 188

Earnings, 151
Earnings per share, 155
Equities, 4
Equivalent production, 99, 100
Expenses, 9, 11
  Accrued expenses, 9
  Direct expenses, 86
  Unrecorded expenses, 25, 26
Export documents, 187

First-in, first-out (FIFO) method, 58, 82
Flow of funds, 65–7
Folio, 15

Gearing ratio, see Debt ratio
General journal, 12
General ledger, 54
Going-concern assumption, 49
Goodwill, 240

Hire purchase, 176, 185
Horizontal analysis, 150

Idle time, 86, 138
Income statement, see Profit and loss statement
Income tax, 46
Inflation, 47, 170
Internal rate of return method, 168
Inter-service department transfers, 90
Inventory, see Stock
Investor method, see Internal rate of return method
Invoice, 12, 188, 192
Issuing bank, 186

Job order cost accounting, 95

Last-in, first-out (LIFO) method, 58, 82
Leasing, 185
Ledger, 8, 15
Letter of credit, 186–9
  Confirmed LC, 188
  Irrevocable LC, 188
  LC at sight, 188
  Red-clause LC, 188
  Transferable LC, 188
Leverage ratio, see Debt ratio
Liabilities, 4
  Current liabilities, 65
  Long-term liabilities, 65
Limited company, 202
Linear regression, 127

Management by exception, 126, 133
Margin of safety, 108
Marginal costing, 113–6
Matching principle, 50

Material requisition form, 81, 82
Materiality, concept of, 50
Merchandising firm, 52
Monetary principle, 49
Mortgage loan, 185
Moving average, method of, 127

Negotiating bank, 186
Net present value method, 167

Objectivity principle, 49
Operating cycle, 64
Operating statement, 145
Overdraft, 184
Overheads, 80
   Administrative overhead, 86
   Factory overhead, 96
   Fixed overhead, 134
   Production overhead, 86
   Selling and distribution overhead, 87
   Variable overhead, 134
Owners' equities, 4, 65

Packing list, 189, 194
Partnership, 200
Pay-back period method, 166
P/E ratio, see Price-earnings ratio
Period cost, 114
Periodic inventory system, 56
Periodic simple average method, 82
Periodic weighted average method, 82
Perpetual inventory system, 59
Posting, 15
Prepayment, 8, 64
Present value, 166
Price-earnings ratio, 155
Prime rate, 184
Process cost accounting, 95
Profit and loss account, 37, 39–40
Profit and loss statement, 45
Profit margin, 152
Profit/volume graph, 109–11
Profit/volume ratio, see Contribution/price ratio
Profitability index method, see Internal rate of return method
Purchase requisition, 80

Purchases journal, 52
P/V graph, see Profit/volume graph

Ratio analysis, 150
   Acid-test ratio, 153
   Borrowing ratio, 154
   Current ratio, 65, 153
   Debt ratio, 154
   Debt service ratio, 155
   Debtors' ratio, 154
   Debtors' turnover ratio, 154
   Gearing ratio, 154
   Leverage ratio, 154
   Liquidity ratio, 153
   Price-earnings ratio (P/E ratio), 155
   Profitability ratio, 151
   Quick ratio, 153
   Stock market ratios, 155
Realisation principle, 50
Remitting bank, 189
Retained earnings, 12
Retained earnings account, 37, 40
Return on capital employed, 151
Return on investment method, 166
Revenue, 9, 11
   Revenue apportionment, 25, 27
   Unrecorded revenue, 25, 26

Sales journal, 52, 53
Salvage value, 170
Shipping guarantee, 198
Simple average method, 82
Sinking fund, 177
Sole proprietorship, 199
Sources and application of cash, 73
Specific identification method, 58
Specific invoice price method, 58
Standard costing, 133
Standard price method, 82
Statement of changes in financial position, 67
Statement of costs, 99, 103
Statement of evaluation, 99, 103
Statement of owner's capital, see Statement of retained earnings
Statement of retained earnings, 46
Statement of sources and application of funds, 67

Stock, 8
  Buffer stock, 82
  Closing stock, 56
  Economic reorder quantity, 83
  Finished goods inventory, 96
  Holding cost, 82
  Minimum stock level, 82
  Opening stock, 56
  Reorder cardiogram, 83
  Reorder level, 82
  Stock evaluation, 58
  Stock ledger, 59
  Stock turnover, 85, 152
Store ledger, 81
Subsidiary inventory ledger, 59
Super-profit, 240

T-account, 5
Term bill, 197
Term loan, 185
Time card, 85
Time-period principle, 49
Time sheet, 85
Time value of money, 165

Transfer pricing, 209
Trend analysis, 150
Trial balance, 19, 24
  Post-closing trial balance, 40–1
Trust receipt, 197

Variances, 133
  Cost variance, 135
  Direct labour cost variance, 138
  Direct material cost variance, 137
  Fixed overhead variance, 139
  Price variance, 134
  Sales variance, 134, 135
  Variable overhead variance, 139
  Volume variance, 134
Vertical analysis, 150

Weight list, 189, 194
Weighted average method, 58, 82
Withdrawals, 9, 11, 37
Work in process, 96, 97
Working capital, 65
Worksheet, 30